The Explorer's Daughter

The Explorer's Daughter

A Young Englishwoman Rediscovers
Her Arctic Childhood

KARI HERBERT

VIKING
an imprint of
PENGUIN BOOKS

For Mum and Dad

VIKING

Published by the Penguin Group
Penguin Books Ltd, 80 Strand, London WC2R ORL, England
Penguin Group (USA) Inc., 375 Hudson Street, New York, New York 10014, USA
Penguin Books Australia Ltd, 250 Camberwell Road, Camberwell, Victoria 3124, Australia
Penguin Books Canada Ltd, 10 Alcorn Avenue, Toronto, Ontario, Canada M4V 3B2
Penguin Books India (P) Ltd, 11 Community Centre, Panchsheel Park, New Delhi – 110 017, India
Penguin Group (NZ), cnr Airborne and Rosedale Roads, Albany, Auckland 1310, New Zealand
Penguin Books (South Africa) (Pty) Ltd, 24 Sturdee Avenue, Rosebank 2196, South Africa

Penguin Books Ltd, Registered Offices: 80 Strand, London WC2R ORL, England

www.penguin.com

First published 2004
1

Copyright © Kari Herbert, 2004

The moral right of the author has been asserted

Set in 12/14.75pt Monotype Bembo
Typeset by Rowland Phototypesetting Ltd, Bury St Edmunds, Suffolk
Printed in Great Britain by Clays Ltd, St Ives plc

A CIP catalogue record for this book is available from the British Library

ISBN 0-670-91374-x

Contents

PART ONE: A Long Way Home

PART TWO: Return

Author's Note

Since my childhood I have known the people of Thule as 'Polar Eskimos'. However the Polar Eskimos have recently begun to refer to themselves as the *Inughuit*, meaning 'The Real People' (although many of the local people still call themselves 'Eskimo'). In this book I have chosen to use the name that they were historically known by – Polar Eskimos or Eskimos – in any historical context, and as Inughuit when I talk about the people in the present day who are, in some ways, a different people to their ancestors.

Eskimo words, unless otherwise indicated, are from the Inuktun dialect of Northwest Greenland, although there is some crossover with the West Greenlandic dialect which is in common usage throughout Greenland. Inuktun words that are in common usage in English – such as 'kayak' – are not italicized; other Inuktun words that are used many times throughout the text – such as *angákoq*, meaning shaman – are italicized only on their first occurrence.

Some names in the text are written as pronounced, such as Paulina – 'Baali'.

List of Illustrations

experienced hunters would dare to get so close to these unpredictable animals.

PART TWO: Return

Picture Credits

1–6, 8, 10–12, 13, 14: reproduced by kind permission of Sir Wally Herbert.
7, 15, 17–27: Kari Herbert.
9: reproduced by kind permission of the *Daily Mail*
16: reproduced by kind permission of Laurence Blyth.

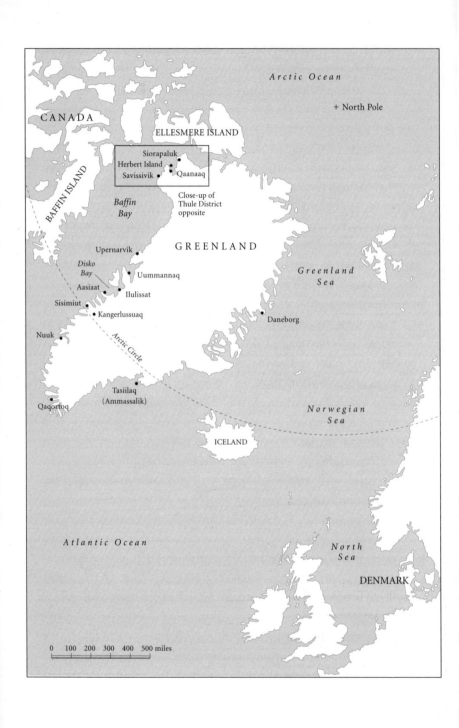

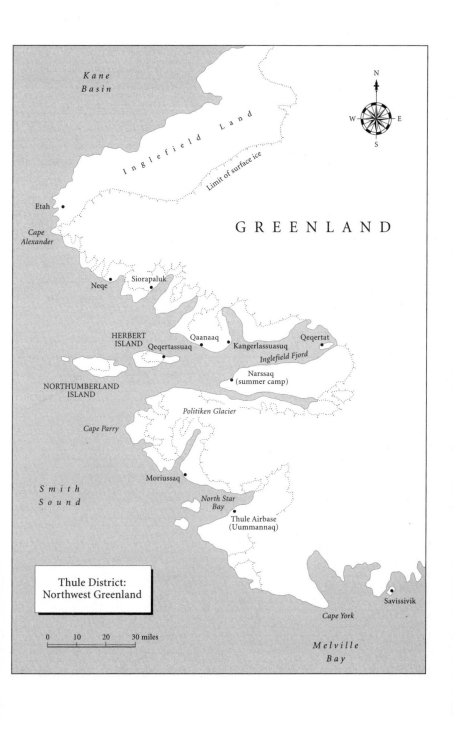

Kane
Basin

Inglefield Land

Limit of surface ice

N
W E
S

Etah

Cape
Alexander

GREENLAND

Neqe   Siorapaluk

HERBERT
ISLAND   Qeqertassuaq   Qaanaaq   Kangerlassuasuq   Qeqertat

Inglefield Fjord

NORTHUMBERLAND
ISLAND

Narssaq
(summer camp)

Politiken Glacier

Cape Parry

Moriussaq

Smith
Sound

North Star
Bay

Thule Airbase
(Uummannaq)

Thule District:
Northwest Greenland

Savissivik

Cape York

0   10   20   30 miles

Melville
Bay

PART ONE
A Long Way Home

'The land itself was a desolation, lifeless, without movement, so lone and cold that the spirit of it was not even that of sadness. There was a hint in it of laughter, but of a laughter more terrible than any sadness – a laughter that was mirthless as the smile of the Sphinx, a laughter cold as the frost and partaking of the grimness of infallibility. It was the masterful and incommunicable wisdom of eternity laughing at the futility of life and the effort of life. It was the Wild, the savage, frozen-hearted Northland Wild.'

Jack London, *White Fang*

1. The Beginning

I still remember the sound of the wind shrieking through the ventilation trap. The baying ghosts of the Arctic storm were running riot, and I stood transfixed in the flimsy hut, clutching the side of my wooden cot. To my left the squat dark oil stove whispered and sputtered to itself. Packing crates, strange one-eyed film cameras, leggy tripods, harpoons and throws of fur seemed to shift in the uneasy light; a window protested at the force of *Sila* – that overpowering High Arctic spirit of weather and nature – that searched for a weak spot to enter our warm sanctuary, the glass bending as it valiantly held sentry. Close by the dark figures of my parents lay on their platform bed, limbs casually entangled in sleep. The storm hadn't blown into their dreams.

I was too young to notice that this was my initiation into the life of the wilderness. Perhaps it was innocence that prevented me from crying out with a child's fear of the unknown, but I like to think that, even then, I felt I belonged in that harsh and untamed place.

When I was ten months old my father took my mother and me to the wilds of Northwest Greenland to live with an indigenous tribe of hunters then known as the Polar Eskimos. At the time it had seemed the most natural thing in the world for him to do. Throughout his life my father, the pioneering polar explorer Sir Wally Herbert, had been drawn to those places on the planet that seemed beyond reach, and the Arctic held for him a particular fascination.

As the son of a soldier and a country girl there was little hint in my father's early life of the direction in which he was heading. As a child he travelled in the wake of his father's military career, and spent his formative years in Egypt and South Africa, playing under the warm guidance of tribal women between the palms and frangipani trees. Few events of that time have left a mark on his memory; nevertheless he rode the up-draughts of these childhood experiences to find that he was born to travel.

My father took his first steps towards the Polar Regions at the tender age of twelve when, for a bet of five shillings, he walked across the River Severn on ice that was barely thick enough to support his meagre weight. It was the first great triumph that he can remember, and one of the most painful: the diminutive hero of this river crossing was given a beating when he returned home for having ventured out on the dangerous ice. It made him only more fascinated with the thrill of adventure.

It was not long before Fate made a decisive move. After three years with the Royal Engineers working as a mapmaker in Egypt, my father hitch-hiked back to England to wait impatiently for some 'sign' that would point towards his future. It was delivered, quite literally, into his lap. One morning as the idealistic twenty-year-old surveyor lurched his way miserably on the bus to work at a small airfield beside the Solent, an abandoned newspaper fell from the overhead luggage rack. It was open at the appointments section, and one vacancy immediately caught his eye: 'Expedition to Antarctica' the heading said; 'Keen young men required.'

My father spent a total of five years in the Antarctic travelling with dog teams and mapping forty-six thousand square miles of new country, and giving over one thousand place names to the then almost entirely uncharted continent of ice. Two geographical features were named after him: the plateau along the spine of the Antarctic Peninsula upon which he was the first to set foot, and the mountain range which forms the western wall of the Axel Heiberg Glacier – the route taken by Amundsen to the South Pole. His passion for exploration had started in earnest.

In between his two expeditions to the Antarctic he hitch-hiked solo from Montevideo in Uruguay back to Britain, and made his first forays into the Arctic – the first a solo expedition around the coast of Spitsbergen and the second to the west coast of Greenland to buy dogs, which he transported back to the Antarctic, and then drove for three thousand miles.

By 1964 his focus had finally settled on his real 'mission': to make the first surface crossing of the Arctic Ocean by its longest axis. By then the highest mountain in the world had been climbed, the Antarctic had been crossed, and the first tentative explorations of the oceans and space made; only one great pioneering journey was left to be attempted on the face of the planet – the journey across the top of the world. That epic trek by four men and forty dogs took sixteen months to complete, and was hailed at the time by Prime Minister Harold Wilson as 'a feat of endurance and courage which ranks with any in polar history'. Indeed, the British Trans-Arctic Expedition (BTAE) is now widely regarded by polar historians as being the first to reach the North Pole on foot, since the claims of both Commander Robert Peary in 1909 and Dr Frederick Cook in 1908 have both been discredited. More than thirty years later my father's shoulders felt the weight of the royal sword of approval when he was dubbed Knight Bachelor, Sir Wally Herbert, in the Millennium Honours ceremony.

An accolade equally cherished is a certificate that was presented to each member of the expedition on reaching the Royal Navy's ice patrol ship off the north coast of Spitsbergen on 11 June 1969 by Captain Peter Buchanan on behalf of the officers and ship's company of HMS *Endurance*. Others had witnessed my father's party set out from Alaska on their journey – these men had witnessed the completion of that journey. In ancient script the certificate reads: 'Wally Herbert is hereby admitted to the Ancient and most Honourable Order of the Threadbare Mukluk – in recognition of the fact that on 21st February 1968 he did, whilst claiming to be of sound mind, leave Point Barrow, Alaska,

in pursuit of some forty Husky Dogs which he finally caught off
the North Coast of Spitsbergen on 29th May 1969.' It was a fond
nod of the head of those sailors to this expedition that has since
been described as 'The Last Great Journey on Earth'. In return
my father presented the Royal Navy ship with the original
engraving which had been in Sir Ernest Shackleton's cabin at
the time he died, and which my father had carried as a talisman
on his sledge for 3,620 route miles across the Arctic Ocean. It
has kept the *Endurance* safe ever since.

Experienced as he was in the polar wilderness, it was my
father's extensive journeys with the Polar Eskimos in Northwest
Greenland in the winter and spring of 1967/68 as he trained for
this Trans-Arctic expedition, which had most honed his skills
and developed his sense of being in tune with the polar desert.
It was during this time that he formed deep bonds with the
hunters, and grew to understand the reasons why the Polar
Eskimos were a breed apart. Theirs was a unique legacy, and his
distress that their traditions and folklore should disappear without
record spurred him into writing several books and filming a
documentary about these people for whom he had developed a
great admiration and respect. There was never a doubt that his
young family would go with him on his return four years later.

Our destination was, rather appropriately, Herbert Island –
named by the explorer Captain E. A. Inglefield in the 1840s after
one of his crew – a remote sliver of land off the coast of Northwest
Greenland which supported one of the last surviving hunting
villages of the Polar Eskimos, and was the second most northerly
continuously inhabited settlement in the world. Even as late as
the early 1970s, life for the islanders was not far removed from
that of their forefathers. The community had no running water
– ice from freshwater icebergs was melted for daily use – and the
entire family would sleep on a single wooden platform covered
in skins and pelts. Labour was still divided by gender: the men
were the hunters, and could be absent from the community for
weeks at a time as they hunted polar bear, seal or walrus by

dog-sledge during the dark ice-bound months, or narwhal – the single tusked whale fondly nicknamed the unicorn of the sea – by harpoon and kayak in the summer; the women would stay at home tending to the children, preparing skins, curing meat and fish, collecting ice and generally keeping the home fires burning. It was a community on the brink of civilization, utterly in tune with their environment and wholly respectful to the animals with which they shared it. The Polar Eskimos did not feel superior to the animal kingdom, only to other men who did not know how to live in accordance with nature.

At only ten months old I was blissfully unaware of the adventure upon which we were embarking, but for my mother, Marie, the prospect was both thrilling and terrifying. She too had enjoyed an exotic childhood: leaving Dublin at the age of three and a half for Cambridge, before moving to Ceylon as a six-year-old to live with her adoptive father (an eminent professor of veterinary science), his godly wife and four of their six sons; travelling from the age of twelve by plane, train and then by stomach-churning bus to be schooled at the convent of Kodaikanal in the hills of Tamil Nadu in India. The nights of her childhood were haunted by the mocking laughter of roaming hyenas, and her days by the stout discipline of the starched Presentation Nuns who despaired at her unquenchable enthusiasm for music-hall songs.

As she came of age, the young Marie McGaughey arrived in 1960s London, studied drama, coaxed her hair into beehives, crowned them with tiaras, and danced the twist with some of the best dancers on the youthful theatrical circuit. By the time she met my father she had experienced enough of the world to know that she craved a life of adventure, and he personified her dream. She told me once that she recognized immediately the glint of distant horizons in my father's eyes, and the moment she felt the fire of his ambitions she knew that she had found her soul mate.

My parents met when my mother was working for Prince

Galitzine's public relations agency: the young explorer had enlisted their services to help raise funds and publicize his forthcoming British Trans-Arctic Expedition. Their romance flourished amongst the pre-expedition chaos. My mother vividly remembers his invitation to go boating on the Serpentine at midwinter; the way he gallantly rowed her across the lake, and the way her fingers froze as she took down shorthand notes of the fundraising letters he dictated to her.

To my mother, the Arctic was at first as alien and forbidding as it was to the Greeks in the earliest days of exploration, and yet it still called to her. By the time my father returned from his expedition sixteen months later she felt that she had already lived through the most extraordinary feats of Arctic endurance via telegraph and newspaper reports. They married shortly after his return on a mild Christmas Eve, the young bride wearing a micro mini skirt, long white platform boots, and a fur jacket that skimmed her thighs. Little did she know that her young husband would propose a two-year trip to the High Arctic as she nursed her firstborn in a hospital bed just a few hours after giving birth.

'Without my realizing it, he gradually built up in my mind a colourful mosaic,' she reminisced, 'until all that was needed to make the Arctic come alive was the lament of sledge dogs and the laughter of Eskimo children.' My father had won her over with the romance of polar travel, describing our destination as 'a pocket of good hunting territory about ninety miles north of the US Strategic Airbase at Thule in Northwest Greenland. To their east,' he had said, 'is a desert of ice: to the north not a living soul of their race.'

Aboard the annual supply ship from Copenhagen, the enormity of the journey on which they were embarking started to dawn on my mother. Until then her mind had been filled with careful planning and logistics; between the two of them my parents had to ensure that there would be enough food, clothing, medicines, books, film and camera equipment to last for two years of isolation, and there was little time for excitement. It was only when they had their first chance to relax on the ship that my mother began to wonder what sort of life she was taking her baby into: would we be able to stand the isolation and cold? What would we do if there were an emergency? But she was soon mesmerized by the Arctic's beauty and possibilities, and she relinquished her fears to its magic, until she first saw Herbert Island:

I felt a tug at my sleeve and a dark figure leaned over the bunk. 'We're just passing Herbert Island,' whispered Wally. 'It's worth a look.' I shot out of bed, my heart pounding. We were in sight of our destination. I scrambled into my clothes and went quickly up on deck. Peering out of my parka, I saw mountains capped with snow, and glaciers spreading like ravenous tongues around them. 'Is that Herbert Island?' I asked, half asleep. 'No, I'll show you in a second – you had better tie your shoelaces first.' Wally guided me round towards the bridge.

'Darling, there's your island,' he said.

A razorback ridge of featureless rock stretched on either side. No light shone on it or was reflected back. The bleak monotony of it was broken only by the scars and scratches of the cutting winds which had swept it clean. There seemed no space for man or beast on this barren rock: and this was where I had brought my baby to live for two years. My vision blurred. I thought I would choke. I could say nothing.

Sensing my distress Wally said lamely, 'It looks better in daylight.'

I nodded and hid my face in my parka.

The following day the weather had brightened somewhat, and Herbert Island softened in the light as the launches left the ship and headed towards our new home, heavy with equipment and supplies. It seemed a vast cargo; Dad was insistent that we should be self-sufficient and not a burden on the small community, which meant that we had huge quantities of dried and canned food, including a ton of baby food sponsored by Heinz, as well as film equipment, books and heavy winter clothing.

The small village of Qeqertassuaq had woken early in anticipation. A rumour had reached them long before our arrival that a young white family were coming to live with them, and the small huddle of Polar Eskimo villagers gathered on the rocky shoreline, drawn by both politeness and curiosity, murmuring among themselves and sizing up the new arrivals. However, the sight of a white child cradled in the arms of my mother dissolved any distance between us and as my mother recalls, 'a chorus of exclamations and friendly laughs filled the air. As I looked for a footing on the slimy green rocks, a young woman stepped down to steady me. I handed you to her, and several pairs of hands reached down to take you to safer ground. For a couple of minutes we all stood grinning at each other, rather embarrassed. A little circle had gathered round the woman holding you while you gurgled appreciatively. The ice was broken and I knew that I would be happy there.'

The little red hut, which was to be our home for the next two years, was suffering from years of neglect. Although it was right in the centre of the village, the hut had until now only been used as a shelter for visiting hunters. Dad was well used to the unkempt living conditions endured by the hunting community, but it must have been quite a disappointing welcome for my mother. Piles of rubbish were strewn both inside and out, decaying walrus heads clung to the roof and a grimy dog skin was pinned to the outhouse. Layers of yellowing blubber greased the path to the blistered doorway and huskies lay sprawled among bleached bones and dusty boulders. The hut inside was little better: remnants of filthy clothing hung from hooks in the cramped porch, leading to a small kitchen that was smeared with layers of blood and discarded blubber. Through another doorway was another larger room, which was furnished with a single wooden platform, serving as both seat and bed, a small chest of drawers painted pink and a makeshift table constructed from packing crates. The walls were dark blue and stained with old blood and grime, the windows were cracked, there was no toilet and an all-pervading smell of seal and walrus and general squalor hung on the air. 'We had to paint it immediately,' Dad told me laughing, 'to seal in the smell.'

The fourteen-foot by eleven-foot hut immediately became the focus of much attention. Visitors flowed continually in and out of the tiny space, sitting to drink tea or coffee, or partake of any food that was on offer as they watched my parents transform the squalid hunter's hut into a welcoming nest. The local children were a daily part of the scene, staying for hours to play with their new little friend.

The new life was hard, for my parents at least. Each morning ice had to be collected and melted for both drinking and washing, coal had to be brought in, the fire cleaned and rebuilt and fuel for the lamp and oil stove had to be bought. Very soon my parents realized that the traditional clothing was by far the warmest option, so after every journey, however small, the furs had to be dried and hung up, and every evening the liners of the traditional kamiks had to be separated from the sealskin outer of the boots to dry out and the boots themselves softened – in the old days the women softened the skins by chewing them, but by then they used a blunt steel tool – the following morning the boots would have to be reassembled with dry tundra grass or moss carefully stuffed in between the layers for extra insulation.

Although communication was initially quite difficult – in those days there were no local language dictionaries to refer to – after a time and with the aid of Dad's thumbnail cartoons, Mum and Dad started picking up the local dialect, and slowly friendships were forged with many of the villagers, in particular with our neighbours Avatak and Maria Qaerngâq and their seven children. Avatak was the grandson of an *angákoq* – an Eskimo shaman – and was a fine 'long-distance' hunter; it was with Avatak and another great hunter Peter Peary (grandson of the polar pioneer Commander Robert E. Peary), that my father shared some of his most memorable journeys in the Arctic. Avatak and I had a special bond; it was as though we recognized each other somehow. I called him *Ataata* – Greenlandic for Dad.

While Avatak and my father were travelling, Maria and my mother spent much of their days together, Maria helping Mum with her *Inuktun* – the local dialect of Greenlandic – and teaching her how to flense skins, handle dogs and generally survive as the Polar Eskimos have done for centuries. And in the mean time I fell into the ways of the other Eskimo children. Soon I was eating seal, walrus and other local foods, and speaking only in Inuktun. I believed that the children of Avatak and Maria were my siblings; Ilannguak and Arquenguak were my brothers, Najannuaq, Louisa, the twins Magda and Paulina (pronounced 'Baali' by the family), and little Edo were my sisters. And I was adamant that Avatak's father, the wonderful old man Taitsianguaraitsiak was *Aata* – my granddad – and that his gentle wife Suakunguak was *Aana* – granny. Another neighbour Migishoo also became regarded as 'granny', but it was not just my privilege to call her so, she was granny to everyone.

Migishoo was the lively old lady of the village, who lived in the most traditional of all the houses – an old wooden hut reinforced on three sides with stones and turf – and whose eyes disappeared completely whenever her soft face crinkled in laughter. She had a particular passion for liquorice. Migishoo was the mother of five grown-up children, and was the guardian of a sixth, a small reticent boy not much older than myself called Niels. Her husband, suffering from 'bad hands', was no longer a hunter and the old woman had to shoulder the responsibility of bringing in the food for the three of them herself. It was difficult for any woman with no hunting skills or equipment to provide for her family, and particularly one of her age and generation. Migishoo was a child of the ancient age of the Polar Eskimo, and was a compact bundle of memories. She remembered her mother's stories of the time, not so long ago, when the white men first came to the area bringing strange deadly weapons that cracked and boomed and smoked, which could hit a beast of water or land from great distances. Now everyone in the community had these 'rifles'.

When Migishoo was a child the community had little in the way of outside influences, and she had been brought up to know only the role of an Eskimo woman, learning how to flense skins, make clothing and keep it serviceable. She had to prepare meat and dry fish and became adept at the many other skills that were essential for a woman to bring to a partnership in order to survive. In those early days, and even when we lived there, there simply was no role-swapping, except in extreme circumstances. Each partner knew exactly what was expected of them; that's how the people survived. Migishoo now had to make the best of her situation. She knew how to catch birds, find eggs and berries and how to fish, and sometimes she cast nets under the ice to catch seal, but often she would have to find other ways to earn money so that she could buy food to feed her family.

Like Migishoo, Aata had also experienced a childhood that was 'primitive'. When I was old enough to understand, the old man took me on a slow walk to the north of the present village to a place where he had lived as a child. Embedded in the ground was a scattering of rudimentary dwellings, which looked more like deep traps for animals than the remnants of old houses. I remember Aata holding my hand with his warm rough paw, pointing with the other to where he and his family had slept on the platform bed, and how high the roof had been before it had collapsed; and then he turned and gently made me face the fjord as he sighed, his body stooping with the weight of age, his dark basin haircut barely moving in the breeze. Yes, this was a beautiful place.

My mother and I stayed mostly with the community during the following two years, joining them on the cool sun-drenched beaches of summer camp and occasionally visiting other small settlements such as Siorapaluk, just north of Herbert Island, but mostly we stayed in the village, particularly during the four dark months. The winter generally confined the women to the villages, whereas the men would often use the good ice conditions to go on long-range hunting trips, travelling as far as Canada or beyond Inglefield Land. It was rare that women accompanied them – save for the exceptional wife with no children to look after, who could take care of the skins of animals caught en route, and ensure that her husband's clothing was kept in good condition. My father, unlike us, quite often left the confines of the village with Avatak and Peter Peary to travel over glacier, fjord and icecap to film them hunting; they travelled by both moonlight and the sun.

On one occasion, however, Mum was to accompany Dad on a long sledge trip to the American airbase to pick up Geoff Renner, a family friend who was to stay with us for three months and was planning to do some travelling with Dad in the area. Although hunters often did the ninety-mile sledge trip between the airbase and the area around Qaanaaq, the route over the Politiken Glacier was well known as being an option for only the very best dog-drivers. It could be a perilous trip, made all the more hazardous if the weather closed in, and not a journey on which to take a young child unless it was absolutely necessary. The best option for all of us was to leave me back at the village with Maria and the children.

The preparations for the forthcoming trip took the best part of two weeks; new harnesses had to be made for the dog team as well as sleeping bag covers and a double-lined tent. The clothing for the journey had to be in its best possible condition, and Dad's *tugto* – reindeer – parka had already been used on several trips and had to be carefully checked and reinforced in places; three pairs of kamiks and another parka for our friend Geoff Renner had to be ordered from the women in the village, and several pairs of sealskin mitts had to be made, as they wore out quickly with the rigours of sledging.

Almost every day Maria and the children would collect me and take me to their house so that my parents could prepare for the trip with no distractions – my inquisitive little hands were always playing with something either hazardous or valuable – and as our hut was so tiny the likelihood of an accident was high.

I felt completely at home in our neighbour's house. Polar Eskimo children have always been indulged in a way that would horrify other European or American mothers. Their open attitude to child-rearing has evolved from two beliefs: the first is that the child is a reincarnated soul and is not only naturally wise to the world, but could also be their father, mother or grandparent – in the past for instance, it was not unusual for parents to call their small child 'Aata' (Grandfather), or the name of another member of the family who was recently deceased; the second belief was that the best lessons were learnt through experience. If a child was playing with a sharp knife the parent would at best murmur '*anganga*' – it's dangerous – for the child would soon know how painful a cut could be. In comparison my parents were understandably more protective of their child. With expensive and irreplaceable camera equipment scattered over the house, and paraffin lamps at arm's reach from our low ceiling, Mum and Dad were constantly shrieking 'Be careful!', particularly when the children swung me around the room, with my head just an inch from the floor. The children soon learnt what this meant and would call out 'Bee-carr-full!' to one another as they were playing.

The children in the village responded well to the relaxed attitude of the settlement, as did I, and although I remember few things vividly from those first couple of years, I do remember the joy of unrestricted childhood. I would happily sit on Avatak's knee, twiddling the knobs on the radio and chatting to him in my childish Inuktun, or play with the children on the floor, making games out of thin air.

The journey to the airbase was expected to take two days, and would entail sledging down the fjord and then up over the glacier and a frozen riverbed for about eighteen miles before descending 2,500 feet to the sea ice. Normally two sledges would travel together over the glacier for safety, but on this occasion my parents would be going alone. The villagers were anxious; even though they respected my father's skills as a dog-driver and polar traveller they were worried that no white man could ever know their land as well as they did. My father had completed the trip many times before but they still shook their heads – it simply was not safe, they insisted. My parents, being who they are, respectfully thanked them for their concern, and gently advised the villagers that they would be leaving the following morning.

We still have film footage of the moment when my parents left: my mother hands a large furry bundle to Maria before walking towards the sledge. She turns to wave and anxiously checks that I am OK. She was exhilarated at the prospect of an adventure with her husband, and although she was sad to leave me behind, she knew she could trust Maria and Avatak to take good care of me; the trip should only take four days to the airbase and back, and it would be a great experience for us all. My puzzled face peers out of the furs, with two huge dark eyes watching the departure. Maria holds my hands as I waddle down the few outdoor steps. The camera angle changes and my father struggles into his stiff parka, looking like the reverse of a strange beast shedding its skin. And then the sledge is off, crashing over the tide crack with the children of the village helping Mum to steer it. The camera switches off as Dad rushes back to retrieve it from its tripod.

The journey to the airbase was apparently exhausting and hair-raising. The glacier rose up in front of them like a biblical task, a vast slick of turquoise-dappled ice, with little snow cover in which to gain a foothold. The way up was difficult, and in places an ice axe was the only way to gouge clefts in the ice to scramble upon. My parents struggled as much as the dogs to get the heavy sledge to the top, climbing each of the four mammoth tiers of the glacier with the dogged hope that each one was the last. As they neared the summit the blue of the afternoon disappeared beyond a high mist, and with alarming rapidity the visibility deteriorated to just a few yards. Unable to see their way forward they made camp for the night, and were finally lulled to sleep by the weight of solitude.

By the time they reached Moriussaq, a small settlement just four hours' travel from the airbase, Mum had experienced some of the most exhilarating moments of her life, but a sudden blizzard prevented them from travelling any further and they sought refuge with a hunter by the name of Kaviarssuak, whose name my father had been given by Orla Sandborg, the personable Danish Administrator in Qaanaaq. Kaviarssuak and his wife Bibiane were amazed to see two frosted white strangers outside their door and hurriedly made them welcome. 'Bibiane had the essence of the Queen of Tonga,' my mother recalls with a smile; 'she was such a wonderful woman.'

On arrival at Thule Airbase the following day my parents found themselves swept up into a world that seemed quite incongruous in comparison to the ice-bound wilderness outside. They drove their team of dogs down roads lined with marker flags that ran between sprawling modern buildings. Cars sped past, the uniformed drivers dipping their heads in greeting. The Danish Administrator pulled his car up beside them, welcomed them warmly and drove them to his home in comfort.

The luxury of the Officers' Club seemed more than a little extravagant after their few months of frugal living, but still it was a welcome change. By virtue of his accomplishments and contacts in the area my father was always given a hearty welcome – particularly it seems on this occasion, for he had a dance dedicated to him by a young buxom entertainer who commanded the stage dressed in hot pants and a low-cut top. My mother couldn't help but wonder what the villagers would think if they had seen what was going on inside the Officers' Club.

Geoff was in his element as they left the airbase on their return home to Qeqertassuaq. With his fine-boned features, gentle manner and his love of Latin American dancing, it was easy to mistake him for a meekly ambitioned man, but in fact he had a particular affinity with the desert, be it of ice or sand, and had not only already travelled extensively in the Antarctic, but would also later complete several crossings of the Sahara.

But the weather in the High Arctic is at best unpredictable, and the three companions were soon swept up in winds that froze any exposed skin, and made progress impossible. 'With each breath I felt my lungs choked,' my mother wrote. 'All sound was muffled. We slid through a nebulous world like phantom figures driving a white hearse. All colour was lost behind a thick veil. The dogs all looked the same, transformed by the snow.'

There was no choice but to make camp. The dogs' traces had to be untangled and anchored to the ice, the sledge unloaded and turned on its side to provide a windbreak – anchored with long guy ropes threaded through small tunnels that had been chipped into the ice – and the tent erected in the lee of the sledge and nailed with pitons to the ice so that it wouldn't blow away in the storm. Thick layers of snow clung to their furs and found their way inside, chilling them to the core; masks of ice set over their faces, narrowing their nostrils, cementing their eyes and gagging their mouths if they tried to speak: 'It was like a slow burial.' It took my father over an hour painstakingly to melt the ice off his face and beard over the Primus stove when they finally managed to rig the tent; another fifteen minutes and it would have suffocated him.

They had snatched moments of sleep. My father and Geoff alternated shifts to look after the stove as the storm beat the tent and threw mounds of snow at the canvas so that the sides of the tent bulged inwards from the weight, as if some wandering animals had got lost in the snow and were huddled against them for comfort.

The tent was almost lost in drifts when they escaped the next morning, and as the blizzard lifted they realized that they were only three hundred yards from the village of Moriussaq. They rounded up the dogs and staggered back to Kaviarssuak and Bibiane's house with their clothing wet and limp. The furs would have to be fully dried out before they could continue. Once again they were welcomed, and the wet furs were strung up around the small house and in the homes of accommodating neighbours.

Many people had returned to the village during the storm, and Bibiane and her husband had stayed awake until three in the morning in case they came back, and hadn't slept from worry. 'The ferocity of the wind had surprised them,' Mum said, 'even though they were used to violent storms.' They would later discover that the wind recorded at the nearby airbase was the second highest recorded on the face of the earth at that time – 207 mph.

The journey back to Qeqertassuaq was fraught with high winds and terrifying moments. The uncompromising weather delayed them day by day, pinioning the three travellers and their dogs to the ice, and making it impossible even to rig a tent so that they had to nail it flat to the ice and crawl between the layers. The cold claustrophobia and the agony of their imprisonment atop the glacier was almost too much for my mother, who was seized with a fear that they would not make it back to the village at all.

Constantly they had to check each other for the white spots of frostbite, pausing only to rub their faces vigorously to get the circulation moving. There was no respite from the wind, and they plunged out of control back down the glacier, sledge, dogs and humans somersaulting one over another. It was a hopeless situation. With doubts that they were on the correct glacier, my father went on ahead to find a safer route only to find himself picked up like a rag doll and thrown slithering over the burnished ice. He clawed at the ice helplessly with his pickaxe, but the ice was as cold and hard as iron, and the wind too strong to fight. It seemed an eternity before he found a bearable route.

It was ten days before they returned to the village, battered and exhausted – they were supposed to be back in four. Dad had dislocated his shoulder and his wrist was sprained from his falls, both he and Geoff had weather-sore faces and they all were aching and bruised. Overwhelmed with relief to be alive, the three of them were choked with emotion as they saw the tiny settlement, my mother sobbing as the villagers ran out to meet them in waves and helped guide the weary travellers towards Maria who clutched me, warm and oblivious to the gravity of events, in her arms. 'I am so happy to see you,' she said quietly as Mum hugged me fiercely. 'We thought you were dead.'

Over the next few days after the stories of the journey were exhausted, Maria related the agonies that they had gone through in their concern for my parents' safety. She had paced the floors holding me, she said, sometimes weeping, and at other times laughing, trying to make nonsense of her fears. They knew that Dad was experienced in the Arctic, but the storms were like nothing they had seen, and they had lasted so long. Avatak had gone to Qaanaaq, hoping that we had made it to the town and were waiting for the weather to break, and he had met Peter on the way who had had similar ideas, but confirmed that the three companions were still on the glacier. The women of the village had urged their men to send out a search party, but the men were hesitant; it was considered an insult to go in search of a man of my father's skill, and besides, they had never seen a storm like it, they would have risked their own lives going out in it.

As the days had progressed with no sign of my parents the people of the village had had to confront the inevitable question: what if Marie and Wally did not return? Avatak and Maria had agonized over it. Maria finally confessed to Mum that even though they would have wanted to keep me, they knew in their hearts that I would be taken away. 'We wept and hugged her,' Maria continued; 'we wondered who her new parents would be, and whether she would have anyone to care for her at all. We blamed ourselves for letting you go on your own.'

This story deeply affected me when I heard it for the first time, not only because of the thought that I could have lost both my parents, but also because it is one of the most significant turning points of my life. The return of my parents made me what I am today; but if Fate had dealt another hand, who knows how long I would have stayed in the community, and what would have become of my future? One thing is certain – the dangerous journey my parents took to the airbase in the winter of 1972 established an enduring bond between myself and the Qaerngâq family.

Moving back to England in 1973 uprooted my world. Dad has since told me that he had hoped to stay longer with the hunting community of Herbert Island, but by the end of two years I was becoming so like the other children in the aboriginal tribe that both my parents had concerns that I would find it increasingly difficult to fit into a 'civilized' society on our return; already I was speaking to my parents only in the local tongue, and I was growing up fast. It was best, in many respects, that we return to the UK, and that I be introduced into the way of life in which I would be fully educated.

We returned to a colder and greyer social climate than the one to which I had grown so accustomed. Friends of the family were bewildered by the wild creature that my parents brought home; by turns I amused them with my knotted rebellious curls and my fascination with running water, and shocked them with my guttural conversation and bloodcurdling shrieks and imita- tions of a cracking whip whenever I saw a pet dog. I have particularly fond memories of my godparents' docile golden labrador Daisy, whom I terrorized immediately with my cries. Yet we did, after some time, become the closest of friends.

From my point of view, England was far more inhospitable and brutal than the place I had just come from. Although my parents were deeply loving, the general attitude to children in England seemed stand-offish compared to the warmth of the tribal hunting community. Now I look back and I realize how spoilt I was in Thule. I had been treated as a little princess – the little white girl who had the tongue and the spirit of the Polar

Eskimos; back in England I was a volatile, confused, distressed and unremarkable little girl.

Mum and Dad sat me for hours in front of the television to encourage me to speak English, and soon I did, fluently, but to the detriment of my Inuktun, which I didn't hear again until our return to the area several years later. My memories, dreams and the language of Thule went into hibernation in the face of the strange new world in which I found myself.

It was seven years before we returned to Northwest Greenland, along with my younger sister Pascale, who celebrated her second birthday there. By that time I was a British schoolgirl, and I had lost all of those words, images and memories of the smells and sounds of my early years. I was shocked to see those faces that had lingered only in my imagination, and the warmth and love with which we were greeted was overwhelming. We were pulled from one home to another; squeezed, pampered and cried over. But there were some faces missing. Alcohol, introduced into the area around thirty years before, had claimed many lives through association: in a blinding tragedy, Avatak had been shot by Maria, who had subsequently been taken away by the authorities; in remarkably similar circumstances, my father's other close sledging companion Peter Peary had also been killed. The community would never be the same again.

As a naive nine-year-old I left the gravesides confused, cheeks glistening with tears, but I had a child's aptitude for the letting go of grief, and moved on quickly to simply revel in the fact that you could have Heinz tomato ketchup on your seal meat, and frozen chocolate bourbon biscuits afterwards. Some things, however, had not changed. There was still pride in the faces of the hunters, icebergs were still melted for the boiled stews of meat, and dripping carcasses of seal were the gory welcome on entering any of the huts, which was enough to turn the stomach of any young girl who had forgotten the past. The old women still grinned gummy smiles, teeth worn to stumps from chewing skins to soften them for clothing; the air was thick with the heavy pungency of blubber and punctuated by the calls of the semi-wild huskies; children still ran around clamouring for attention, rubbing noses and sniffing each other in affection. It was only later that I realized that the very fabric of the hunting way of life was wearing thin, families were being torn apart, and some were already lost to the seductions of a modern alternative.

One person who didn't seem to be yearning for a life elsewhere was Patdloq, one of my old playmates, about fourteen years old at the time, who happily took me with her on the chore of collecting ice for cooking and drinking. Most children in the community knew how to handle dogs and sledges from a young age, and Patdloq was particularly skilful. After negotiating the ice rubble of the tide crack we sped across the sea ice on her miniature sledge behind two huskies that she had been allowed to train since they were puppies. For me it was an expedition to the heart of my earlier memories: the playful flurries of ice that shot up from behind the dogs, a burning cold ice drop hesitating on my lips, the ice breeze catching in my throat and the languorous *swhhhhhhhhsssh* of the runners on the hard packed ice. A couple of miles away we stopped beside a magnificent cobalt and emerald-green iceberg and chipped away at it until we had filled our buckets. Patdloq indicated that we needed more, and as I turned my back she shrieked with delight and disappeared on her sledge, leaving me alone on the ice.

I could see the settlement, but it was cold and it was polar bear country – unlike any local nine-year-old I had no idea what to do next. The snaking tracks of the sledge were barely visible, easily forgotten whispers of a passage back across the pack ice. Hot terrified tears burned my face until finally the silence calmed me almost to a trance. The huddle of the settlement huts dwarfed by the towering rocky outcrop behind it gave an aura of protection, and I sank into the vastness of ice and sky. I was cradled by its magic. The missing passenger was soon noticed and I felt a surge of excitement as hollering villagers streaked out in formation to pluck me from my reverie. I returned to the settlement with mixed feelings for my companion, who showed no remorse, and took great delight in mocking my running after the sledge; nevertheless that day I truly felt at home and that night I went to sleep with my old 'grandfather' Aata stroking my head and my nose as he used to when I was tiny and couldn't sleep. We left the following day, and I never saw Aata again.

Throughout my life I have been surrounded by the memorabilia of Arctic travel. And although I often felt alienated in school as a consequence of my history and experiences, I still gathered around me one or two friends who loved the adventure that our home offered. With both parents being writers, books overtook the house, and Dad seemed to be constantly occupied with building shelves to accommodate them. Packing crates from Dad's British Trans-Arctic Expedition were utilized in various ways, such as steps into an attic office or chairs at the dining table (chairs on which I have sat to write some of this book); prizes of walrus and narwhal tusks from hunting trips lay next to small games of skill fashioned from bone; drawings and paintings of daily life for the Polar Eskimo hung next to a rifle with the sight still attached through which my father first viewed land after sixteen months on the ice (he used to joke that the rifle had one bullet left to terrify prospective boyfriends); in pride of place was a harpoon draped with the tattered Union Jack which was pitched on the North Pole for one day.

Sometimes we would take summer picnics in the garden, resting our drinks on the fifteen-foot sledge that lay retired and redundant on the lush green lawn, and my friends and I would take it in turns to retrieve ice cream from the chest freezer which was mostly filled with still-serviceable Arctic fur clothing that had to be kept at temperatures below freezing to prevent them from rotting, as there was always the possibility that Dad would be off on more travels. Before one of his longest expeditions – an attempt at the circumnavigation of Greenland – there were so many supplies in our tiny home that Cadbury's chocolate bars spilled out from every space in our kitchen cupboards. It was a child's dream.

As I grew older I suspected that I was being haunted by something but, not being sure what it was, I put it down to my adolescent bewilderment. But in 1994 Greenland came to my rescue. Dad was lecturing on ships going to the Arctic and the Antarctic, and an opportunity came up for both my parents to lecture on a new High Arctic cruise which was to travel through Thule. Determined to join them, I got my first writing commission from *Traveller* magazine to write about the trip, and accompanied my parents on our first return to the district for fifteen years.

The moment I glimpsed my first sight of pack ice from the window of the plane I had a flashback to my last flight to the Arctic, and was transported back to the same childlike excitement. But it was not the ice that I remembered; it was the light – the blue-white blinding light. And then I caught the inexpressibly subtle scent of fresh snow. The return of these prodigal memories brought me to believe that some fragment of myself had been lost between these two worlds.

It was the fifth day of our sea voyage when we anchored a mile from the main administrative town of Qaanaaq. We had smashed through thick ice in order to get there, the ice groaning and splitting; behind us the still seething rubble filling the black wound, which in a few hours would show little indication of our path. The day was bitter but clear and the Zodiac boat ride to shore gave us ample time to take in the significant growth of Qaanaaq since our last visit. The scattering of old hunters' huts was lost among a sprawl of brightly painted wooden houses hovering between snakes of steel pipes; a large satellite dish sat awkwardly on the hillside and whale-backed Herbert Island lay silent, tantalizingly close.

There to greet us on the shore was the usual mêlée of children eager to make new friends and to beg a ride on the boats. My 'sister' Baali was there waiting. All my fears that I would not recognize any of the family, or that I would be rejected, disappeared instantly. She ran straight to me and we shared an embrace that in its tight grasp held all the time, and all the family that we had lost: three years previously my fifteen-year-old sister Pascale had tragically died in an electrical accident at home. It was still a raw wound for all of us. In Thule Avatak, Aata, Aana and many others in the community had also died. We gathered ourselves together and headed up to Najannuaq's home, the eldest sister who, like all of the girls, now had children of her own.

To our great surprise we learned that Maria, who had been exiled from the community since the night she had shot her husband Avatak, was in Qaanaaq with a special dispensation to spend a few days with her children. It was more than we could ever have hoped for and the atmosphere was electric. The happiness of reunion mingled tangibly with loss as she stood in the doorway of the hut, a gulf of never-shared experiences between us. I sat bewildered on the hard bench. Maria was suddenly weeping inconsolably in my lap, my mother beside me, stroking her hair, an audience of trembling, sniffing siblings around us. As we recovered we reminisced, laughing, crying and playing with the children who were determined not to be left out. It was an unending cycle of glistening dark eyes and wild toothless grins in desperate absorption of each other.

Everything had changed considerably since our first trip. The huts, modern and with double glazing and central heating, no longer had to be insulated with layers of newspaper; in the early 1970s it was not unusual to see posters of Christ gazing down in benevolent perpetuity at the layers of incongruous images from women's magazines used as makeshift wallpaper. Plastic furniture had replaced the uncompromisingly hard sleeping platforms, and the children ran around in leggings, glossy wellington boots and DKNY T-shirts – gifts from cruise-ship tourists. Baali's six-year-old daughter Little Tekummeq had a Walkman plugged to her ears, her cousin Suakunguak played a small bleeping computer game. The tea, however, was the same; brewed in the kettle, weak, sweet, black and aromatic. Still, the pungent smell of blubber was heavy in the air and husky pups outside gambolled around their mother.

We communicated in our silence, my hair pulled just as before, but at least not cut: my parents had spent our first few months in Greenland wondering why my hair never seemed to grow, until finally they discovered that the Eskimos had been cutting off and keeping my curls as protective amulets. The children continued to kiss Eskimo fashion, our old friend and guardian Migishoo, wizened and frail, now in the small retirement home, still presented me with liquorice. Her hollow face was wild with delight as she called to my father, 'Ooaallee!!' while she softened a piece of imaginary sealskin between her fingers. Her traditional *ulu*, a curved knife used for flensing skins, lay next to her pillow, the handle worn smooth from years of handling. Down at the beach an old hunter proudly showed the tourists how to use a harpoon in a kayak, and up on the darkening hill the plastic flowers continued to splash colour on the ordered graves that look across to the pale pinks of Herbert Island.

We left Maria sitting immobile with her thoughts in a hard wooden chair that she had dragged to the centre of the living space. She was the same age as my mother, yet her face looked ancient and had the landscape of one who has lived in grief and in exile from a loving life. Her eyes were glassy and unseeing as we walked away; the only expression was in her hands, which grasped her legs in agonized claws.

The whole community seemed to be in shock at Maria's return, and our appearance had compacted time and awakened their memories. Avatak had been shot shortly after our departure from Herbert Island, and seeing both Maria and our family in Qaanaaq was too much for some. I was still reeling from my encounter with Maria when I heard a desperate wail emanating from a figure on the path back to the beach. The woman was keening, tearing at her heart and her clothes and grasping at her head as if her soul was leaving her and she was desperate to hold onto it. Suddenly she leapt at me and clasped my face in a fierce grip before looking desperate and questioning at the rest of the entourage that we had accumulated. '*Kaari-ngaa* . . . ?' ('Our Kari?') she croaked, and I nodded as best I could as she went to my mother and stroked her cheek. It was Benina, Avatak's sister.

We left after just a few hours, the ship was to head south and the captain was on a tight schedule. We departed as our old friends wept on the beach, not knowing when we would next see them. At that moment I pledged that one day I would return and spend some time with these people who had once accepted me as their own.

Over the years word reached me that the community had changed almost beyond recognition. Now Herbert Island is virtually deserted, with only one die-hard hunter and his daughter in semi-permanent residence; alcohol flows freely and insidiously through the veins of the people, and the rise in unemployment and the changing roles of men and women are affecting the balance of what was once a harmonious, albeit harsh, way of life. Children are brought up on a diet of violent movies and imported hotdogs, and yet they still have the imprint of the hunting traditions in their daily lives. Cultural confusion haunts their future. They too, it seems, are lost between past and present.

Finally, thirty years after my first visit, I returned to Thule to see for myself what had changed in my Arctic homeland, and more importantly, to rekindle the relationships with the people of my childhood, rediscover my past, and in a sense continue a family tradition − to document the lives and dreams of this extraordinary community on the precipice of change.

2. A Long Way Home

Greenland is a peripheral place; nudging the edges of our world maps and cloaking itself under icecaps as if playing a game of hide and seek. For most of the world whose imagination cannot journey further north than Iceland, Greenland, the largest island on earth after Australia, barely seems to exist at all. This was illustrated quite succinctly by a customer service operator who, when asked if I could use my mobile phone in Greenland, answered, 'Greenland . . . Is that in Scotland?' The mystique of the North has a long tradition. Captain York, skipper of the explorer Knud Rasmussen's ship *Sokongen* on the 1921–5 Arctic journey, said: 'For you and me, the word "Greenland" used to evoke little more than whiteness and cold. Just to live there must have called for a kind of daily heroism; in a word, to us "Greenland" meant more or less the North Pole.'

The island is a place of incomprehensible proportions and bewildering statistics: it is nine times the size of the British Isles, and of its 848,484 square miles of landmass, less than one-sixth is ice-free. The length, north to south of the country, is equivalent to the distance from the tip of Scotland to the Sahara Desert. Its glaciers alone produce around ten thousand icebergs every year; its icecap contains approximately 10 per cent of the world's fresh water, the weight of which (five miles thick in places) has sunk some of the land to 1,180 feet below sea level. On top of that, if the 2.5 million cubic km of icecap should melt, the surface of the seas worldwide would rise up to six or seven metres, with catastrophic consequences for some of the world's greatest cities (London, New York, Hong Kong and Sydney to name but a few) and would change the shape of every coastal country.

The country is known to the Inuit as *Kalaallit Nunaat*, meaning 'White Earth', and as one they believe that this place is Nature's dominion and that the vast Arctic is a realm bigger than the dreams of the people who walk within it.

From as far back as 330 BC explorers, poets and great thinkers have sought to map and define the Arctic wilderness. For them all it seems to become an exploration not just of its vast and complex beauty, but also of their own relation to it.

This boundary of the known world was christened *Ultima Thule* – 'the furthest place', or 'unknown land' – by the Greek explorer Pytheas of Massalia who edged the southern shores of Greenland in 330 BC, and who spoke of a place where the summer had no night, and 'where neither earth, water, nor air exist separately, but a sort of concretion of all these, resembling a sea-lung, in which the earth, the sea, and all things were suspended, thus forming, as it were, a link to unite the whole together'.

In 1618 Pierre Bertius, cosmographer to Louis XIII, spoke of Greenland in ominous terms:

The cold there cannot be defeated . . . and . . . several people have been killed by it. The winter lasts nine months without rain . . . The very rich protect themselves . . . with fire; others can do no more than rub their feet, while some seek warmth in caves . . . This whole country is full of cruel bears against whom the inhabitants war continuously. Also . . . if what is said is true, there are unicorns. All maintain that there are men called pygmies . . . The pygmies, it seems, have a human form, with hair that falls to the tips of their fingers and beards that reach to their knees, but they are brutes with neither language nor reason . . . they hiss like geese . . .

For the Europeans and Americans that followed two centuries later, the Arctic held different promises: adventure, wealth and even fame. But the Arctic did not care for these whims of 'civilized' man. These fair-skinned conquerors perished in their hundreds; the Arctic respected neither rank nor goodness of heart, and as their ships were crushed by ice, and as their bodies rotted both inside and out with frostbite and scurvy, both officers and crew grew wild with madness, fighting both the light that blinded them, and the darkness that struck them with unknown terrors. Some, such as the ill-fated Franklin expedition of 1845, succumbed to the unimaginable horror of cannibalism.

The lucky ones returned home with stories of derring do, and to their fascinated audiences they waxed lyrical about the mythological beasts such as the narwhal, which they described as being both unicorn and mermaid, and the magnificence of the icescape. Here, for instance, is William McKinlay aboard *The Jeanette* in the Canadian Arctic Expedition of October 1913:

Huge ice-blocks larger than houses were being tossed about like pebbles! What stupendous forces must have been at work with millions of tons of ice on either side trying to make way in opposite directions! As we watched this terrifying work of Nature, we noticed that the area of contention was creeping slowly but surely towards us, & we fell to wondering, with a shudder, what would be our lot . . . To the East, West & South, are seething masses of ice battling for supremacy, grinding, crushing, groaning, roaring ice . . .

They told tales of the primitive peoples they encountered, whose tools were as rudimentary as Stone Age implements, whose vocabulary had no alphabet, whose skin shivered with lice and whose women were traded as freely as their fine furs. They told the public on their return that the Arctic aborigines were as innocent and uncultured as the animals they hunted, and as such should be treated as children; and yet these people whom in their ignorance their visitors dismissed as no more than curiosities or even savages, had survived for centuries in this wondrous, desperate place, and had in fact saved many a polar hero.

Returning to Thule had been something that I had wanted to

do for thirty years, even if for the most part it had been a childish
passion. But now my dream had defined edges. It had solidified
into a Plan; manifested itself in schedules, budgets and a growing
conviction that this return to my 'roots' was less about choice
than it was about destiny. The enormity of the project began to
overwhelm me.

These days it takes, on average, about four days to reach Qaanaaq
from the UK, and all four days are weather dependent. When
we first travelled up to Thule things were not so easy. A passage
aboard either the annual supply ship or the coal ship could take
between ten days and a month to reach Northwest Greenland,
and the only other alternative was to fly courtesy of the military
to the American Thule airbase at Pituffik (requiring special
permission from the US government); the final ninety miles
north to the administrative town of Qaanaaq was either by
helicopter, boat or dog-sledge. In comparison this journey would
be easy; a new airstrip had recently been built at Qaanaaq and I
was now able to fly direct, albeit with a number of refuelling
stops and aircraft changes.

Everything around me was glaring white: the starched tablecloth, the origami napkin folded into a preening bird, the fine
bistro crockery. It was like having a preview of the absolute
whiteness awaiting me. I sat transfixed by the lump of ice floating
in my glass of mineral water, recalling a lesson from a dull
geography class over fifteen years before: 'Four-fifths of an iceberg lies *under* the water.' It had been the most interesting thing
I had learnt in geography. I could almost hear the rasping voice
of the teacher whose tweed jacket smelt faintly of Old Spice and
whose classes were an exercise in the statistical analysis of crops
and populations, never the nature and the life-blood of the
countries we studied. My father despaired of my lack of understanding of where different countries lay in relation to one
another, but it was always hard to explain that I passed my exams
knowing how to colour in a pie chart, not by expressing the

complexities of a pygmy's dietary habits, or the climate of Siberia.

'Excuse me, Kari Herbert?' A voice broke into my reverie and I looked up feeling slightly foolish. The fastidiously groomed receptionist smiled and handed me a large brown envelope. I thanked her with my single word of Danish, ordered an emergency glass of wine from a passing waitress and opened the envelope. My fingers recoiled instantly from the unexpected texture of the object inside. The sealskin folder flashed silver in the bright light of the restaurant, and I caught the eye of a lone Nordic businessman, who was tenderly stroking a gin and tonic with perfectly manicured hands, openly watching me.

For the last three months I had been in constant motion preparing for this, the biggest project of my life so far, a dream come true, while I was also forced to confront the failing health of my father. The years of sheer bloody-minded endurance in the Arctic had taken their toll, and his body was now dealing with a different set of challenges – diabetes and heart disease. With the long journey ahead of me I wondered if I was abandoning my responsibilities. If there was an emergency at home it could be at least a week before I could get back.

I was shaking at the enormity of it all. I was making my way to the very edge of civilization, a place lost in its own concept of light and darkness. And then there was also the arrival in Thule to consider; my parents had confessed to me years before that they were very worried that if I ever returned to the Arctic I would be hugely disappointed, that the magic would have disappeared. Of course, since I started this project in earnest they were both full of encouragement, even when Dad was at his most fragile in a hospital bed. They were both determined that I should not cancel my plans, and I could still see the glow of the Arctic in their eyes whenever I spoke of the trip. It was that more than anything that encouraged me to take a leap of faith and leave.

I caught sight of myself sitting in the luxurious Copenhagen Hilton Kastrup finding strength in a glass of chilled Chablis, a

sealskin folder at my side containing my airline ticket to Greenland and a postcard of a polar bear from Greenland Tourism
wishing me an exciting trip. I was growing increasingly terrified
of the possibility that I would find myself alienated from the
people I had always assumed to be a fundamental part of my life.
I feebly comforted myself with the thought that the Inughuit are
warm and hospitable people, even to strangers, so how could
they turn away from someone who had lived with them and
whose first words were in their tongue?

I retired to the snowy plateau of my hotel bed and slept fitfully,
dreaming of missed planes and fragile bridges of glassy ice over
chasms of thunderous waters, and woke with a cold terror as the
bridge desiccated and disappeared beneath my feet.

As is only to be expected when travelling to the High Arctic,
my journey started with a delay. I had arrived at the airport pale
from lack of sleep and nerves at five o'clock in the morning, and
spent the next six hours staring at the departures board and
watching portly Danes knocking back jugs of frothy beer for
breakfast. The plane was delayed, it was pointlessly confirmed,
but no one had any idea how long it would be before we could
leave. A woman nudged me at the information desk: 'Do you
know that this airline is called "Ammaqqa Air" – Maybe Air?'
She shook her head and stumbled off to the snack bar. The final
call was announced with such a tone of authority that it felt like
we were on the brink of a national emergency.

Kangerlussuaq is home to the only international airport in
Greenland, and is little more than a cluster of sombre buildings
that hark back to the days when air travel was purely for the
transportation of mail, emergency supplies and the occasional
governmental worker or explorer. Sondre Stromfjord – as it
was known before it reverted to its Greenlandic name – was
established along with several other airbases in the Second World
War as a line of defence against possible German attack. The
mastermind behind the construction of these airbases had been

Colonel Bernt Balchen, the pioneer aviator who had been an aircraft engineer with Amundsen during his historic trans-Arctic flight across the North Pole from Spitsbergen to Alaska in 1926, and the pilot of Admiral Byrd's sixteen-hour flight to the South Pole in 1929. My father knew him well – in fact, he even named a mountain after this modest 'giant' of a man, overlooking the icefalls of the Axel Heiberg Glacier down which he had flown on his return from the South Pole. The mountain is part of the 'Herbert Range' and thus the bond between them was established.

There was also a bond, of sorts, between Sondre Stromfjord and my father, for it was at this place that he had brought the dogs ashore after his journey up the west coast of Greenland in 1960, buying huskies for the New Zealand Expedition to the Antarctic. The only thing that marked the place out in my memory, however, was its ability to breed gargantuan mosquitoes, which were eight times the size of their southern cousins. I clearly remembered the horror of the hotel room walls weeping with the blood of previous occupants and the suffocating clouds of airborne predators with their incessant high-pitched humming.

The airport itself has changed considerably over the years, and is now a modern complex housing two curio shops, a duty-free outlet, an overpriced hotel complete with a canteen serving hot-dogs and Danish pastries, and a five-star restaurant for wealthy patrons whose planes are delayed. With a couple of hours to kill I wandered outside to join the ranks of thickset outdoor types in matching fleeces baring their solid calves to the +3°C heat. We watched the small Dash 7 aircraft busying themselves on the tarmac, and I felt thankful that the plague of insects was nothing like my memory, and for the fact that I was spared rushing to the shop to buy thick stockings sprayed with insect repellent to wear under my trousers.

I brushed a long-legged mosquito from my face and gazed up at the sky, bleached with the summer sun. A sign cast a weak

shadow on my hand resting on a dark railing: London 3 hours
25 minutes, New York 4 hours, North Pole 3 hours 15 minutes.
I smiled and thought of my father, visualizing the almost entirely
disintegrated Union Jack flag over the fireplace at home that was
for one moment 'the North Pole', and was overcome with a
sense of familiarity. A tinny voice squawked from the sound
system announcing my flight to Ilulissat, and I shouldered my
rucksack, now filled with hope, and headed towards the waiting
plane.

The legendary Eric the Red gave Greenland its name in around
986 AD to entice settlers from his Icelandic home, from which
he was exiled after being pronounced a murderous outlaw. Five
years after first setting foot on this great mass of land and ice, the
Norse chieftain returned with twenty-five ships, of which only
fourteen survived, carrying five hundred hopeful pilgrims, who
established a farming community which thrived, for a time, in
Southwest Greenland in the present district of Godthåb. It is
generally believed that he made up the name 'Greenland' in
order to entice prospective real estate buyers, but in fact the
southern part of Greenland to which the Nordic settlers sailed
would have been verdant and therefore enticing in the summer
months, and so perhaps Eric wasn't quite the conman as has been
supposed. A promotional video shown on the plane showed
gently rambling fields of lush crops and rippling grass, and was
far more reminiscent of the lowlands of Scotland than the desolation of its reputation. Further north, however, the landscape
changes dramatically.

It was a barren grey desert that stretched endlessly beneath us as
we headed north of Kangerlussuaq. Vibrant pools of improbable
colour punctuated the hills of monotone – toxic lakes of copper-
and viridian-green, interspersed with deep pools of peacock- and
azure-blue – and beyond, shimmering to the east, the icecap
shrouded the land. Nowhere was there any indication of life.

We were greeted in Ilulissat by a lethargic signalman who

vaguely motioned the Dash 7 aircraft towards the terminal building, swinging a pair of wheel blocks like censers. Behind me a
six-year-old suddenly babbled in Greenlandic and I felt another
quiver of familiarity.

Logistically I had to spend a night at the West Greenlandic
town of Ilulissat before continuing my journey to the Thule
district – now known as the municipality of Avernassuaq – the
following day, and it was a welcome stopover. Ilulissat is beside
the Ice Fjord, a place of extraordinary beauty, and the home of
Sermeq Kujalleg, the world's most productive calving glacier. This
one glacier alone, moving at an average speed of up to thirty
metres per day, produces around 10 per cent of all the icebergs
between Greenland and Canada. It is likely that it was a rogue
iceberg from Sermeq Kujalleg that sank the *Titanic*.

A passing acquaintance in London had put me in contact with
a Danish architect living in Ilulissat, and he had kindly invited
me to stay with him before the next leg of my journey. I much
preferred the idea of staying in someone's home rather than in
an impersonal hotel, so I had gratefully accepted the offer. Kjeld
Kemp looked every bit the architect, with a polished brow, sharp
black shirt and perfunctory but generous manner. He shook
my hand fiercely and without hesitation installed me in his
Scandinavian-style house.

The towns of western and southern Greenland have been
heavily influenced by European settlers, and on first impression
seem little more than an annexe of Scandinavia. Doll's house
architecture dominated the dusty streets, sprinkling bright
primary colours throughout the miniature urban sprawl, the
cheerful homes holding their own against the long shadows
of the four-storey apartment blocks that stand as sickly grey
monuments to the scandalously unimaginative housing for the
poor.

Kjeld's house was an airy creation of polished wood and clean
lines, with vast windows on two sides overlooking the Ice Fjord
and a veranda that hung precariously over a smooth drop of rock.

This was the home of a hard-working bachelor; the largest room was given over to the office which bristled with computers and plans for new buildings, the music system piled high with CDs of Tina Turner and Whitney Houston, the fridge stocked with a couple of bottles of Tuborg beer, out-of-date condiments and a small fresh assortment of cold meats for his guest.

'Use the phone, use the Internet, make yourself at home!' he exclaimed with open arms. 'I have to go and work, but we will have dinner at a friend's house later.' The door clunked behind him. 'Use the phone!' he called from outside, and then he was gone. I walked down the narrow corridor to the room he had allocated for me. The room was functional and an addiction to work had spilled over into this tiny office-bedroom too. A desk dominated the room, on which an A4 piece of paper prominently shrieked 'use the phone!' once again; the cordless handset rested on the paper. The single bed was perfectly made up with one corner of the duvet turned down precisely, a bottle of mineral water, an apple and a bottle opener had been placed on the bedside table. I wondered vaguely if this would be the last time I would lie in a proper bed with a duvet until my return home, and whether this would be the last piece of fruit I would see for the next seven weeks.

The ice called and I quickly escaped the house and made my way to a small deserted jetty on the edge of the fjord. The dark water growled from below, protesting at the shards of ice that pierced its liquid skin. The ice in turn rolled and circled over the surface as if it was being stirred by an unseen teaspoon. Small fishing trawlers and solitary fishermen negotiated the choked waters in brightly coloured boats, sending dull hollow thuds ricocheting off vast icy amphitheatres as small boulders of ice struck the hull. An occasional clap of thunder in a pristine blue-sky day belied the instability of the huge ice mountains as they partly collapsed in great ten-storey tower blocks, sending shockwaves through the water, which in places was the consistency of porridge. I was mesmerized by the icebergs, slowly dancing at the whim of invisible currents and felt my skin prickle with the conflicting warmth of the sun and the icy breath from the fjord.

I finally crawled into bed, exhausted after an evening with Kjeld's friends, where for most of the evening I couldn't even focus properly let alone participate in intelligent conversation. I had been awake for over twenty-four hours. Our host had been a gentle bear of a Dane with a rampant beard and rebellious hair whose life of teaching in Greenland had promoted a consistent affair with the bottle in whose warm forgetfulness he had perhaps lingered to avoid the pain of a too sensitive heart. His fresh-faced nineteen-year-old daughter had talked eagerly to me all evening over the coquettish giggles of three bottle-blonde Danish women.

We had returned to the house in the early hours of the morning, still bathed in light; there would be no more darkness for me until my return to Copenhagen. At that moment I wished that I had gazed longer at the stars at home. Often, travellers from the temperate zone find that the rhythms of the Arctic confuse both body and mind. We are so accustomed to the ebb and flow of light and darkness that the uncharted passing of time makes us uneasy and we teeter on the edge of primeval disorientation. For me the absence of the moon and stars holds an even deeper significance. Throughout my life, whenever I felt the first pangs of nostalgia or homesickness I would gaze up at the stars and imagine the people I loved at home looking up simultaneously at the same constellations.

Kjeld bade me goodnight and suggested I lock my bedroom door: 'My neighbour sometimes pays unexpected visits if he has had a little to drink. He is a Greenlander and shouldn't be any trouble, but just in case . . .' But although I was dog-tired I had another restless night. I had for months dreamed of Greenland, every single night, and this was no exception. The icebergs of the fjord ground into my subconscious. Suffocated by the light, I woke thrashing in the coils of the duvet that had wound itself tightly around my legs. For the last six years I had been travelling the world in my capacity as a photographer and writer, and in all that time I have never experienced such a tremendous bout of nerves.

In no time at all Kjeld's voice roused me from my light sleep, calling me for breakfast. Again he was dressed immaculately and at 5.45 a.m. had laid out a spread of English Breakfast tea – 'I thought tea was appropriate' – and fresh hot rolls with jam. I was too excited to eat but managed a few mouthfuls to be polite before rushing to the airport, promising to tell him some great stories on my return.

The airport was utterly deserted. I was thirty minutes early and no one had arrived yet. Before long the doors burst open and two young men struggled into the small building carrying a large box between them that was emanating loud shrieks and twitters. They smiled and then dashed off again, leaving me alone with the box, inside which something was flapping about frantically. I waited uncomfortably for the men's return; the container looked far too flimsy for this internal assault and I prepared myself for the imminent escape of the mysterious creature.

A few relays and a couple more luggage bearers later and the group of four travellers sank wearily into the hard airport lounge chairs surrounded by boxes and bulging duffle bags. They were scientists, 'but sort of ornithologists really', going up to the Thule airbase from which they could study falcons. I asked them what was in the box. 'Pigeons,' the team leader answered straight-faced. 'We heard that the postal services are not so good up here.'

We chatted amiably about our respective projects as we waited for the small aircraft to fire up. I was grateful for the company, and I was starting to get a sense of the uniqueness of this journey. The further I travelled north, the more the people changed. The last couple of flights had been filled with a mixture of business people and outdoor enthusiasts, and the odd pensioner couple whose freedom and adventurous spirit had been paid for by a lifetime of savings. This last leg to Qaanaaq via Upernavik had a different clientele: returning Inughuit who had been visiting family further south, the scientists, and me.

The stout Greenlandic stewardess smiled beatifically at her charges, who took up only eight seats at the rear of the tiny aircraft, and elegantly mimed the safety procedures, indicating with a sweep of her hand where we could find the 'polar suits' should we crash anywhere over the uninhabited coastline or icecap between Ilulissat and Qaanaaq. The safety card showed a cartoon of someone looking immobile and perplexed sitting on the ice. There are two flights to Qaanaaq during the week, if there is clement weather, and as there is only one supply ship to the area each year, the flights are used as much for the transportation of mail and fresh supplies as they are for fee-paying passengers. In this case half of the seats from the front of the plane had been removed and in their place was a bulky mountain of goods – fresh food, mail-order clothing, baggage and scientific equipment – covered by tarpaulins and lashed to the floor in suspiciously loose looking knots. The stewardess pushed a small trolley down the amputated aisle, serving tea, coffee and sweet biscuits to the passengers.

We landed briefly at Upernavik to refuel and exchange some passengers. The short runway grazed a high rock promontory, around which glacial Arctic waters moved in a satin shimmer. Fluid mountains soared upwards in permanent ecstasy. Hearing the boarding call for the last leg of the journey I returned to the terminal building. A seven-year-old girl hurried up to me and with great sincerity gave me a dissected fly as a parting gift.

The young Greenlander smiled as he sat next to me, squeezing his long legs into the limited space of the Dash 7. He is tall for a Greenlander, I thought to myself briefly before gazing out again at a lone iceberg floating majestically in the sound.

'Have you the time?' he asked quietly in Greenlandic. I didn't quite understand, and he grinned. 'Danish, English or Spanish?' he added.

'English,' I replied and smiled, but looked away again, preoccupied with my destination.

'I am worried that they will not understand me in Qaanaaq,' he offered in return, and introduced himself as Martin. We didn't stop talking until we landed.

Martin was in his mid-twenties, and although he had lived his life so far in Upernavik, he liked the idea of travelling the world, and last year had gone on holiday to Spain. He had loved it there and was desperate to go back, but this holiday he had decided to spend a few days in Qaanaaq; he had never been there before and people all over Greenland talked about Thule. 'I have heard that that place is the real Greenland,' he said, and I smiled thinking inwardly that it was strange hearing this from someone who lived as far north as Upernavik.

Martin was an engaging companion, with a dress sense straight out of London and mannerisms that were more than a little camp. 'I am a very gentle and spiritual guy,' he informed me, 'but more in a New Age sort of way than a traditional Inuit way.' He paused. 'I can see that you are spiritual too, which is why I know I can talk to you.' I was flattered by his description. 'I have seen auras,' he continued, 'since I was a little boy, but never really thought anything of it; I presumed that everyone saw what I saw, and it was only later that I discovered that I was "different".' His brow furrowed gently. 'Suddenly it was something to be scared of, and I had a lot of problems with my gifts until I met a western woman, a healer. Do you know what a healer is? It was her who taught me the goodness of these qualities and encouraged me to work with them.' He looked into the middle distance dreamily. She really changed his life, he murmured quietly. 'Now I meditate all the time, and I can feel illness in people when I stand close to them.'

The frankness of the conversation had taken me completely by surprise. The Inughuit of the Thule district have always been in a sense a spiritual people, but their ancient beliefs are rooted in animalism and certainly not in what is now branded as being

New Age philosophies. Hearing about healing, meditation and clairvoyancy from a Greenlander was not at all what I was expecting to encounter in the Arctic.

'Do you have asthma?' Martin asked with a knowing look.

'Um, no I don't,' I replied, almost wishing I did so as not to disappoint him.

'Anything wrong with your lungs?' I shook my head.

'Ah, it must be someone behind me then.' I turned and looked around, but no one seemed to be short of breath. Martin was unperturbed. 'Sometimes,' he continued, 'I have clear pictures in my head of something happening in someone's life.' He pulled out a pack of tarot cards from a record case under the seat. 'Do you know what these are?' he asked, watching me carefully to see if I would be insulted or shocked at them. I nodded, amused; I had spent the latter part of my childhood living in Totnes in South Devon, which for decades has been a hangout for all sorts of alternative practitioners. I didn't think a pack of tarot cards was likely to faze me. Two of the scientists across the aisle looked over, suppressing giggles. I gave Martin my full attention. The tarot cards were colourfully illustrated with every conceivable sort of angel. 'You can't be frightened by angels,' Martin murmured, although his tone suddenly made me not so sure. He shuffled the cards over and over again and finally, after expertly cutting and dealing, the cards lay in formation, bunched up on the small airline table in front of us. The reading, he said, would be for the next three months.

'You are to have a vision. Your trip has great purpose —' he made a sound as if it was all becoming clear — 'there will be a gifting but,' he added darkly, 'also a loss of power.' He squeezed my hand reassuringly and gave me the faintest wink before studying the cards again. 'Don't worry, something new will emerge from this loss of power, for which there would be rewards and finally . . . a soul mate and children.' He sat back silently, perhaps in honour of the angels, and looked satisfied before closing his eyes and meditating on the moment. As my father said later when I told him about the reading, 'Well, that just about covers everything.'

I had been so distracted by Martin and his psychic delving that I had completely lost track of where we were, and as the plane came into Qaanaaq I felt my heart leap into my throat. Below us was Herbert Island, the place in the Arctic to which I felt most strongly connected. The sun was high and soft, barely casting any shadows, and Herbert Island itself looked pale, rigid and uncompromising.

We touched down and I was paralysed with excitement and fear. I wanted everyone to get off the plane first so that I could deal with whatever was there to greet me in my own way, under my own steam. What if no one was there to meet me? . . . What if everyone was there to meet me? The scientists patted me on the back encouragingly and Martin walked on ahead after reminding me of my guardian angel. I hovered towards the back of the group as they filed one by one through the doorway to the new terminal building. Peeking over their shoulders I could see a small gathering of faces on the other side, casting their eyes over the new arrivals, some embracing, others standing awkwardly shaking hands. A face raised itself over the throng and looked anxiously at the scientists in front of me, studying their faces briefly before moving further down the line, and then we caught sight of each other.

It was Magda, Baali's twin sister. We shared the uncomfortable moment of seeing each other but being too far apart and with too many people in between to connect us. Then we were in front of each other and clutching each other in a tight embrace. Magda heaved great sobs into my shoulder and all I could do was soothe her and wait for my own tide to break. She looked away, embarrassed at her emotion, and I asked her if she was OK. She nodded and held her face in her hands for a moment before speaking rapidly to me in Greenlandic. I didn't have the first idea of what she was saying. All I could make out was something about Louisa – one of the sisters with whom I should be staying – being ill, that she was in Nuuk and that something was seriously wrong. Louisa's husband was introduced to me fleetingly before he fled into the throng again and I stood in a whirl waiting for my luggage, wondering what on earth was going on.

A warm hand rested reassuringly on my shoulder for a moment and I heard someone say 'welcome' to me behind my ear. It was Hans Jensen, owner of the hotel in Qaanaaq, whom I had met briefly once before in Nuuk and with whom my father had spent some time on his various trips to Qaanaaq. 'It looks as though you have been well received,' he said smiling and I felt as though I was about to explode with tears. I had no idea that I had got myself into such an emotional state. I was relieved that he was there, and he relayed what Magda was telling me in English. 'Louisa has been taken ill,' he told me, looking at me with concern. 'She has been rushed to hospital in Nuuk, maybe it is something to do with her baby, she is pregnant you know.' I was confused and worried; it must be something serious as there is a hospital in Qaanaaq, and others even better equipped between Qaanaaq and Nuuk. The flight to Nuuk itself would take an entire day at least. I had many questions unanswered but Hans Jensen left all of a sudden to attend to his waiting guests, and I was left hauling my luggage off the carousel with Magda, both of us with streaming eyes and bitten lips. How sick was Louisa? And where was I going to stay now? I shook off my worries knowing that now Magda was there I would surely be all right, and would find a floor somewhere where I could sleep until I could learn more about the situation. I shook hands with the scientists, wished them good luck and followed my 'sister' out of the airport.

A pickup truck was waiting outside and Magda and I scrambled into the back seat, my bag slung into the back with Louisa's husband sitting unceremoniously on top. 'Welcome to Qaanaaq!' a voice bellowed at me in English, and I looked up stunned into the round face of the driver; he grinned happily and I laughed and thanked him as Magda's hand found mine and clasped it in a fierce grip before folding herself into the crook of my arm.

The convoy to town kicked up plumes of dust from the single-track dirt road that wound along the coast, casting thick veils over the dark embrace of mountains and the hungry tongues of glaciers lapping the clear waters of Inglefield fjord. I could see Martin in the back of the pickup in front, squashed in between other visiting Greenlanders and stony-faced Inughuit workers; covering his face from the dust with an immaculate black sleeve, he seemed so out of place in this rugged landscape.

Magda crushed my hand again and pointed towards Herbert Island. 'Home,' she said.

3. Lifting the Veil

The pickup truck ground to a halt outside a smart dark-green house overlooking the church and a modern assembly of swings, slides and other playground games. Magda finally freed my crushed fingers from her grip and nimbly leapt out of the truck, disappearing into Louisa's house. I scrambled after her and automatically pulled off my boots and parka in the hallway.

It was not the home of a hunting family. In fact it was quite the opposite. Blond polished wooden floors swept through the main living space, frilly burgundy curtains hung from wrought-iron poles framing new double-glazed windows, and exotic plants basked in the steady 28°C heat provided by modern radiators. An enormous wide-screen television dominated the room. The home had modern femininity stamped all over it, and none of the homely frugality of the huts of the past. This place was devoid of smells and fresh meat, and was neatly ordered.

Magda's wiry frame flitted from one side of the room to another with restless excitement, not knowing quite where to put herself and what to show me first. She sat down abruptly at the dining table and indicated that I should join her, and then instantly changed her mind and scuttled up the stairs, beckoning me to follow. I skidded inelegantly in her wake, my thermal socks finding no purchase on the wooden floor.

Magda knocked softly on one of the two bedroom doors before opening it to reveal a bedroom that could belong to a teenager anywhere in the world. Plastered all over the walls were glossy posters of Britney Spears and magazine pullouts of various boy and girl bands. Pink gauze curtains gently moved in the fresh Arctic breeze. Sitting on the bed were two girls in their early teens who looked up at me curiously, but with little emotion.

Magda introduced the more aloof of the two as Karen, Louisa's daughter, whose room I would be sharing for the next few weeks. She gave me a sullen look, and flashed me an ironic grin for good measure. Her cousin Suakunguak looked torn between following her friend's example, and being friendly. She gave me a coy smile. Magda pointed towards a thin foam mattress in one corner of the room resting on a low wooden support, where I would be sleeping. This was more than I had hoped for, and I turned to smile broadly at the girls. Karen ignored me, and Suakunguak's eyes fluttered downwards in embarrassment. I looked at Magda and she lifted her eyes to heaven and shrugged.

Magda led the way back downstairs and poured me a cup of tea from a tall white Thermos flask. No battered kettle on the stove now, no having to go outside to chip ice off an iceberg to melt for your tea. Most of the houses in Qaanaaq now have running water, which is either drained off the inland ice in summer or melted at the water plant from icebergs collected by digger from the ice field in winter and spring. The tea brought me back to my senses and its aromatic warmth filled me with nostalgia in the midst of so much modernization.

Magda and I sat and looked at each other, beaming idiotically, wanting to say a million things and not knowing how to say them. We stop-started sentences, talking over each other in tangles then ground to a halt and giggled foolishly before taking it in turns to try out snippets of Greenlandic on each other, but to no avail. I had naively thought that I would be struck by a tidal wave of remembered vocabulary and instead I was riding a wave of lost voices.

In an attempt to find a common thread of discussion I delved into my rucksack and finally found a small album of photographs that I had hastily put together before leaving London. It was a strange compilation of images, many from when we first lived on Herbert Island; pictures of the Qaerngâq children and myself as we were growing up and moments of time with Maria, Avatak,

Aata and Aana and other characters of the community, to all of whom I had once felt kin. Magda pointed to each person in each picture, telling me their name and asking me if I remembered them. I did. Here was a picture of the eldest sister Najannuaq feeding me with baby food, there a picture of me gazing up at big brother Arquenguak, seated in miniature polar bear pants and a chunky sweater that made my arms stick out at right angles to my body. Baali, she told me as we pointed at her twin sister in one of the pictures, was hunting with her husband further down the fjord; Ilannguak too was away. Then we reached a black-and-white portrait of Maria. In it she looked serene and thoughtful. It was taken when she and Avatak were happy together.

'*Anaana* . . .' I ventured, '*Naniitoq*, where is she, is she here in Qaanaaq?'

'*Nu-uh*, No,' Magda replied, touching the image briefly before looking up to hold my eyes with a glimmer of heartbreak. '*Anaana* dead.'

I felt my knees buckle slightly. I felt for the chair and sat down heavily. Over the years I had imbued the memory of Maria with perhaps impossible qualities; she was the key-keeper to part of my life story. If she had not been in Qaanaaq I would have travelled the Arctic to find her.

I sat in numbed silence as Magda explained to me that her mother had died of a heart attack the previous year. I looked at her in bewilderment, searching her eyes deeply, but not a tremor seemed to pass through her body as she continued to flick through the rest of the pictures. Death comes all too often to this community for it to wrench continued heartache from its inhabitants.

'*Agiri*, come,' she said softly, and pulled me off my seat. She spoke rapidly in Greenlandic and I lost her thread. She laughed at my confused expression and repeated herself slowly. We were to go to her house, I finally understood, and from there she would call the others on her telephone. Well practised myself in cauterizing grief, I took a deep breath and fell out of the door behind her.

The town was quiet and sleepy in the afternoon haze. Husky pups tumbled across the streets and children in bright urban clothing played in the dirt or hung nonchalantly off the wooden railings of the stairs and walkways that zigzagged across town, crossing thick insulated pipes that service most of the homes in Qaanaaq. I wondered vaguely where the children got their modern clothes from, and then remembered that even when we lived on Herbert Island the children often wore western clothes that had been bought from the rudimentary stores in Qaanaaq or were presents from the Americans at the airbase.

In the distance Qaanaaq's generator rumbled persistently, providing electricity to every home in the town (many of the smaller villages in the area still do not have electricity). The huts seemed to hover above the ground on their stilted platforms. Most houses in the Arctic are raised off the ground, for two reasons: first, so that the warmth of the house does not melt the permafrost on which they are built and cause subsidence, and secondly, so that drifting snow cannot seal up the doorways and hold the occupants to ransom. The brightly coloured houses clustered together like a crowd of gossiping grand-dames, picking up their skirts so that their hems would not be dirtied by the dog faeces and forgotten debris that had been uncovered by the summer melt of the snows and blown around their ankles.

Qaanaaq had become houseproud. Lace curtains fluttered at the windows, rubbish was mostly contained within black plastic binliners, and piles of ageing blubber added character to only the most traditional of houses. On first impressions the inhabitants of Qaanaaq seemed to have doused their lifestyle in disinfectant.

Magda's house was one of a long line of grey-painted shoe-boxes. Inside and out her home was much more humble than her sister's; plain linoleum covered the floor and the few pieces of simple furniture huddled at one end of the room. A small collection of medals, won from various hunting contests, were strung up on colourful ribbons enlivening one whitewashed wall. It was frugal, but clean and clearly the home of a modern hunter and his family. Once again tea was poured and Magda visibly relaxed; she was now free to be the hostess she had wanted to be from the start. Still full of energy, she leapt to the phone and plucked at the dial, talking rapidly into the receiver. Disembodied voices sounded surprised on the other end of the line. Magda chatted eagerly, looking at me and grinning as she spoke. I perched on the side of the sofa and nibbled a biscuit while Magda busied herself lighting small candles on the coffee table and preparing more hot flasks of tea and coffee for the expected deluge of guests.

The telephone calls quickly galvanized the family and in just a few moments there was a hurried bustling in the hallway and Najannuaq, the eldest of the family, and her eight-year-old son Orfik bundled in. She grinned and gathered me in a tight embrace before letting go abruptly and sitting on the couch adjacent to mine. Her son hung back bashfully, his eyes flashing inquisitively under a reddish mop of hair. Najannuaq steadily poured herself a cup of tea and then leant back to study my face. 'How was your trip?' she asked in English. I almost choked. I hadn't expected any of the sisters to be able to speak English and I could have hugged her again with relief. I babbled. She listened, ran a hand through her wiry hair and distractedly stirred sugar into her tea. Her face flickered between amusement and boredom and . . . something I couldn't quite pinpoint. My conversation petered out in the face of her apparent uninterest.

'I work at the, agh . . .' She struggled for the right word in annoyance, and between us we concluded that she worked at the Post Office. 'I have lunch break. I go now.' She walked away, preoccupied, but as an afterthought she turned, her eyes momentarily bright. 'Good to see you,' she said, leaving me all the more bewildered. Magda seemed completely oblivious to the fleeting visit, and then also left to go to the store.

I stood in the centre of the room uncertainly, not knowing

what to expect next. Then Arquenguak arrived. The younger of
the two brothers, Arquenguak had always been in the shadow
of his big brother Ilannguak. Both Maria and Avatak had on
occasion confessed their concerns to my parents that the young
boy seemed too sensitive for the life of a hunter, but he had
nevertheless followed in the tradition of the male members of
his family. Now his bulk filled the doorframe, and he smiled at
me from across the room with shy, liquid eyes. Overcome with
embarrassment at his obvious emotion, Arquenguak painstakingly took his time to take off his thin Goretex jacket and pull
his socks up carefully. I could hardly bear it, and crossed the
room myself to greet him. He smiled, his full mouth trembling
ever so slightly and returned my hug with a quick tight squeeze
before clearing his throat and looking helplessly at his wife for a
second before picking up a plastic bag and bolting for the sink.

'Hello.' I smiled warmly at his wife Tukúmek, who nodded
at me with the briefest of smiles before sitting down. Arquenguak
busied himself with slicing something up in the kitchen. Tukúmek was a beautiful woman, with light caramel skin, flashing
doe eyes and a wide sensuous mouth. Her long ponytail of raven
hair slid enigmatically over one shoulder. She bombarded me
with questions in Greenlandic.

'I cannot remember the language,' I said, colouring with
embarrassment and shifting under her hard gaze. I remembered
that she spoke English from the last time we met several years
ago, but also I knew that, quite naturally, she resented speaking
in a language that was not naturally her own.

'What are you doing here?' she repeated impatiently, this
time in English. I explained that I had wanted to meet my
'family' again, and that I was writing a book. She raised a wary
eyebrow.

Arquenguak stood by the window, looking uncomfortable,
his eyes searching every surface to purchase a hold on something
that wouldn't give his emotions away. He carefully smoothed
his thick fringe to one side.

'I need to learn Greenlandic again,' I added.

'Yes,' she said brusquely, 'you do,' and left me alone at the table. I was utterly deflated.

Arquenguak returned to the sink. I got up to join him, and he smiled beatifically at me brandishing a worn knife. '*Neri*, eat!' he offered encouragingly – in the sink was a plastic bag filled with raw whale blubber from which he was cutting small chunks and popping them in his mouth. Tukúmek leant over his shoulder and cut off a lump for herself, slicing thin slivers off it and chewing noisily, the *mattak* crunching between her brilliant white teeth.

'Are you hungry?' she asked with her mouth full, pointing to the blubber.

'Er, no thanks, I have eaten,' I replied and they smiled knowingly at me. It would take me a couple of days to adjust to the local diet. Tukúmek looked out over the fjord, the light glancing off her high proud cheekbones, her primrose-yellow vest echoing the sunlight. Her body had thickened from having children and her posture was worn down slightly from an outdoor life, but she must have been stunning as a young girl. When she smiled she radiated.

Before long Arquenguak and Tukúmek left in order to prepare their boat for a trip later in the day, and once again I was alone. For a while I just sat there, feeling as if I was sitting on the edge of the world.

Magda finally returned, panting, grinning from ear to ear with a bag of food which she quickly packed away before coming over to me and briefly squeezing my hand. As if they had sensed that food was imminent, her family threw themselves through the front door. Her son Rasmus leapt on the couch and switched on the TV eyeing me mischievously. Her husband nodded in greeting and sat down at the table, heavy with confidence. His hair fell in a soft quiff over a strong dark brow and a well-proportioned face. He looked like an Inughuit James Dean. Magda looked at him lovingly. 'Gideon, my husband,' she cooed and looked at me in delight. '*Kusannaq* . . . he is beautiful!' she whispered loudly and nudged me for my approval.

Gideon talked in firm conversational tones, which I gathered to be something about hunting and the state of his boat. Magda commiserated, making concerned noises. It was not long before I felt that I was overstaying my welcome; after briefly acknowledging my presence Gideon had demanded all of Magda's attention, and I could see that she was torn between being with me and indulging her husband's demands. By then I was craving some time to myself to muddle through the experience so far, and I left with relief promising Magda I would see her the following day. I was still reeling from the shock of hearing about Maria's death, and I had to make my peace with the news before I could do anything else. I let my feet take me on the familiar dust track out to the cemetery.

PLOT 98: Avatak Qaerngâq

The grave was slightly shabby and unkempt – life had continued without him, and eventually the colour had faded from the wreath of fake flowers, and with it the grief. But at that moment I felt it acutely. The four-day journey, the long-nurtured expectations, the disjointed reunions and stark revelations had all taken their toll and I was awash with emotion.

I thought back to the last time I saw Avatak, my memory of it now merged with the story my parents told me of our dramatic departure from this place and its people that we had grown to love so deeply.

We left the village on the edge of twilight, amid tears and fierce embraces. Avatak led the way with his sledge loaded with our belongings; we followed behind, our sledge heavy with the rest of the equipment, and me inside a shelter that Dad had constructed at the back of the sledge, lit by a single hurricane lamp. Maria rode the sledge with us over the pressure ridge and away from the village as a final gesture of friendship. Arquenguak and Ilannguak ran alongside. Out on the ice Maria whispered a soft goodbye to my mother, touched her arm and slipped off the sledge and into the darkness with her sons. The dying flicker of her torch nodded to us as we grew further apart. We travelled in velvet darkness under a vast canopy of stars; the hurricane lamp glowed like a Chinese lantern: a pinprick of orange light in a sea of black.

The journey to Thule Airbase was hazardous, and familiar to my parents as being the one that almost claimed their lives nearly two years before. This time we had the comfort of having Avatak with us, who knew the route as well as he knew the lines on his hands. But unlike Avatak who was driving dogs we were using a skidoo, which is notoriously more difficult to control on uncompromising glacial surfaces.

The start of the journey had been smooth over the unbroken ice, but as we rounded the moraine at the foot of the glacier my parents found that it had changed dramatically from when they were last there. Where there had previously been smooth hard ice there were fractured chasms. The moraine was shifting; it was alive and did not take kindly to travellers passing over it. The two men struggled to manoeuvre the sledges over a precarious ice bridge, beneath which a boiling cauldron of black water roared as if from hell itself. The dogs grew mute; sensing the gravity of the situation, watching the men claw and strain at the sledges and the ice until they finally made it to firmer ground. In an instant the bridge exploded behind them, collapsing in a drama dimly lit by the single lamp still bobbing in the shelter.

We had no choice but to press on up the glacier, and there was no chance of rest until both sledges were in a safer and more sheltered position in case we were overcome with bad weather. I was frightened and distressed and pleaded incessantly to go home. All three of my guardians struggled to ignore my cries, until finally Avatak found a moment of respite from their struggle and popped a knob of frozen butter in my mouth. It soothed me immediately.

It was twelve hours before we had the chance to make camp. The two sledges were placed together, the packing boxes placed side by side to make a platform, and the tent pitched over the top for our shelter. I was full of exuberance after being cooped up for so long, and danced in abandon over the platform before settling beside Avatak, chatting happily in Inuktun and sharing chocolate and hardtack biscuits. The bond was clear between us, and my mother has since written that she realized at that moment it would be hard for Avatak to let me go.

The next indigo day presented more troubles. The usual route down to the sea ice was impassable, and instead we had to turn to a more hazardous route to continue the journey. The skidoo was almost impossible to move over the sharp rocks and vast boulders spewed out by the glacier and the exertion nearly broke the men and strained every muscle in my mother's body.

After another uncomfortable night in an old hunter's hut, which was both filthy and airless, we were off again, but by now we had crossed the glacier, and as we descended to the smooth ice of the fjord the skidoo roared ahead. Somewhere in the darkness we passed Avatak and his dogs – the journey to the small village of Moriussaq close to the airbase took only an hour and a half by skidoo instead of the usual four hours by dog sledge.

A wobble of lanterns greeted us as we neared the settlement as the villagers scrambled out of their houses to greet the mysterious visitors; they had heard our approach from miles away, and immediately we were welcomed into the home of Bibiane and Kaviarssuak, who had given my parents shelter when they were stranded by the storm on their last trip from the airbase. It was some time later before an exhausted Avatak arrived, and I ran to him in delight to be scooped up into his arms.

The next morning we went to collect Avatak for the very last leg of the journey. He was staying in one of the neighbouring houses, and still looked tousled and half asleep as the hosts clattered about making coffee. I scrambled into his lap and talked happily to him, smoothing down his hair. Mum looked at the two of us caught up in our own little world, and found herself fighting back her tears. The difficulty of the journey had distracted her from the heartbreak of our imminent departure.

The airbase was shimmering with light at our approach, and the hitherto hushed Arctic was shattered with the sound of jets screaming overhead. We stopped on the periphery of these disparate worlds and unloaded the equipment from the wooden sledges to a waiting heated vehicle. As Mum wrote in her book *The Snow People*:

As Wally held Kari Avatak stepped forward and buried his head in her neck. My hand reached out to comfort him. '*Inudluarit*, Avatak, Goodbye.' The door slammed and the car sprang into life. I leant out of the window. 'Some time soon we will be back.' But as the engine roared, a weeping man turned away, and my words were lost in the night.

We never saw him again.

My knees gave way beneath me as I choked on the hazy memory. I held a tiny golden Arctic poppy between my fingers – the tundra had taken over Avatak's grave – but I reminded myself that according to Inughuit legacy, his soul still lives on. In his case, it is said, in his grandson.

The horrifying moment of Avatak's death was witnessed by his eldest daughter Najannuaq. The pregnant teenager ran to her father as he collapsed from the shot from his own rifle and she cradled him in her lap as her mother howled with grief and regret and the world spun crazily around them all. His last breath – his spirit they believe – he breathed into her belly. The child became the name, Avatak.

Reincarnation has always been a fundamental part of the belief system of the Inughuit, and the continuation of life in another body is not just the sole preserve of humankind, but of animals too. Time and time again, the Inughuit believe, the spirits of the dead seek a body through which to express themselves. Each spirit has a name, and that name is an essence in itself. The handing on of names therefore holds particular significance for the Inughuit. A baby cries out when it is born, it is said, because it is crying for its name, for without a name a person is incomplete and vulnerable. The newly named is thought to have an intimate bond with the one after whom they were named; therefore if a daughter bears the name of her grandmother, she may be called 'mother' by her father – rather confusingly a daughter could also be named after her dead grandfather in which case her own father could call her 'father'. This does not happen in modern Greenland, but people are still superstitious of names. It is still believed that people sharing the same name have some sort of spiritual bond.

Fake flowers rippled in the midnight sun and I found more familiar graves: a couple of crucifixes away was the last resting place of my father's other solid friend and travelling companion Peter Peary, the Inughuit grandson of the great explorer Robert E. Peary; dead within a couple of months of Avatak, rumoured also to have been shot by his wife, although the official line was suicide. My father and Peter Peary had journeyed together over much of the High Arctic, and the two men together had faced death several times; as my dad once said, 'We survived to laugh at the very fear which drew us closer together.'

I sat quietly on a rock, tinged with the same sombre grey as the earth. Plots of impossible colour from plastic flowers carpeted the ground and I looked up slowly to the name on the new white crucifix. Maria Qaerngâq: In: 18.12.1940 Toq: 09.06.2001.

A family quietly ambled through the graveyard, visiting their deceased family members one by one. The tour ended at the most recent departure, just two graves away from where I was sitting. At each they paused, rearranged a flower or a small stone demarcating their plot and shook their head solemnly. Two girls in modern hip-hop gear clung to each other, inseparable in their teenage friendship. Their mouths worked in unison chewing gum. They gazed over at me blankly, aloof. Two of the older women came over to the grave, looked down at me and then up at the inscription. 'Ah Maria!' one of them exclaimed softly. The other nodded and shrugged her shoulders. They tut-tutted in sympathy, looking at me with open curiosity and walked away, finally leaving me alone with the bitter Arctic breeze curling around my thoughts and memories.

A figure was weaving towards me as I started my walk back to town. The only destination on this path was the graveyard and a flat, deserted piece of earth scattered with oil drums – once the rudimentary landing spot for helicopters from the American airbase, now a dusty football pitch. The woman swayed with each step, squinting at me peculiarly as we neared each other. I greeted her in Greenlandic and she stopped unsteadily.

'*Kinatit?* Who are you?' she slurred.

'Kari,' I replied.

'Eh?' she spat back, wrinkling her nose and turning her ear towards me. I repeated my name and watched a dim light flicker in the recesses of her memory. Something clicked and she babbled incoherently at me in Greenlandic, frequently interspersing the excited diatribe with a slow '*Ajor*' of astonishment and repeated mentions of my father's name. She soon wore herself out and bent over resting her weight on her knees. I bent down with her and asked her if she was OK, only to find her face pressed up against mine, her breath sour and reeking of whisky. She pinched my cheek hard and snorted with what could have passed as a giggle. '*Kaari-gnaa*, our Kari,' she breathed slowly, her fumes making me dizzy, singing: '*Illit Angiho*, you are so big!' She swayed backwards and I lunged to pull her back on her feet. She grasped my hand and yelped, suddenly becoming animated again. I hadn't taken my gloves with me on my walk and my hands were freezing. She rubbed them vigorously with calloused fingers and slapped me hard on the back urging me back towards the town to get warm. Then she turned and giggled and continued weaving her way towards the graveyard.

Louisa's husband was sitting on the sofa talking to his wife on his bright yellow mobile phone when I returned to my new home. The room was thick with the smell of boiled chicken. I could hear Louisa berating him from her hospital bed, and his reply was a constant '*soo, soo* – yes, yes' in West Greenlandic. The distant voice sounded tired and worried, and as I heard the odd tinny word that I recognized it seemed that she was more concerned that I had arrived safely and was being welcomed than about her own situation. Hans flicked his eyes towards me nervously.

Hans seemed most uncomfortable in his own skin, and completely terrified in my presence. His eyes were perpetually watery and I wondered how serious Louisa's condition was. I asked if she was going to be OK and he shrugged, nodded and rubbed his brow fiercely. I wondered if I should be staying there at all, but by now it was nearing midnight, and too late to make other arrangements.

Hans did his utmost to entertain me, pulling out piles of photographs of the family over the years, constantly whistling three notes in the same repetitive order and drumming his fingers on the table as I went through endless repeats of the same pictures. Every time I said something to him he jumped slightly in shock, and then would revert back to tapping his foot agitatedly on the floor and constantly shifting position. Finally I managed to discover that Louisa was supposed to be returning in two days. I sighed with relief; things weren't as critical as I had supposed, and I resolved to talk to Hans Jensen at the hotel the next morning to see if he could give me any more details.

At well past midnight, Karen the thirteen-year-old daughter was still not home. Hans didn't seem openly concerned, and sat staring blankly at the television. I had been awake for twenty-one emotionally charged hours and I was boss-eyed with exhaustion, but I didn't know whether to go to bed, or whether I should stay up until the teenager returned, as I was sleeping in her room. Finally no amount of resolve could keep my eyes open and I staggered upstairs to sleep.

Just as I was crawling into bed Karen returned with a group of friends who ploughed into the bedroom laughing and chattering loudly. The group pulled itself up short as they saw me and whispered urgently to each other, Karen looking darkly in my direction. A boy of fourteen smiled and waved and said something briskly to the others and disappeared into the parents' room with the others in tow. Karen stomped around the bedroom, shot me a chilling look and walked out with her portable music system.

I gazed up at Britney in her pink boob tube and hot pants looking down on me like a blessed Angel of Pop and began to wonder if returning to Thule had been a big mistake.

4. Dawning

I woke feeling disoriented, with Britney still watching over me. I glanced over to Karen's bed; her Coca-Cola duvet was undisturbed and I found myself vaguely worried where she was. Downstairs Hans was already having breakfast and indicated that I should join him. He still seemed a little lost, thrown into a situation he wasn't used to. Louisa probably usually dealt with guests and their teenage daughter, and he was faltering. The wood veneer table was strewn with crumbs, small livid smears of jam and dollops of margarine. He gave me a lopsided smile and shyly handed me a wedge of bread.

It was a beautiful Arctic summer day. The sky stretched endlessly above; infinite space had turned cornflower blue. I felt my cheeks flush from the summer chill as I walked past the colourful houses of the town towards Hans Jensen's small hotel. All around were delicate carpets of wild flowers: white heather was scattered like light snow amongst the bright yellows of Arctic poppies and the lilacs and purples of the saxifrage. Husky pups ran around my feet, yapping and tugging on the hems of my trouser legs with their sharp little teeth. Snow buntings rose in clouds into the air as I passed.

Hans Jensen greeted me warmly and we sat together on the steps of the hotel in the cool sunshine catching up on news and watching the diminutive snow buntings flit back and forth in front of us flashing their white breasts under perfect dark wings. I looked at him fondly; his stout hotelier's frame thinly disguised the mischievous boy beneath. Jolly eyes twinkled behind his glasses. He told me a terrible joke that I immediately forgot.

Hans Jensen had been my first point of contact when I first started planning my return to Thule – he had given me his telephone number when I met him at the Arctic Winter Games in Nuuk a few months before, and he had been wonderfully supportive of my idea to return. He had forewarned the Qaerngâq family that I was going to spend the summer in Qaanaaq, the result of which had been the invitation to stay in Louisa's home.

I asked him what I should do about staying with Louisa considering the new circumstances and he was adamant that I should stay where I was: 'Louisa would be so disappointed if you left now,' he said; 'she told me you were her little sister and that there was no question that you should stay at her house. You are family.' He patted my knee reassuringly and promised he would tell me if he thought that at any point I should make myself scarce.

We were joined then by two men: an American in a leather pilot's jacket and an Englishman in a sensible outdoor coat, who were doing a tour of the Arctic in their private plane. They glowed with enthusiasm about their trip. The American brandished a plastic bag at us: 'Mattak anyone?' The Englishman said, 'I'd prefer chocolate, thank you,' and bit into a Snickers bar. I looked at him enviously, but instead was handed a chunk of wet blubber. It was dense, and too big a mouthful. My jaw started to ache after several minutes of chewing. It tasted something like avocado. The American in the mean time seemed to chew each piece just twice and swallow the chunks whole. The Englishman grimaced.

An ageing Greenlander paddled her way up the steep slope towards us, her eyes downcast as if looking at the ground might make the journey easier. Her flat pink cheeks puffed in and out with the exertion. She looked momentarily startled as she looked up and saw us watching her, then smiled winningly and paused to catch her breath. Two strands of greying hair escaped her floral headscarf and fluttered in the breeze.

As she heaved her way up the steps she glanced my way and paused, as if I reminded her of someone. She seemed familiar.

She looked at the men I was sitting with and thought better of making an introduction and meekly went inside. But as the tourists left to go to the airport she quietly slipped back through the door: 'Kari?' she asked, and as I nodded, still trying to place her, she pointed a thumb to her chest: 'Uanga Naja!' Instantly my memory was brought into focus.

Naja was the widow of Orla Sandborg, the great-hearted Viking of a man who had been the Danish Administrator of the Thule district when we arrived in the early 1970s. Orla had learnt to speak the Thule dialect fluently and had done much for the community; he had also been a great friend and supporter of my parents. He died many years ago, but Naja now stood in front of me in Technicolor. She had come to Qaanaaq for a holiday she told me; she lived in Nuuk, but had so many happy memories here. You could see them dancing in her eyes. I finally left Naja waving at the hotel window, and made my way down to the store to buy food for the house.

Although there had been a great deal of trade between the whalers and the Polar Eskimos throughout the 1800s, the Polar Eskimos were still extremely naive to the benefits and pitfalls of trade until well into the twentieth century. For centuries the whalers – and occasional passing expeditions – had exploited their innocence, often giving meagre contributions of metal tools and food in exchange for stunning furs and ivory, with which they would make a vast profit on returning home. It was not hard for the visitors to take advantage of the Polar Eskimos; but whereas the fair-skinned traders assumed that the indigenous people were primitive and inferior in intellect, in fact the Polar Eskimos simply had a different attitude to possessions and trade.

The Polar Eskimos were not possessive of their belongings: since time began their possessions had been shared, lent and borrowed without question. Meat and fur were also shared; quite often men would hunt in small groups – the hunter who had 'first harpoon' had the choice cuts. Each subsequent 'harpoon' had rights to the meat, but would have to make do with whichever part of the animal corresponded to their throw. Even when the animal had been skinned a hunter could symbolically 'hit' the carcass with his harpoon for a share. It was in this way that the small communities were able to survive the periodic curse of famine.

A form of trade between different communities existed in the Arctic long before the white men came, but it was not trade as we know it, rather a chance to share and barter for things that were lacking in each specific community. One area might have too much polar bear and no seal; another area might have plenty of seal but no auklets from which to make the delicacy of *kiviak*.

With the arrival of the white men things were inevitably going to change, and change they did with the arrival of the Eskimo-Danish explorer Knud Rasmussen. Already Robert E. Peary – known to the Polar Eskimos as *Piuli* – had spent many seasons in the area between 1891 and 1909, and had had a significant impact on the small population. In return for their services as guides and helpers on his various expeditions he had supplied them with guns, ammunition and metal goods, which they could not create themselves. However, when Peary left the area his supplies, on which the Polar Eskimos were now dependent, disappeared. By the time Knud Rasmussen arrived it was clear that there was an urgent need to put in place some guidelines for trade so that the Polar Eskimos could get hold of the equipment on which they were reliant, and so that they would no longer be taken advantage of; it also occurred to Rasmussen that as a result there would be the opportunity to make a good enough profit to finance his anthropological and archaeological research in the Arctic. The trading post eventually financed seven scientific expeditions in the Arctic and the publication of his research. His relationship with the Polar Eskimos was based on mutual respect. Half Eskimo and born in Jakobshaven (now called Ilulissat), Rasmussen was really the first outsider, along with the Dane Peter Freuchan, who truly appreciated the quiet dignity and intelligence of these polar hunters, and who made his home in Thule.

Rasmussen set up the first trading post in 1909 on the site where Thule Airbase now stands. The store was a place where the Eskimos were encouraged to bring their furs and ivory, and in exchange could choose from rifles, ammunition and knives as well as a large selection of European goods such as tea, coffee, sugar and modern fabrics which in no time the locals adopted quite as their own.

The trading post – or *pisiniarfik* – became a place for more than just trade; it became the focus for the community. Life for the Polar Eskimos up until then had been pretty bleak, with little entertainment except for the occasional trading meet, summer camp and the continuous rounds of visiting. The *pisiniarfik* became the social hub of the community where the inhabitants could gather on common ground and not be tied to the constrictive traditions that bound host and visitor. Here they could share news, exchange gossip, and openly show off or admire the results of a good hunting trip, and watch the inevitable disputes between husbands and their wives about what goods should be purchased; it was a stage for local drama.

By the time we arrived in the area in 1971 the Danish government managed stores all over Greenland, and there was even a small store on Herbert Island. It was the closure of the store in 1979 that prompted the residents finally to leave the settlement of Qeqertassuaq and move permanently to the mainland.

Even to this day the shop in Qaanaaq has a buzz about it. Often there are small crowds of people either hanging on the railings outside, or gathered inside the bare foyer looking at notices for the sale of dogs, a party, or the new cash prize for the winner of next week's bingo. A motley collection of individuals stood outside the store that morning: a couple of pensioners in thin grot-stained jackets and old sealskin kamiks, an Inughuit worker in blue overalls and wellington boots and a small group of teenagers sporting homespun bleached hairstyles. They watched me with interest as I mounted the stairs to the heavy doors and returned my greetings politely before whispering conspiratorially to each other.

The shop itself was larger than I had imagined it to be. A hotdog stand doled out bright orange frankfurters in floury rolls to teenagers and governmental workers in their uniform blue overalls. Beside it was a Danish bakery with a small selection of sweet pastries, and opposite was a news-stand with a thin range of pornographic and teenage magazines and a handful of Hollywood generated DVDs and videos. A group of grinning children queued with grubby hands at the bakery for boiled sweets and orange ice-lollies.

The store sold everything from tomato ketchup to furniture – at four times the price of their equivalent in the UK – but supplies were running low and the shelves were frugally stocked. The supply ship to Qaanaaq still only comes once a year – although there are plans for two ships a year as the demand for consumables constantly increases. I walked around the store, fingering the rack of rifles and empty boxes of ammunition, wandering past the bare shelves for electrical goods. One shelf held a glistening pile of sealskins that had been colourfully dyed in vivid blues, reds and orange. A Mongol-looking woman stood at the counter and raised her almond-shaped eyes. For a moment I could have sworn I saw her ebony topknot bedecked with strings of turquoise and amber and her body swathed with a heavy silk *chupa* of an ancient and far-distant plateau. She smiled and looked down again to her small coarse hands resting on the glass counter, and the fleeting vision was gone. I bought one of the two last remaining lumps of cheese, some dry crackers and a few tins of sardines for lunch as well as a large packet of expensive Danish biscuits for the girls and headed home.

The house was filled with teenagers when I returned, all piled on top of each other on the long sofa like a litter of puppies. They communed in their boredom; barely talking, the girls checked their chipped nail polish and kicked the air as the boys feigned sleep.

As I prepared some food Karen plucked a DVD off the shelves and smiled at me – the first time her look hadn't been hostile. She swished back to her friends in her hipster flared jeans and *Britney Spears Live* soon flashed on to the TV. The teenagers sang in bad English, staring blankly at the screen. Eventually bored with Britney's antics, two of the boys started play fighting. They had obviously been watching some Jackie Chan films and suddenly legs and arms were flailing all over the place as the boys did imitation martial arts moves. Then Edo walked in. As the youngest of the Qaerngâq family she was only a couple of years older than me, but she had aged quickly. Her shoulders stooped and her breasts wobbled free and low under a thin T-shirt. She smiled. 'Wel-com to Qaanaaq!' she said slowly and then threw her head back with a 'ha-ha!' Her voice was gruff and nasal. She gave me a brief hug before joining the others on the couch, whereupon she also stared at the TV set. I opened the biscuits, offered her tea and fumbled around the kitchen to find a kettle and teabags. A couple of heads poked around the corner observing me, the children sniggering as I opened cupboard after cupboard in my search before one of them pointed to the stained coffee percolator and said 'tee'. By the time I returned to the table with the hot flask the teenagers had devoured every last biscuit. They looked at me with angelic innocence, their cheeks bulging with chocolate and butter shortbread. I sat down next to Edo, who also was smacking her mouth from gorging; she laughed abruptly, and then her face fell back into non-expression as a young teenage girl with peroxide bleached hair walked in. The girl came up to me confidently and shook my hand and introduced herself with a stilting 'Are you hungry?' as if she were saying 'How do you do?'

As she left, Edo had insisted that I go and visit her that evening and scribbled her house number on a piece of paper before telling

Little Suakunguak and Karen that they should help me find it. I felt obliged to go, even though it was later than she expected. I regretted it as soon as I arrived at her house. I heard a murmur from inside as I knocked on the door, and remembering that there are no closed doors in the community I pushed my way inside. When we first arrived in Greenland my mother was bewildered by the lack of privacy, even in one's own home – children lived with no boundaries and constantly bundled their way in and out of other people's houses. Finally at the end of her tether, my mother had taught the confused children how to knock before entering. It took some time for them to remember, and they would often come hurtling into the house unannounced, and then run back to the door and give it a cursory knock.

The hallway was a jumble of boots and coats and Edo sat directly opposite the door on a couch with a man I hadn't met before. 'Hello!' I exclaimed happily and found myself rooted to the spot by the silent, expressionless faces that stared back at me from within. Although the Inughuit seem extremely relaxed on the surface there are many rules of social engagement that can change the atmosphere from friendly to hostile in a matter of moments. It can be bewildering for the uneducated visitor: although the Inughuit rarely knock on doors they generally give the hosts some warning of their imminent visit by coughing or stamping the snow off their kamiks before going inside. But if a visitor does not sense some invisible sign that the occupants are not in the mood for a visit they can often be given a frosty welcome. Then, on entering the home, one usually stands until a seat becomes available, or until one is invited to sit. Apparently when white men first came to the area they used to blunder into the homes of the locals and without being invited would take the best seat and take over the conversation. The Eskimos found this very insulting.

My predicament was that I knew some of the old rules, but assumed that along with the modern lifestyle the visiting customs had relaxed, but I had no idea which ones and to what extent. I hovered between joining Edo and her friend, or forgetting the whole thing and coming back another time – but then it would be rude just to turn and leave. The two of them looked at me blankly, giving me no encouragement to come further inside. I took that as my cue and indicated that I would come back another time. I was just turning to leave when Edo got up from the sofa and offered me a glass of orange squash. I awkwardly took off my boots and sat on a chair opposite the couple.

We sat in an uncomfortable silence for a few minutes, Edo looking first at the man and then at me, her face an expressionless mask. Maria too had occasionally looked like this. I felt as though I was intruding on an intimate moment, although there was nothing in their body language to suggest it. I attempted to make some conversation, but I was not feeling confident and struggling for words, so I sought refuge in my little West Greenlandic phrasebook. West Greenlandic is the common language for the whole of Greenland, but although the Thule dialect is very different, most people in Qaanaaq can get the gist of what is being said. Edo's friend, who until that point had been watching me silently, suddenly became animated and asked to see the book. He was an imposing character: a bulky fair-skinned man, with a gruff manner and brutal looking hands. It was difficult to tell if he was entirely Danish or of mixed blood. He scraped a hand over his coarse stubble – it sounded as if he was sanding wood – and focused on the book. He flashed me a theatrical look and loudly launched into a string of strange and incongruous phrases in English. I laughed as Edo's face finally broke into a smile. It was like seeing the sunshine through a fog. The ice broken, we continued in our hesitant conversations cheerily as they both drank their beer and smoked with nicotine-yellow fingers. As time wore on the phrases he picked out became more pointed and lascivious. I laughed them off and decided it was time to take my leave. 'Do you wan' go home with me?' he called after me; Edo snorted next to him and elbowed his thick arm. Derisive laughter followed me out of the door.

Hans seemed more relaxed by the time I returned and he told me gaily that Louisa would be returning the following day. He was clearly excited at the prospect of seeing his wife again, and finally it seemed as though he was starting to drop his guard. Tearing himself away from the excruciating adverts on the television, he pulled a traditional Inughuit game off the wall and handed it to me as if it were a peace offering. In the days before TV these games were not just the only entertainment but also a way of keeping the mind active during the months of winter darkness when the weather was impenetrable and conversation had run dry. The long piece of bone had three holes bored into it, and strung between them were two bone figurines threaded on sinew. The 'female' hung on one loop, the 'male' on the other. The task was to get one of the figures to join the other on the same loop. Hans sat on the edge of his seat watching me closely as I struggled with the game. Two white lines were drawn on either side of his face where the arms of his glasses had blocked out the glaring Arctic sunlight. Finally he could contain himself no longer and had to show me how to do it – it was extremely complicated, but I slowly mastered it (more by fluke than skill) and he laughed for a moment before checking himself and retreating back into his shell.

At 11.15 p.m. the sun was as high as it had been in the morning. The sun had swung around in a lazy loop and the cast of the shadows was the only indication that time was passing at all. Children were still running around outside, and a hut a few doors down was throbbing with thrash metal. The only time the town is silent in summer seems to be between 3 and 6.30 a.m. After that the occasional person can be seen on the street of sand and rubble, before the morning tide of people sweeps down to the shop to get their daily bread before it has sold out.

My body was flummoxed by the lack of darkness and I left the house to walk off my restlessness. I made my way through the boggy tundra, the ground pulling at my feet, reaching hungrily for company and making strange sucking noises as I walked on it. I found refuge on a rock polka-dotted with orange lichen, and felt myself drift on the haunting refrain of the dogs singing to the wilderness. Herbert Island looked as enigmatic as ever.

Magda was expecting me and had piles of photographs waiting on the coffee table when I arrived the following morning. She had promised to take me out there on Gideon's boat, but the '*motori ayorpok*' – the engine was broken, so I had to be patient. She refilled the Thermos with fresh tea and sat down beside me on the sofa, with one arm hooked tightly around my waist, and encouraged me to go through the envelopes of pictures. She chuckled to herself as she pointed out birthdays and Christmases and confirmations. There were hundreds to go through, but as we ploughed through the second pack Magda gently put her hand over mine and stopped me at a picture of a slim teenager. '*Irniq* . . . my son,' Magda said, and knelt on the floor to look into my face. '*Tuqungahuq* . . . he's dead.' Her son had committed suicide. I looked at Magda in amazement, and held her face gently between my hands as her eyes brimmed with tears. She looked back at me in response to my silent question: Why?

I saw more pictures of her son. He was her eldest, and was a tall and gentle looking boy from another marriage. He looked so untroubled in the photographs. It was touching to see him in all his finery at his confirmation; sparkling white anorak, kamiks and new polar bear pants, standing with his grinning family. More family members came and went through the photo albums. Killed by a walrus. Drowned in his kayak . . . We talked about Maria, and she told me that Edo had taken a picture of her when she was dead so that the spirit would go through the picture to one of the newborn members of the family. With the help of drawing pictures, miming and using the few Inuktun words that I knew she told me that the souls had flown from Maria, Avatak,

Aata and all the others, that they were not gone, they were not with their bodies: I should not be sad.

After two hours of looking at photographs and being steeped in melancholia I had had enough and Magda quietly put them away and stood by the window looking at Herbert Island. She would find a way to get me out there, she said, and added quietly that she only has to look at Herbert Island to make everything OK. When the family first moved to Qaanaaq she had to keep checking it was there every morning, terrified that the island would desert her. She misses it terribly in the winter. Her lips trembled as she spoke.

By the time I left Magda's house I was feeling decidedly out of sorts, and longed for some privacy so that I could get my head around all the news I had been told. Louisa's house was filled with teenagers again, and the only place I could think of where I could be alone was the cemetery.

As I neared the cemetery I paused and took out the mobile telephone that I hadn't yet tried out, and called my parents. I was feeling vulnerable and confused and needed to talk to the people that knew this place and myself most. As soon as I heard my mother's voice I cracked. Nothing had been what I had been expecting, and hearing the tales of all the people that had died had only compounded all my feelings of disorientation. My parents were as startled by the news as I had been. As I hung up in tears I watched the Thursday plane fly overhead, and knew that Louisa would be on it.

Louisa was home when I got back. I kicked off my boots and was struggling out of my outer layers when I saw her moon-like face peer around the doorway with glistening eyes and an expression of great expectation. I was absorbed into her soft body within moments and we both heaved with a mixture of emotions. Finally I felt at home.

Louisa is the mother hen of the family and she welcomed me wholeheartedly into her nest. Her laughter was contagious, and it rolled with freedom and genuine amusement. Hans sat on the

sofa gazing at his pregnant wife, his eyes glistening with ador-
ation. Louisa's brow furrowed as she realized that I had forgotten
my Greenlandic, but she was patient with my few words and
somehow we managed to muddle through.

Soon the house was alive: Arquenguak and Ilannguak arrived,
just back from hunting, and filled the room with their presence.
Then Magda came in with Gideon, who was transformed among
his friends and was as playful and energetic as a springer spaniel.
The brothers were docile in comparison and regarded him with
faint amusement. Ilannguak pulled me into a rough and heartfelt
hug. Although broad and physically strong he had soft and lively
eyes with which he studied me with a look that can only be
described as intense brotherly love. His wife Arnarulunaguaq
followed shortly after, her small wrinkled face twinkling in the
doorway as she pulled off her boots. The family moved around
the house freely, opening cupboards and helping themselves to
food, eating sardines in tomato sauce out of the tins with their
fingers, slurping and chatting through mid-chew and sprawling
over the floor, commandeering the space that the teenagers
usually took up.

It was hard to believe that I was in such a remote area of
Greenland when I was in the modern confines of their home.
Hans is a West Greenlander, originally from Ilulissat, which is
where Louisa and Hans met, and where Karen was born. As a
consequence their lifestyle, language and choice of possessions
reflect more of the cosmopolitan lifestyle of the city than the
traditional hunting culture of Thule.

Above the sofa a faded triptych of the Manhattan skyline
dominated the wall, beside which a giant pink plastic doll sported
the traditional West Greenlandic dress, which Karen had once
worn as a baby. On the other side of the room two plaster
figurines graced the dark shelving unit with their immaculate
halos next to a new Bang & Olufsen music system. Miniature
pairs of sealskin kamiks and mittens were pinned to the wall
between the surround-sound speakers. Drawing pins in the ceil-

ing still skewered the remnants of the previous year's Christmas decorations.

The celebration of Christmas was quickly adopted by the Eskimos when the missionaries first arrived in Greenland; the Eskimos loved celebrations and parties, particularly during the dark winter months when there was little diversion from the bleak monotony except storytelling and eating, and preparations would begin several weeks before the festive period. Traditionally everyone would get a new anorak and a new pair of kamiks, which would mean a great deal of work for a mother who had several children. Seal, fox and polar bear skins – whichever were available – would have to be scraped, stretched, dried and then softened and sewn into garments or boots. The man of the house would be busy too; meat for family and guests was needed, and it was a pitiable hunter who was unable to provide enough skins with which to clothe his family at Christmas. The night before Christmas clean newspaper would be stuck to the walls and fresh candles placed in all the holders.

Christmas in Greenland started on 24 December. All the women and girls dressed in thigh-skimming white sealskin kamiks trimmed with polar bear fur, blue-fox fur knickers and colourful anoraks, and the men and boys in white anoraks, polar bear pants and short kamiks to the knee, and they all scrambled up the steep hillside to the church in the ebony-skied morning, torches dancing over snowdrifts and dogs. In the church on Herbert Island, the villagers shook hands vigorously, wishing each other '*Juurli Pidluarit!*' before settling in the pews, the men on one side, the women on the other, to hear the catechist give his sermon. Later, Santa Claus would fly to the settlement in a US helicopter to deliver presents to all the children from the people at the airbase – when my parents told the children that Santa really came from the North Pole and that he delivered presents from a sledge pulled by flying *tugto* (reindeer), the children laughed. Everyone knew, they exclaimed patiently, that *Nihima* (Santa) was an American soldier and came by helicopter.

Visiting was the essential pastime over the few days of
Christmas, and the Qaerngâq family were always the first visitors to our little hut. Gifts were immediately exchanged over
piles of food. One Christmas my father received a pair of sealskin
mittens from Maria and a large pair of walrus tusks from Avatak,
which his friend and sledging companion had spent hours
polishing; there was a beautifully crafted miniature sledge for me
from Avatak and a large prepared sealskin for my mother from
Maria, as well as another unusual gift. Mum wrote about the
present in her book *The Snow People*:

. . . What I had kept to the last, and what really intrigued me, was a
large parcel I had shoved behind me on the bed.

'I worked all night on that,' said Maria as I picked it up. I noticed
one corner was a bit soggy and it seemed very heavy. I couldn't think
what it could be. Bit by bit I began to uncover a gorgeous white fox
fur. 'Oh Maria!' I exclaimed. 'How clever of you. How did you
manage to stuff it?' I had unwrapped the whole parcel. 'It looks so
real.' Everyone was convulsed with laughter, rolling around in their
seats and looking at me. I suddenly realised to my horror that the fox
I was holding was frozen stiff, straight out of the trap. I let out a shriek
and dropped it, more in fun than in earnest, and they howled with
delight.

I wondered what Christmas was like in Qaanaaq now, but
again my photographs had been pulled out and the family were
engrossed in the pictures of us all as children. Louisa laughed as
she pointed to pictures of Avatak and me and teased me: 'You
used to call him *Ataata*, and I would say no, he's my dad, not
yours, and you would burst into tears and stamp your feet
insisting that he was your dad!' The same was repeated with
Maria. The others joined in with the story, pinching my arms
and talking over one another with nostalgia. And then once
again we came to my sister Pascale's photograph and the house
fell into silence. I felt the recent flood of emotions rise up again

and stick in my throat. I suddenly had a desperate yearning for her to be there and to share in it all with me. It was one of the many journeys we had talked about as children. How different this trip, my whole life, would be if she were still here. Louisa sensed the change in my expression and rubbed my back roughly. I looked up and found five pairs of liquid eyes fixed upon me.

The crowd left as quickly as they had arrived, as is the custom of the hunting community. Louisa sighed quietly and sat back on the sofa; she looked well and happy, and it was hard to picture her being rushed to hospital. She read my mind and smiled holding her belly. '*Uanga* OK!' she said laughing.

Together we prepared some food for dinner. Although the store was low on fresh produce there was still plenty of frozen meat, and pork was to be the meal of the evening. I found it strange that of all the meat they could have in the store the most commonly bought was pork and chicken, meat that the Thule people would never have eaten traditionally, and I imagine has only recently been introduced to farms in southern Greenland.

Louisa talked throughout the meal. One memory led into another, all of which she found hilarious, some to a point where she would grip her sides and wheeze with so much laughter that both Hans and I kept trying to make her stop in case we had to take her back to hospital again, our concerned faces only making her laugh more. She told me how the kids had used me as their little gopher. Mum and Dad had boxes of supplies for our two-year-long trip, including stacks of Cadbury's chocolate. When Mum wasn't looking the girls would get me to go into our stores and grab as many bars of chocolate as I could carry and bring them out to where they would be hiding outside. This plan had gone perfectly a couple of times until I slipped on some ice and my armfuls of chocolate spilled all over the floor. 'Marie came out hearing you crying and was so confused why there was so much chocolate all over the ground!'

Louisa had exhausted herself, and after the evening meal the colour drained completely from her face and she slipped off to bed with Hans guiding her up the stairs. It was 9 p.m. and I was still buzzing from the day and escaped quietly out of the door towards the beach. I took my time, strolling between small beached icebergs that glittered in the cool light. Not far away dark silhouettes of meat racks crouched in grotesque shapes holding up their dismembered carcasses like crude sacrificial offerings to the heavens; their wooden struts looked like swollen and disfigured limbs with years of accumulated blood and fat. On either side forgotten boats lay in their idle state of decay. At their rotten bows dogs were tethered in dusty teams, yawning with boredom in the dry Arctic heat; it would be months before they felt the freedom of speeding out across the ice.

In the distance two figures seemed to be waving at me. As I neared I realized that it was Magda and one of Avatak's sisters; the eyesight of the Inughuit is remarkable, and they had seen me approaching long before I could even see their figures. They led me to a group of people hanging around an upturned fibreglass boat. Najannuaq grinned and asked me if I had had a good day; it was her husband's boat, she told me, and needed repairing. It was a convivial atmosphere; the women sat chattering amiably in the sunshine watching the children play on the beach while the three men industriously worked on the hull of the small craft. Najannuaq's husband didn't pay any attention to his audience; the ponytail of his 1980s hairstyle snaked down his back over dark blue stained overalls, and his face was dark and set in concentration. An older man helped with a broad grin, cutting up sheets of fibreglass with a practised hand. Gideon played up to the female crowd.

'Do you have trees in London?' he asked me loudly, and Najannuaq interpreted his question casually.

'Yes,' I replied, 'they are bigger than these houses.' I swept a hand over the large warehouses on the beach. Gideon looked thoughtful for a moment and then kicked the huge log that was supporting the boat, which had probably been washed ashore by the currents that wind their way from Siberia.

'*Ammaqa* . . . maybe this tree came from London!' he laughed.

With a start it occurred to me that this was the first real scene of everyday life that I had experienced in Qaanaaq over the last few days. It dawned on me that I had left the house without my camera, something I never normally do. I raced up the steep hill to the house to find that Louisa was up again and dressed and about to go out. I told her that everyone was down at the beach and she nodded saying she would meet me down there.

In the short time it had taken me to return the breeze had sharpened and the crowd was starting to disperse. Louisa and I accompanied Najannuaq back to her house, just two doors down from where I was staying. Puppies played in the dust outside with Orfik who looked up with a cheery English 'hello!' As we entered through the kitchen I nearly tripped over two dead guillemots lying on the floor with a surprised 'Oh!' prompting a chorus of 'Be carr-ful Kaari!' to ring out behind me. The familiar call from when I was a little girl had the girls giggling and nudging each other as they guided me into the centre of the home. The small living room was homely but simply furnished with a small outdated television set sitting in the corner and a battered radio on a plastic-covered table. Light danced on the walls, filtered through the lace curtains.

'Do you want a drink?' Najannuaq asked me. 'Tea, coffee' – she leant into me whispering conspiratorially – 'wine, beer, whisky?' she laughed heartily. Louisa shot her a disapproving look. 'Tea,' I replied laughing with her, wondering silently who among the sisters drank alcohol. 'Are you hungry? Well help yourself then!' Najannuaq said and pointed towards a fried egg left over from breakfast swimming in grease in a frying pan on the hob. We feasted at midnight on doorsteps of white bread smothered in liver pâté and the town's last piece of Emmental cheese, drinking sweet tea and sharing more memories. Najannuaq's husband sat at the table looking pained at the chattering conversation of women. Finally he cleared his voice, and silenced us all. He talked directly to his wife, not looking at me once, and asked through her how long I was staying and what did I need to do while I was in Qaanaaq. He was concerned, he said sagely, that I had come a long way and they must help me. I was surprised and grateful, and felt a lick of guilt that I had assumed he was ambivalent to my presence. I told them that I really wanted to get out to Herbert Island, but apart from that I just wanted to spend time with them. They talked among themselves, discussing various possibilities.

'Maybe you could go out with Arquenguak or Ilannguak to Qeqertassuaq,' Najannuaq offered seriously, and then carried on teasing me about my curly hair, saying that she had to keep perming hers to get it to curl like mine.

Louisa and I returned to the house slowly, with my arm under hers to give her some support. 'Arquenguak came to visit you,' she murmured as if she was thinking out loud. I felt a gladdening in my chest and dearly hoped that I was finally finding a place here again.

5. Village of Ghosts

The siren went off at about 4 a.m. It was a deafening, gut-wrenching sound. The old wartime air-raid siren ricocheted off the mountains and shook the foundations of the house. I shot up from my bunk and instinctively leapt over to Karen's bed to rescue her from the unknown threat, but the bed was still empty. Throwing open the window I clutched at my ears and tried to steady my pounding heart that was threatening to leap out of the window before I did. As Hans slammed out of the front door and disappeared into the perpetual light, I hallucinated wildly that this was the end of the world. Since the 1950s the American airbase at Thule has been used as an early-warning missile station, and in my disoriented state I assumed that the base had been targeted and that the siren was the bugle call of imminent vaporization.

The scene outside was confusing. The siren seemed to be having no effect on the town itself. Perhaps everyone had been warned to stay indoors if they heard it. A solitary man belted down the street rubbing his eyes and pulling his jacket over one arm, then he was gone. And then there was silence. A heavy, ominous silence that comforted my ringing ears but not my thoughts, which screamed through every possibility. I wearily sank back into bed and slept fitfully, dreaming of bombs dropping from flying sledges, barely hearing Karen slipping quietly into bed. The following day I was to discover that the siren was the fire station calling the hunters to duty.

Greenland – and in particular the Thule area – became the focus of strategic interest during the Second World War. In 1941 the first American–Danish Agreement on the Defence of Greenland was signed, and a joint Danish–American weather station was installed next door to the ancient village of Uummannaq in the shadow of table-topped Dundas Mountain. By 1946 the weather station had grown considerably, and some locals believe that it was designed to conceal the true nature of the agreement that had been signed, which had specific military intentions. Six years later, those military intentions became a reality.

In April 1951 a further defence treaty was signed between the Danish government and the US military, and later that same summer the inhabitants of the small settlement of Uummannaq saw the land of their ancestors being assaulted by the unstoppable American military machine. The people of Thule watched as supply convoys totalling 82 ships carrying 6 million tons of cargo anchored offshore in North Star Bay. Over the next two years a construction force of no less than 19,000 men swarmed over their beaches. The Inughuit and their land shuddered with the sound and vibration of 'Operation Blue Jay' as it gouged out the heart of the Pituffik valley with its thundering machinery; the pale-skinned men built a vast temple to War on the land of the ancients in just ten weeks.

Throughout the Cold War, Thule Airbase was the eyes and ears of the armed forces, its state-of-the-art Ballistic Missile Early Warning System (BMEWS) enabling the American people to sleep at peace. In 1987 the BMEWS was upgraded to a Phased Array Radar – currently Thule has the same capability as similar installations in Clear, Alaska, and Fylingdales, UK – but the intentions for the development of this miniature America (clocks in the airbase are set to the same time as New York) do not stop there. Plans are afoot for the construction of a new 'Star Wars Shield' which the military believes will protect them from attack from so-called rogue states, or large terrorist organizations. But the Inughuit, who have every reason to be deeply concerned, are meeting the proposal with dismay and anger. The issue, although complex, has its roots in an event half a century ago that sowed the seeds of distrust and outright opposition to the base and those people that operate from the shadows of power.

In 1953, just as the anti-aircraft battery was completed, the villagers of Uummannaq were informed they were no longer entitled to live on the land that they had continuously inhabited for hundreds of years. The fact that it was one of the richest hunting areas in Greenland held no sway, and the Inughuit were told they had less than a week in which to gather together their belongings and leave. The orders were given with a threat of immediate violence. If the Inughuit didn't leave, their homes would be bulldozed, if they returned they would be arrested. The Danish government told them that provision had been made for them at a new settlement ninety miles north called Qaanaaq, where they would be given new homes. They were promised a new life, with the benevolence of an iron fist. With no choice, and with no protection from the Danish government (there is pointed irony that they were due to become Danish citizens only one week later), the community took as many belongings as they could carry on their sledges, and men, women, children and elders embarked on the difficult journey across the Politiken Glacier to their new home – the same journey that my parents undertook in the storm of 1973. When the exiled villagers arrived there was no accommodation as had been promised, only a handful of tents that were handed out to the first arrivals. As winter came fast upon them, the exiles were forced to make do with what shelter they could find in Qaanaaq and the surrounding settlements. That time is still raw in the hearts of the people who live there now.

The dream of having a space-based missile system – hence the label 'Star Wars' – was the brainchild of former US president Ronald Reagan, and although it violates the 1972 Anti-Ballistic Missile (ABM) treaty, George W. Bush has renewed the plan with vigour, and in the meantime has unilaterally withdrawn from the ABM, so that America is free to develop his National Missile Defense system (NMD), without international intervention. With the recent escalation of 'Terror', Bush has increased funding on a phenomenal scale, and the development of the NMD has been accelerated. Negotiations between US military and the Danish government concerning upgrading the airbase are at a critical stage, but the Inughuit, naturally a quiet and peaceful people, resent the fact that they are being dragged into a world of politics with which they have no direct involvement, and are finally fighting for their rights, terrified that if the systems are upgraded at Thule Airbase, they will become a natural target for a first strike. It is distressing to hear this small hunting community discussing their fears of a global arms race.

I had been staying at Louisa's for almost two weeks, and was just starting to find my feet. Daily I met more people from my past, who squeezed and pummelled me as I walked through the dusty tracks of the town, and others whom I didn't know from before began to recognize my face and wave and call greetings to me wherever I went. The place still felt strangely alien to me, but then Qaanaaq was never my home. Often I gazed at Herbert Island and wondered how different this trip would have been if the family still lived there.

The community crafts shop in Qaanaaq was open as I walked past, and I took some time to plough through the endless plastic boxes filled with small *tupilaks* and carvings etched from bone and ivory, created by artists throughout the district. A tupilak was traditionally a miniature ivory carving depicting a monster that was made and magically brought to life by an Eskimo who wanted to rid himself of an enemy. The tupilak was completed in an isolated place and sent out to attack the enemy in whatever form it had been made to represent; as a walrus it would capsize the victim while in his kayak; as a bear it could attack him on a hunt. Typically, as of all spirits, the tupilak had no sense of loyalty and could be turned against the man or woman who created it by an angákoq. This type of witchcraft had died out by the time we lived in Greenland, but tupilaks are still a fundamental part of the creative identity of the Polar Eskimo. As children my sister and I were given gifts of tupilaks intricately carved from walrus tusk. The grotesque faces and forms were strangely comforting, and for years I believed that they were actually protecting us from other less tangible and darker spirits that lurk in a child's imagination.

I was fully absorbed in the boxes in the small back room when I was disturbed by a commotion coming from the main shop. I ignored the noise, and it was only when I saw a huddle of people nudging my peripheral vision that I looked up. Baali was standing in the doorway. Before I had a chance to move Baali had crossed the room and was gripping me tightly. We squeezed each other until we were breathless, both of us on the verge of tears. Her husband Kristian stood grinning a couple of feet away; a twelve-year-old girl hung at his side, watching Baali and myself curiously from under a knitted blue hat – here were two women in their thirties who looked so very different, but whose faces were awash with old friendship.

Baali and Kristian had changed considerably over the years. The last time I had seen them they were still fresh with the innocence of young married life. Kristian had been a lanky youth, with the whisper of a moustache and an awkward manner. The Kristian standing before me now was manly and confident, with broad shoulders and strong hands. There was a constant chuckle hovering about his lips. Baali stood beside him looking radiant. The structure of her face was now clearly defined, with broad high cheekbones and almond eyes that crinkled in amusement, echoing the humour of her husband. With a start I realized that I recognized their daughter too; she was the younger of Baali's two children, and the last time I saw her she was an affectionate six-year-old with a runny nose that she wiped continually on her sleeves. Now she was a young woman.

The family was tired and their faces were creased and darkened by the sun. Baali squeezed my arm tightly; she had to go and visit Louisa, and unload their gear from the boat, she explained. Baali turned as they walked away, and held onto the doorframe to look back at me with a rush of warmth before disappearing without another word.

I found the family again a couple of hours later at the store, standing beside the hotdog stand with Magda and Gideon, leaning against the counter and chatting as if they were at a bar. Magda called to me as soon as she spotted me; she had good news: 'Baali and Kristian will take you to Herbert Island later today.'

'But we would have to wait until high tide,' Kristian added in sign language after I squeaked with delight.

'When is high tide?' I asked them; they all shrugged in unison, and had a short conference before all agreeing that it would definitely be sometime later. They giggled as I jumped on the spot in excitement. I felt like a five-year-old again. I ran home to get my gear sorted out; the boat journey would be cold and I needed to find my thermals and get my camera gear together. I could hardly contain myself, and it was infectious: Baali arrived at Louisa's just half an hour later to pick me up.

We were in high spirits as we walked through Qaanaaq. Kristian laughed saying that he would be falling asleep at the tiller on the way home because he was so tired. Baali's younger daughter Naduk skipped around us, grinning then running on ahead blazing a trail in her blue bobble hat.

Baali and Kristian's house was identical in design and layout to Edo's, and was only one row of houses above, which confused me momentarily, until I realized the decor was ever so slightly different: a different pattern on the upholstery, a slightly larger music system; another version of Christ in pious benevolence hanging on the wall. Almost all of the houses in modern Qaanaaq are 'kits' ordered from the Danish government, which arrive once a year on the supply ship. The challenge is to personalize the houses using the limited resources available. I wondered how everyone was able to afford the televisions and music systems that so far had been in every house I had visited.

Baali was in her element, finding waterproofs and warm

clothes for everyone and throwing together some food for the family as they were all ravenous. Kristian wandered around relaxed, clutching a sandwich in one hand and binoculars in the other. He studied Herbert Island, the state of the water and the tide. He murmured something to Baali and she joined him at the window, and looked over his shoulder at the fjord. I caught snippets of their hushed conversation: '*Ammaqa* . . . maybe . . .' then something about bad weather, but it didn't seem serious; they looked at each other, turned to smile at me, and got dressed for the journey.

A tractor rolled past us as we walked down to the beach and it ground to a stop as the driver exchanged cheerful conversation with Baali and Kristian. On hearing that we were on our way to Herbert Island he frowned and looked towards the island, extending his arm and flicking his hand from side to side as if swatting a fly. 'The water is getting rough about half-way out,' he said. My heart sank at the prospect that the trip would be postponed again. I looked nervously over to Baali and Kristian to gauge their response, but they had already noticed the choppy water and had decided to chance it. The man shrugged and then nodded his head in my direction.

'*Kaari-gna*,' Baali called up, 'from Herbert Island!' The old man's eyes opened wide and he flashed a toothless smile in approval: '*Ajor*.' He chuckled and drove off casting back an exaggerated salute.

Baali unlocked a small wooden shed on the beach where they kept their fuel, skins and hunting and travelling accessories. The boat was still mostly kitted out from their recent expedition, so there was little equipment to get together. Kristian quickly pulled on some waterproof waders and looked down at my walking boots. 'They're no good,' he said shaking his head and pointing at my feet, but before I had a chance to say a word he hollered a war cry, swept me up in a fireman's lift and ran out to the boat pretending to abduct me. The girls ran after us shrieking in mock distress.

Our enthusiasm to get going meant that the tide was still out, and negotiating the labyrinth of sharp rocks took great skill, relying on Kristian's inner compass when the murky waters were impenetrable to the eye. The others were unperturbed, they had navigated this hazardous stretch of water since they were children, and the map of deep channels was clearly etched in their subconscious.

Soon we were skimming the crystal waters with barely a murmur, gliding among majestic icebergs of turquoise and peacock-blue. These impermanent fossils of ice had been in existence for several thousands of years, but as waterfalls cascaded off the floating ice castles in the near-warmth of the Arctic summer, the fjord would soon become a graveyard for many of these great edifices.

But the man in the tractor had been right: a third of the way to Herbert Island the water suddenly changed character and rose in spiteful choppy peaks that ravaged the boat, making us lurch and slam into the waves. The sky darkened, and in an instant the icebergs that had been a glorious crystal gateway to our homeland became grey and ominous, and the further we travelled the more they seemed to crowd in on us. Naduk's brilliant smile froze into a fixed grimace, and Baali rubbed her hands with concern. It was too much she decided, and we had to return to Qaanaaq. We turned away from Herbert Island, beaten. A feeling of inevitability swept over me, the return home had been too easy, and perhaps too soon.

The waters around Qaanaaq were oily smooth, becalmed by an underwater embrace of rocks, and as Kristian stopped the boat to change fuel tanks we took the opportunity to regain some of the breath that had been knocked out of us on the fjord. Baali produced some fresh Danish pastries and bottles of sweet fizzy drinks and we sat silently for a time, gazing with sorry eyes towards the island that lay bruised and purple on the horizon echoing our disappointment. Kristian moved over towards me and showed me his watch. '*Ammaqa unnugu,*' he said softly with an encouraging look. *'Ammaqa imarihuq.'* Maybe we would try again later; maybe then the sea would be calm. He elbowed me encouragingly, Naduk and I cheered and Baali squeezed my knee and flashed a relieved smile; we would get there when the time was right.

I returned to Louisa's house just in time for a delicious meal of boiled Arctic salmon with rice laden with mild, bright yellow curry powder, a flavouring that was originally brought to Qaanaaq to satisfy Danish tastes, but has now been adopted with gusto by the modern Inughuit. The Inughuit are used to strong tastes; the most sought-after delicacies here are the most pungent, and they love the piquant taste of fermented meat. The curry powder here was not so much hot but flavoursome, and gives the 'bland' food of the *kadlunas* some kick. I needed the warmth of the meal. Even though we hadn't made it all the way to the island, we had still been out on the fjord for at least three hours, and the chill had worked its way deep into my core.

About 7 p.m. Hans's bright yellow mobile phone chirruped a tinny techno beat as Baali telephoned to say that I should meet them at the boat, and Louisa had barely mentioned Herbert Island before I was out the door. Baali and Naduk were already kitted out and climbing into the boat as I ran across the beach. By that time I had managed to purchase a pair of thin and glaringly white wellies, at the sight of which Kristian cried out as if he had been blinded and despite my protests ran over to pick me up and carry me to the boat once again.

The water now looked like rippled velvet and it seemed as if some invisible hand had moved the icebergs in a game of chess. Herbert Island looked barren and inhospitable, but my heart went out to it. The island changed constantly with the light: one moment she could be a mirage of pink and lilac, and the next dark and brooding with her sharp ridges slicing through cloud and sky.

Naduk chattered to me urgently as we neared the island's small rocky harbour and spotted Gideon and Magda walking through the village. Gideon had managed to mend his boat engine and they had taken a short trip out to the island in order to tend to their dogs that were still tethered at the abandoned settlement.

I felt a prickling sensation as we scraped the bow to shore. Magda had control of around twenty huskies with a twenty-foot whip which she snaked and cracked so fast and with such precision that it made her look like Medusa. The huskies' tails wagged high and proud as they swarmed over the tundra, tangling their traces and nipping each other; they were excited but had allegiance to the whip, and snapped at the air as if they could taste freedom and adventure.

Baali pointed towards a small red-painted wooden hut, and exclaimed: 'Kari House!' Never in recent years have I felt such a surge of rightness. I was home.

I clambered out of the boat, skidding on the same slippery dark rocks that had greeted my mother when we had first arrived thirty years before. But I didn't have the same reception. The village of Qeqertassuaq was deserted, and the only life on the island was our two small parties; in a couple of hours the only hearts that would beat in this old village would be those of the dogs left behind.

Two husky pups nipped at my heels, tripping me up for attention as we scrambled over uneven tundra and rocks towards the hut. The air was fresh and light, and had more of the scent of spring than midsummer. Baali paused to grab my hand, and together we ran laughing over the last few yards to the door.

The hut seemed bigger than I remembered it. The door was pinned shut with a rusting padlock, but it was not locked and with a little fiddling the door creaked open. It was a peculiar sensation to be there. Tekumeq Peary now 'owned' the hut and it looked as though she had just gone for a walk – the house was littered with belongings: furs, jackets, boots and provisions. In the main room a tin ashtray was filled with nicotine-yellow butts and rings of coffee stained the plastic tablecloth.

I was strangely overwhelmed with a feeling of unease inside this place which I had longed to revisit for many years. I waited for the memories to flood back, and stood in silent contemplation willing them to sweep me away, but they didn't come. I searched hungrily for some sign that we had been there; a picture, a book, a toy that I had discarded in the confusion of leaving that had waited loyally for my return, but the only thing that was left were the shelves that Dad had laboured over, which were now the receptacle for the moments of other people's lives. Pictures and shabby books sat on the pale green painted wood, and none of them was familiar. The place had forgotten us.

I wanted to go out and collect some ice to melt for some tea, load up the fire, scrub the place from top to bottom and start afresh. The place hadn't been looked after; it was dirty, smelly and unkempt. In a sense it was hard to believe that we had lived there at all. Naduk watched me curiously from the open doorway leading to the kitchen.

But we had lived there. I remembered where the cot had been, the bed, and yes, the ventilation trap – the 'nose' – was still in the same place. I stood where my cot was, but the reality of the place was not as magical as the memory. The hut was cold and lifeless.

Naduk smiled her overwhelming smile, and I was grateful for her being there with me; then Baali came in and the atmosphere immediately changed. 'Wally,' she said pointing at the shelves and busily imitated him banging in nails and scratching his head. How many times over the years had I seen the same scene! She plumped up a cushion and sat down matter-of-factly gazing around at the place; she was at home there. She looked at me quizzically, trying to gauge how I was feeling. I wanted to stay there, sleep a few nights, breathe life into the old place and immerse myself in old memories so that I might discover what it was that I was trying to find by coming back.

Slowly we walked out of the house and paused outside while Naduk secured the door against stormy winter and roaming foxes and polar bears. Baali pointed over to Migishoo's place. The old house was stripped of its roof and its turf and rock walls were torn and ragged. It looked naked and pitiful. Her hand swept up the thin valley and there behind our place was the family home of the Qaerngâq family: Maria, Avatak and all the children, just a few metres from our door. What a happy path lay between. But their house too had been looted by the same wind. Torn wallpaper trembled in the brisk breeze, and the roof lay like a splintered puzzle halfway up the hill behind. The door was barricaded with debris and a glassless window frame leant against the outside of the hut. Baali, using the frame as a ladder, hopped into her old home through the gash where the window once fitted.

I crawled up the frame behind her avoiding the jagged splinters of glass and watched her walk in her childhood footsteps and listened to her calling out her memories. Her short laughs and smiles blended seamlessly with frowns and sighs as she rode the many images of her life there.

'This is where we all used to sleep,' she cooed, 'look, look! Ataata, Anaana, Magda, Uanga –' she put me between her and Edo – 'lying just like so,' she said, outlining the figure of what seemed like a little corpse. '*Illit*, you!' she pointed, and started wriggling, punching and kicking, and then mimicked the others as they all howled from the onslaught of my boisterous restlessness.

The cold wind flitting through the gaping roof and windows tugged at our hair as we stood side by side and I pictured where the little table had been, where Avatak used to sit me on his knee and feed me butter to ease my whimpers and tantrums, and cast my eyes over the floor on which we had scrabbled around as children playing with beads, or anything at hand for that matter.

Outside the ground was littered with remnants of lives spent there: a rusting tin of sweetened condensed milk, a bleached packet of tobacco. The little outhouse was filled with abandoned junk – a slowly rusting pair of white ice-skates, a foot pump that

Baali was jumping up and down on, giggling at the squeaky huff-puff sound and old comics given as Christmas presents by the Americans at the airbase. We threw ourselves into childhood fantasy, and Naduk didn't know what to make of it.

We followed the trail of the wind and up onto a small ridge to the church-cum-school. A cluster of graves huddled wind-worn near the entrance, but there were not so many fake flowers colouring this small plot. The tundra had crept up on the scattering of crucifixes and Nature's tenacious fingers were reclaiming the land.

The church was our refuge. Quiet and sheltered, it looked pristine and ready for its ghostly congregation. White paper cutout angels framed a simple altar; Migishoo had made them, Baali told me. But Migishoo had died several years ago and they looked freshly created. The church felt as if it had been embalmed. The air was steady, unmoving, and all sound seemed deadened and very far away.

Baali sat on the small organ chair and started pedalling the air through the old pipes. The sound was momentarily shocking in the silence. But the small building seemed to welcome the simple music, as though it had been waiting for company for many years.

Naduk and I walked round the small interior fingering old hymnbooks and sitting on the worn pews, and together we pushed the door open on the curate's little cell. The dust was the only indication that someone wasn't about to return. A small pile of printed psalms lay on a wooden desk beside the hard single cot. A sprig of plastic flowers bloomed perpetually in the corner beside a small window that looked over the fjord. Beyond lay nothing but wilderness.

The first missionary to arrive in the district was Gustav Olsten in 1909, and by all accounts he seemed to adapt quickly to the way of life of Thule. Olsten was an excellent hunter and kayak master, and a keen promoter of Christianity. By the time Gustav Olsten left his northern ministry in 1927 the entire population of Thule – a few hundred Inughuit hunters, women and children – had been baptized.

We left the church, shutting the large doors securely with their strong bolts and walked round to the school which was housed at the back of the same building, and choked on the stale air as we walked in through the small side door.

Three bunk beds were piled in one corner of the single schoolroom against bookshelves coloured with books written mostly in Danish, and a stack of old *National Geographic* magazines. It was warm inside and smelled faintly of an old library. Stubby fingers of chalk lay in the gutter of the blackboard and polite graffiti adorned the board itself: small scribbles of names in neat lines and the dates of their visitation. Naduk added her inscription. Baali wandered around opening windows and studying abandoned mementoes. She pointed to a couple of board games gathering dust on one of the top shelves. 'Kari's toys,' she laughed; we must have left them there when we headed back to England. I was caught out for a moment – it was proof, if I needed any, that I had been there. They had my tiny fingerprints all over them.

Resisting the urge to take the toys down I reached instead for a globe that sat beside them and took it over to Naduk, placing it on the main table next to the squat dark stove. I pointed to Greenland and she found Qaanaaq and then the tiny dot of Herbert Island that indicated where we stood on the surface of the world. So very far, it seemed, from anywhere else. I traced my finger down to Scotland where my parents lived and Baali touched it as if she could communicate with them through her fingertips. 'Maria, Oowaallee . . .'

The kitchen was well stocked and I felt an involuntary prayer rise in my chest for the weather to turn so that we could stay. There were enough supplies to keep us fed for a couple of days: a healthy supply of English Breakfast tea, hardtack biscuits, Nutella and cornflakes. It had a toilet too, which Baali showed me with a proud '*Anartarfik!*' then giggled as if it was the first time she had ever seen one. It was the only toilet in the village.

The winter snows had retreated and surrendered the ground, which was strewn with old rubbish and items that had long since been forgotten. Tools and items of clothing were scattered amongst plastic bags and packaging from 'civilized' life. Scavenging among the rubbish, when they were not sleeping, were several teams of huskies – there are not enough areas in Qaanaaq to tether all the dogs, and some hunters prefer to keep the teams fairly isolated so that they are kept semi-wild, but still tethered on long leashes, with hunters coming over from the mainland every few days to feed them on the meat still stored on the arthritic meat racks around the village.

Herbert Island is now populated more by dogs than by humans. Bristling with energy, these working dogs are stocky and athletic with thick healthy fur and keen eyes. They are the progeny of the wilderness, at their happiest when they are sprinting through the ice desert, catching the scent of a bear or just the palpable energy of the hunt. Often brought up by their masters from pups, the dogs are essentially faithful and loyal to their owner, but they can be unpredictable. As a child I was taught to fear the huskies. More akin to the wolf than any domestic animal, once loose the dogs behave like a pack, and if they are hungry have been known to tear a child to pieces. In no time I was taught to bellow my little lungs out at anything that had sharp teeth, even though all of us children handled puppies like rag dolls.

The tough dogs of Herbert Island had a different aura about them than most of the dog teams in Qaanaaq; they were thicker set, more alive and wilder than their townie counterparts. And Ilannguak's team was particularly striking. Almost all white, with only flecks of black or brown in their pelts, the dogs were healthy and straining at their leashes to go on an adventure. They were from good stock, bred from Avatak and Aata's teams. Aata's dogs were known throughout the district as being one of the strongest, fastest and most obedient teams. He had spent a lifetime training them to be the best, and had traded out all the weaker dogs.

We walked past the throaty greetings of the Herbert Island dogs towards Aata's house, and at last the memories came back. The house was cruelly weathered, the dark maroon paint blistered and peeling and the house itself was starting to sag like a drunk old man into the pitted ground.

The ghosts of my old friends were waiting on the front step to greet me. As I walked through them I shuddered with an awakening of something indescribable. I felt like a child slipping my feet into Grandpa's still-warm slippers. I instinctively ducked to one side as I walked through the entrance, half expecting a seal carcass to be hanging by the door as it always had done with its blood dripping languidly into a plastic bowl on the floor. But there was no seal, and the house was devoid of people. Only spirits rattled around there now. Aata's faded armchair sat in the corner with his imprint still on the worn cushions. Naduk squeezed past me and plumped herself down in it happily chewing on a thumbnail. I took a sharp intake of breath in surprise, and realized that she had never known her grandfather. Naduk smiled, oblivious to my thoughts.

The two-room house was pretty much the same as it had ever been, only the furniture had moved slightly and there were modern photographs on the walls. The bedroom still had a single bed pressed against one wall. I sat at the table and pictured the time when I was nine years old, doing my school homework on the small wooden table, writing with great concentration in my exercise book, with Aata sitting to my left, watching me with great affection, sucking on his old pipe. I used to love the smell of his pipe tobacco smoke in my hair when I went to sleep at night.

I could close my eyes and remember nights of nightmares when Aata would come to my side and gently stroke my forehead down to the tip of my nose to smooth my brow and ease my fevered imagination.

Baali and Kristian noisily bundled into the main room and broke my reverie. But the contemplative mood overtook them too. We sat in silence for a while, all with contented smiles on our faces, taking in the light on the duck-egg blue walls; the huge tin drum where iceberg chunks would melt for the water supply; the kitchen sideboard without a sink, where an *ulu*, a traditional curved knife, would sit, still warm after hours of flensing seal skin, and above where I sat the portraits of Aata and Aana in their last days. Aata looked directly into the camera, a glint of amusement and wisdom still perceptible behind his sunglasses. Aana looked down coyly in a separate photograph, but still nudging her husband, she looked as charming as she must have been as a young girl. The Arctic breeze whipped the small hut and whistled in warning. In one motion we all got up to leave. Our time on the island was up.

Magda and Gideon had also felt the wind change and their boat soon drew up beside us. Wide and bare, Gideon's fibre-glass boat looked an uncomfortable vessel to travel in; at least Kristian's boat had a tiny wooden platform in the bow that could be covered in canvas in bad weather. Magda took on a pose as regal as the Queen of Sheba, in a yellow anorak. She commandeered the entire bow with her arms outstretched, and with her hands lightly resting on either side of the boat. She grinned at us broadly, whipped off her sealskin mitts and, holding up a newborn pup barely the size of her hand, shouted that the boat was full of dogs and puppies; she laughed, adjusted her fluffy ear-warmers and returned to her original pose. And then we were off in tandem, Herbert Island diminishing darkly behind us.

The ride was rough. Within ten minutes the sea had changed from a rippling pond to a viridian swirling mass. Baali, Naduk and I clung desperately to the hard wooden benches and the equipment for over two hours, trying to keep both the gear and ourselves in the boat as we slammed uncompromisingly into the waves. I wondered if my insides would ever fit back together again, and was amazed that none of us had been knocked out by the violence of our brains rattling against our skulls. A flock of guillemots dived ecstatically around us, wheeling about on the wind and playing with the waves, highlighting the clumsiness of our efforts to ride the elements.

We were in pieces by the time we landed on the beach. A small group of hunters and their wives were waiting for us as we neared the shore, and those with waterproofs ran into the water to guide us in quickly. Magda and Gideon had arrived just a couple of minutes before us and were struggling among terse cries to unload the dogs that were in a frenzy, desperate to jump overboard and reach solid ground. The hunters roared at the dogs to keep them under control as Gideon was almost pulled overboard as he gripped their traces. It was utter chaos. Women ran after the dogs as they broke free from Gideon's grasp and ran amok, a five-year-old screamed and threw sand at the dogs, his brothers and cousins following suit, yelling and making swift arm movements as if they were cracking whips. I ran among them, my stomach still churning from the boat trip, and finally caught one of the more docile-looking dogs and stood on his trace in an effort to help, and then immediately regretted it as I heard a low grumble emanate from his throat. But Magda soon had it under control, cracking her whip unmercifully until they were all in a single panting group.

I was exhausted, and exhilarated. The crowd dispersed quickly and silently and I hugged the twins before struggling back to Louisa's house, to find her reading in a shaft of brilliant sunlight with hot tea ready for me in the flask, waiting expectantly to hear all about the trip. It was 3 a.m.

6. The Reluctant Angákoq

'*Aj-aa-ja, aj-aa-ja . . . ajajeahay . . .*' All eyes are fixed on a bent craggy-faced man as his eyes roll inward and he starts to chant. The angákoq sways hypnotically from side to side, and the voice seems to come from far far away, beyond distance, beyond time. A shallow dish is slick with the oily light of burning blubber, sending macabre shadows dancing on the skins, rock, bone and dark fragrant turf of the ancient dwelling. A child whimpers in a corner and is gathered into a tight embrace by a mother who sits almost naked, her high breasts glistening with sweat, her eyes glazed, unfocused. The tribe move with the ebb and flow of the wiry voice, skin brushing against skin. The air is thick with the heat of bodies, the atmosphere heavy with the weight of the spirits that press down on the knotted group. The angákoq grimaces and twitches, his fingers claw the air and bite into his thighs, his voice rises and falls and starts to fill the room; the spirits are coming closer. The women chant '*Aj-a-ja, aj-a-ja.*' The drum is played, bone on bone – the skin membrane reverberates but is not touched: *tatata-taa, tatata-taa*. The rhythm becomes insistent, demanding, fervent.

The angákoq cries out with ancient tongue that no one present understands – for everyone knows the power of words, and to speak the name of an object or being in a séance could bring untold disaster to those who heard it – he leaps up snarling, foaming at the mouth. A woman suppresses a scream and instead sings higher. The sound reaches fever pitch, and the man collapses. The angákoq is no longer breathing and a single note disappears into the distance; his spirit is travelling. Inside the hut the sound quietens, but the *ajajas* continue so that the shaman can find his way back; they are soft now, murmured and slow.

The journey is a difficult one for the angákoq, but his tribe depends on it. Game has abandoned the community, and the threat of starvation is upon them. Unwittingly the hunters must have offended the animals; perhaps a seal or a walrus was not given water when it was killed, perhaps a woman had walked out on the sea ice when she was menstruating; there were so many rules to observe that it was hard to pinpoint who of the tribe had slipped up. Whatever the mistaken act was, the only way to rectify the situation is for the angákoq to visit Nerrivik, the goddess of the waters and the one who guides and protects the animals that live in her domain.

Nerrivik is angry, and she has cloaked herself in murky waters to show her discontent. The angákoq trembles; she is a fearsome sight. The goddess sits naked on the seabed, her pale bloated body wrinkled and loose from the centuries of living underwater. She looks warily at the angákoq, she doesn't trust mankind, and she still nurses a grudge. Once, she was a young beautiful woman, who danced on the shores of the land and felt the sun caress her skin, but it is a distant memory.

Nerrivik (also known as *Arnaquagssaq*) was an orphan, and like all orphans she was regarded less with pity than with contempt, for she was a burden on the community. One day the community decided to move camp, and once all the boats and kayaks were loaded, they resolved to leave the young girl alone to her fate. But Nerrivik plunged into the water after them, terrified that she would starve at the deserted camp. In desperation she tried to pull herself up on the boat of her guardian, but he pushed her away from the side. Again she pulled on the side of the boat until it almost capsized. Her guardian in his fury took a heavy axe and chopped off a few fingers from each hand, but still poor Nerrivik clung on. Again the man attacked her, until eventually she had nothing but stumps left. No longer able to grip the side of the boat, Nerrivik sank slowly to the bottom of the sea and thus became the goddess of the waters.

The angákoq knows he has to appease the awful goddess of

the waters, and has learnt what he must do from his father, who was an angákoq before him. Nerrivik turns her head towards him and sees that the one who approaches her is a strong shaman. Her long black hair is knotted and vile with the accumulated wrongdoings of humans, and in the knots hide the animals of the sea. She is suspicious of the shaman, but her unruly hair is bothersome and with the vanity of a once beautiful woman, she longs to have her hair groomed.

With soothing words the angákoq speaks to her, and gently combs her hair and cleans her house. She is pleased, and in recognition of his efforts Nerrivik sends the game out into the waters again.

In the dwelling the people wait and chant, and once again they hear the distant eerie whistle of the spirit of the angákoq as he returns. The light is extinguished and the sound grows louder, more distinct. The crowd welcome him back with chants and stamping that make the small dwelling tremble. There is silence. The angákoq breathes hoarsely; the trip has exhausted him. He will need several days to recover.

I was on the search for an angákoq – an Inughuit shaman. Visiting Aata's house had made me realize how much I was missing not only him, but also the intangible thing he represented: the sense of spirit, still so strong in the community when we lived there, and which seemed to have disappeared entirely from modern Qaanaaq.

At his own admission, Aata was 'the *little* shaman', although he would laugh uproariously whenever he said it. His father and his grandfather had both been angákoqs before him and it was in his genes – the son of an angákoq would automatically follow in his father's footsteps, but occasionally an angákoq might see a child unrelated to him that was spiritually sensitive, and it would be his duty to teach that child the ways of the angákoq. But Aata didn't think he was a very good angákoq. I think he was unnerved by the idea of going on the hazardous journeys to the moon to save the odd soul or two, although he did believe that he had a black polar bear as his spirit guide, which was a powerful symbol in Eskimo mythology. According to the Polar Eskimo tradition the brown or black bear is the most intelligent of animals and endowed with tremendous power. No magic is a match for its spiritual strength, and no man could even mention the bear by name without risking its revenge. Unlike the white bear, the black bear's power could be transferred to a strong angákoq, which would be an essential talisman for an old Eskimo shaman when he journeyed through the spirit world.

Before the missionaries came, the Polar Eskimos did not believe in gods as such, but rather imbued everything around them with spirit. The spirits were independent of each other, and no spirit could thwart another, but as a whole they greatly complicated the life of the Eskimo, which was already very hard. The *Inua* was the spirit or the 'living owner' of any one thing, yet somehow they had evolved a belief that differentiated man from everything else around him – man had instead of spirit a 'soul', called *târneq*, which translated means 'something like darkness' or 'something like a shadow', and this soul was vulnerable. The spirits were to be treated with the utmost respect, for if they were angered they could steal a man's soul, and unless it was retrieved quickly by an angákoq the body would fall sick and could easily die.

Only a century ago – when Aata's angákoq father was young – the life of the Eskimo was intrinsically linked with ritual of one form or another; perhaps this grew out of the need to perform their daily duties with great presence of mind, as carelessness could result in injury or death. Rituals and taboos in dealing with hunting were particularly important since the Polar Eskimos believed that each animal had a spirit. Respect for these animals, their only source of food and clothing, was of grave importance, for if it was treated badly an animal's spirit could wreak havoc. Reincarnation was a fundamental belief, affecting both humans and animals, and in order for the hunted animal to permit itself to be killed in the first instance, and then to be reborn (and killed again), the hunter had to treat its carcass with the utmost respect. When we lived in Thule, the true hunters believed this to be true. If the animal had in the slightest way been offended by its treatment at the hands of the hunter it could withdraw its favours and never return to that particular hunter, or worse, it might spread the word to the rest of its kind that this hunter and perhaps all his kin or even the entire community, should be abandoned by its species. Only by an angákoq appeasing Nerrivik – the goddess of the waters – the Polar Eskimos believed, would the animals return. The angákoqs were the medium between the world of the Inughuit and the complex, mystical world of the spirits. Without the angákoq the people would be at the mercy of these spirits.

During my quest to find out if any angákoqs still survived in the area I heard of an old man by the name of Qaviunnguak who, if not a true angákoq, at least had many of the qualities of one. He was, some said, the nearest I would find to an angákoq these days.

Qaviunnguak was now relegated to living in the nursing home, although he seemed younger than the other residents. He greeted me quietly and then, alarmed that a chair was missing from his room, promptly disappeared to fetch one. I wondered why he was in the home at all as he seemed perfectly capable of looking after himself.

'Ah, I can't go hunting any more,' he offered on his return, 'because of my eyes. I got a splinter in my eye and so my eyesight is very bad. And I broke my arm once when I was out hunting,' he added as an afterthought. 'Mostly I just walk, walk, walk. And sometimes I go fishing, when it is clear weather. I fish for some ugly fish!' The old man was lost in amusement for a moment, but regained his composure quickly.

Qaviunnguak's room was spartan; furnished only with a few photographs and a large television set that faced his hospital bed. A handful of hunting memorabilia lined the glossy white window-ledge and a line of boots stood to attention facing one wall. At one end of the row, set slightly apart from the others, was a pair of silver moon boots: Qaviunnguak's special boots.

The old man invited me to join him at a table set up by the window, and offered me tea and orange squash; perhaps I would like a biscuit? He looked happy to have company and a small smile played on his thin lips. A wall-mounted clock behind his head lent him a halo of time.

Knowing that it would be impolite to ask the old man if he was an angákoq himself, I instead asked Qaviunnguak if he had ever met one on his travels. He scratched a patch of stubble on his chin, and then nodded slowly as if he was being asked a trick question: 'There was one angákoq I knew, but then he stopped being an angákoq.' The angákoq had supposedly thwarted the 'evil' gifts by becoming baptized.

I asked: 'If he knew he was going to lose his gifts, why was he baptized?'

Qaviunnguak drew himself up in his seat as he talked of the old shaman. 'He didn't want to have visions again, because sometimes he could sense death around some of the people who came to visit him, and he knew that the catechist said that [having visions] was bad. He used to have some spirits that used to help him, and even after he was baptized they still kept following him, they would not leave him alone. I remember him telling me that when he tried to get away from his spirits it felt like someone was sticking needles in him all over. He said it was very painful. The spirits didn't want to leave him.' Qaviunnguak spoke slowly and carefully, acting out where the man had felt pain.

Being an angákoq was a difficult business, and involved many tasks. The angákoq was a witchdoctor, a seer, and the giver of names when babies were born, and when there was no game, or any other kind of trouble in the community, he not only had to try to appease Nerrivik the goddess of the sea, but also take spirit journeys deep beneath the ice or even into the earth itself through rock and stone to talk with the ancestors. Some of the strongest angákoqs were known even to take the most hazardous journey to the moon.

I asked Qaviunnguak if the angákoq he knew had ever gone to the moon, but he shook his head: no. I teased him asking if he had ever journeyed to the moon himself, and pointed to the silver boots. He laughed brassily. 'Not today,' he said with a twinkle in his good eye, starting to warm to the conversation. 'When you are an angákoq you cannot hunt or kill animals.'

'But then how do you eat?'

'We can hunt on the land, we can catch hare and musk oxen and such, but we cannot hunt anything that lives in water. You have to choose between being a good hunter, or an angákoq. And life for the angákoq is hard.' I wondered if this taboo was something to do with offending Nerrivik. 'Not so much,' he replied; 'it is because those that live in the sea are more heavenly animals. They are not from the air or land. We have to respect them more.' Qaviunnguak poured himself a glass of bright orange squash. 'Not long ago, and your father will know this, if a hunter killed an animal from the sea he would put a ball of snow in the mouth of the seal or walrus or narwhal, to make sure that the animal did not get thirsty on its way to the spirit world. This was important to make sure that the animals would be pleased with the hunter so that they would come back again in their next life to be hunted again.'

Historically the angákoq was the closest thing that the Polar Eskimos had to a leader. In such a hostile environment the people traditionally relied on its simple community-based infrastructure to survive: they helped one another in order to help themselves. The Eskimos of old were communistic in their way of life and there was never any leadership structure; no one individual ever had power over a community, and neither was there a tribal council as such. In the old days if a group of men travelled together to hunt they sometimes deferred to one man's decisions, but that man – who would be the best hunter of them all –

would merely voice his ideas; it was entirely up to the individual either to follow the suggestion, or take off on his own. In the community itself the only person who really had any sway was the angákoq, but even he (or very occasionally she) would be consulted only on certain matters. In such an environment the individual was weak and vulnerable; security for oneself and one's family was to be found only by being a part of the pack; the members of a community never had allegiance to anyone or anything but their clan. The greatest fear of any Polar Eskimo was to be different to everyone else – even being more intelligent than others in their village could sometimes be a burden. The life of the angákoq then must have been very lonely. Qaviunnguak believed that the angákoq he knew was baptized more to avoid this loneliness than because of his fear of seer-ship.

But there was one angákoq who did not fear leadership. Kritlaq was said to be the greatest of all the angákoqs, and was known far and wide for his great wisdom and spiritual strength. But misfortune dogged his tribe of Admiralty Inlet, on the northern part of Baffin Island: there had been no game for some time, the weather conspired to make hunting even more difficult, and the tribe continually faced the threat of starvation. But Kritlaq had a vision of another place where the tribe would be safe and would not go hungry. His spirit went on reconnaissance flights and, assured by the spirits that all would be well, he advised the tribe to follow him. They did. Guiding his followers by the light of the flames that shot out of his head during the long polar nights, Kritlaq led his party north over Devon and Ellesmere Islands and finally made camp in 1864 at Etah, his promised land, just north of Qaanaaq. It had taken them seven years.

The ancestral history of the Polar Eskimos – such as this story of Kritlaq – along with traditional myths and stories of local affairs were communicated orally down the generations through song, and the drum songs, until the missionaries deemed them pagan in 1900, were the heartbeat of the communities. The missionaries confiscated the drums of the Polar Eskimos, along with their belief system, but even as Christianity was finally worked into the modern Arctic, the rhythm of the Eskimo world continued behind closed doors. Aata would on occasion produce a prized plastic dustpan and brush and leap and chant guttural songs and tales with great alacrity – just one example that the old traditions were not so easy to dismiss, particularly when survival itself depended on superstition.

If drum songs were the heartbeat of the communities, then storytelling was the blood that kept the people alive, and sane in the interminable darkness of winter. Eskimo folkloric stories were uniquely gruesome with little observance to moral lessons, serving it seems simply to terrify listeners of any age into a healthy reverence of the spirit world. The stories engrained upon the Polar Eskimo the reassurance that he or she, and therefore all of humankind, was to be ridiculed and should not be regarded above any of the other animals that happened to exist on the face of the planet. Stories of cannibalism, revenge and of relations with animals – there are many stories of women who married dogs or bears and bore strange and grotesque children – were most popular, and the creation myths are uniquely obscure. In all the stories, however, there is an underlying sense that the spirit world – *Inua* – was constantly laughing at the foibles of the human race.

Amaunalik was an old woman famous for her repertoire of stories and Eskimo myths, and during the time my father spent in the Arctic, she told him many tales. 'She used no gestures or facial contortions to dramatize her tales,' my father said, 'only her voice – that soft, expressive, almost magical voice that intoned all stories at the same slow pace, as though each word was feeding on the atmosphere the sound itself created.'

'One of our forefathers,' she would begin, clearing her throat with the customary show of embarrassment at having attracted an audience, 'one of our forefathers, it is told, he used to go out waiting at a seal's breathing hole now and again when he was starving. He, having gone out hunting one day, his wife (fearing that he would eat her when he returned) her sealskin jacket she stuffed it with grass. And when she had stuffed it, she laid it in her sleeping place, and in the igloo passage, it is told, she made a cave, her husband came home, and thinking it was his wife lying in her sleeping place, he stabbed her. But he discovered when he had stabbed it, the sealskin jacket was quite without human being, and when he saw this he began to boil water. And when it was boiling, it is told, his thigh he began to cook it. Then – part of himself he having put to boil – he cried out because he was dying, while in the pot his thigh was boiling!'

'*Ajor!* What a pity!' Amaunalik would exclaim at the end of each gruesome story, and then, looking around at her audience, burst out laughing as though the very indignity of the mutilated man had suddenly become ridiculous. Soon they were all roaring with laughter and with tears pumping from their eyes and their bodies heaving they would eventually slump into a silence broken only now and then by a shuddered sigh. Only then, as the horror of the story crept into their bones and began to work its healing miracles upon the fear within their souls would Amaunalik clear her throat and start another tale more horrible than the last.

The creation myths are singularly bizarre with rarely any plot or logical progress, and all vary considerably.

In the beginning [they say] there was nothing but water. Then suddenly, one day, it began to rain rocks – and that is how land was created. The people, they came out of mounds of earth, but at that time they were only babies, they could not see, they could not even crawl – they just lay there sprawling and feeding themselves with handfuls of mud until at last a woman came looking for them. She had made some babies' clothes in the hope that one day she would find some babies to care for, so she was very happy when she found them and after dressing the babies, she took them all home – and that is how there came to be so many people in the world.

Like other stories of creation around the globe, there is another myth that describes a cataclysmic flood:

They also say that in those days snow could burn and that fire sometimes fell from the sky. They say too that at first, people did not know how to die and in a while became so numerous that they over-populated the Earth. Then there came a mighty flood which swept most of them away. Traces of that flood they say can be found even today on the tops of the high hills where there are shells.

There are many theories on the evolution of mankind in the Arctic regions, but all have established that man was not native to Greenland: the Eskimos of Greenland came from Somewhere Else. But from where these ice-borne nomads *originally* came, and the actual location of that elusive Somewhere Else, is difficult to pinpoint. Most suppose that the Inughuit have a Mongol lineage due to the striking similarities in physical characteristics to their Asian counterparts – short stature with small narrow hands and tiny feet, with narrow almond-shaped eyes set in smooth dark-skinned faces; and their babies – until the Europeans came and diluted the blood line – were often born with the blue Mongolian spot at the base of their spine. But then most of these physical characteristics could just as easily be attributed to natural genetic evolution as their bodies naturally adapted to survival in that harsh environment. What is generally accepted however is that the Bering 'Bridge' – a route between Siberia and Alaska that appeared and disappeared over the course of thousands of years due to the effects of climate change – was responsible for the migrations of animals moving eastwards across the Arctic sometime between 13,000 and 10,000 years ago, and in pursuit were those tribes that depended on them for survival.

The migrations from Canada are well documented through extensive archaeological research and the oral histories of the Eskimos themselves; it is generally undisputed, for instance, that the first wave of Paleo-Eskimo immigrants – known as the

Independence 1 – arrived on the northern shores of Greenland around five thousand years ago. These primitive hunters had their sights on land-based game rather than the rich waters that surrounded them, and soon moved out of the area. The Sarqaq people followed on the heels of these first pioneers to Greenland, and were the first to move down the west coast and, hemmed in by the vast Greenland icecap on one side and the coast on the other, they began to adapt to a marine-based way of life. But with their still rudimentary skills they too soon died out.

It was another five hundred or so years before another human voice was heard anywhere on the 25,000-mile coastline of Greenland. This time the tribes hailed from another culture: the Dorset people. Far more advanced than their predecessors, the Dorset people became fine hunters both on land and at sea, and evolved into accomplished artisans. But this culture too disappeared, leaving only traces of its existence by the time that Eric the Red's settlers arrived in AD 986.

The next culture to sweep across this part of the Arctic can only be described as a phenomenon. It is not known where exactly the Thule culture originated – the name Thule is attributed both to the place and the culture, which is used to describe all historical maritime Eskimo cultures across the Arctic – but from the moment they appeared in the Bering Strait region they dramatically accelerated the cultural evolution of every tribe with which they came into contact. The Thule people had become masters of their environment; they developed highly crafted weapons, *umiaks* (large skin-covered boats) and *kayaks*, made sledges and drove dogs. As their culture developed, so did their need to understand the subtleties of their environment, and soon they imbued it with a wealth of spirits, which would result in complicated superstitions and taboos that were still an essential part of their belief-system right up until Rasmussen and Freuchan came to the area in 1910.

The Thule people flooded into the northern reaches of Greenland from Ellesmere Island via the ice bridge to Smith Sound in the eleventh century AD and by 1300 were pressing down towards the south, where they would finally come into contact with the last of the Norsemen from Eric the Red's colony. Unwilling to struggle for survival, the now-called *Inugsuk* settled happily into their gentler climate, lost their whaling skills and instead concentrated on perfecting the kayak and the umiaq: the Inugsuk became fishermen.

Meanwhile, in the far north small migratory groups still made their way from Canada to Northwest Greenland right up until the eighteenth century. Those that chose to stay in the north were known as the Polar Eskimos, and became the most brave and skilful of hunters.

Few now remember the old stories of their evolution; the mocking laughter of the white man at their stories made the Eskimos feel foolish about relating them, and as there was no written language – until the missionaries came and started to teach their flock how to read and write – the only stories that were not lost were the ones that visitors to the area (such as Rasmussen and Freuchan) wrote down. Sadly, even the ancient tradition of storytelling is rapidly being forgotten now that there is alternative entertainment in the long winter months. In his 1927 book *Across Arctic America*, Knud Rasmussen reports that even then there was a decreasing reliance on ritual and taboo: 'We have forgotten all the old spells and magic songs, and you will find no more amulets sewn up in our inner garments. Our people have food enough and do not bother about their souls.' Today, few people in modern Qaanaaq believe that angákoqs still exist.

I asked Qaviunnguak if there were any angákoqs left. He sighed: 'No, no, there are no angákoqs left, not like in the old days. The angákoq I told you about died of TB. But some people still feel and see spirits and strange things, the psychic ones, but that is different. The world is different now. It is not good to be an angákoq.' I felt that his last comment had been forced on him, and so I just waited for him to continue, which he did.

'When I was a child, maybe about three years old, my mother died and we were very poor. My sister had to grow up with somebody else, so we had different step-parents. We both shared the same father, but he couldn't do much to keep us. So sometimes we would go from house to house, and get new parents to look after us. As I grew up I learnt how to hunt, but I didn't have any hunter's clothes, because I didn't have a mother to make them for me, and I was so poor. I managed somehow, and eventually I had all the things a hunter needed; an old kayak and harpoon, and I went a long way from the settlement to go and hunt for myself and sleep alone. But I had never slept away from the settlement and I got nightmares, I was so frightened and alone. One night I had such a bad nightmare, and I kept telling myself to wake up, but my eyes were already open! In front of me I saw three women, I didn't think they were real, and so I closed my eyes and opened them again, and they were still there.'

From that moment on, whenever the young Qaviunnguak went hunting alone the three women would appear to him in visions to warn him of imminent danger and to protect him from the threats of darker spiritual forces. They stayed with him until they felt he was strong enough to look after himself. As they left one of the women gave him a gift of dried animal blood: 'When I woke up I still had the blood in my hand, then, just as if it was a dream, the blood faded from my hands, as if it had never been there at all!' Qaviunnguak stared at his hands remembering the disbelief. It had been there, he assured me, it was real and then it was gone. He took a sip of tea and carried on with his story.

'I was still young and unmarried, and always I would go hunting with other young men; I forgot about the visions of the three women that I used to have. Then one night I went to sleep as normal and awoke sitting up, and I could feel that something was wrong with my arm, but there was no blood, and I hadn't cut myself as I first thought, but there in front of me when I looked, my arm had turned into the paw of a polar bear. Ajor! I didn't know what to do! I turned away from it; I couldn't look at it because it frightened me too much. I didn't look at it again.' The old man laughed, turning away from his arm as he told the story. 'A long way off I could see the settlement and from then on I knew who was coming and going without seeing them. But I never told my friends about my experience.'

I smiled. It sounded to me as if I had found a reluctant angákoq. But then something in his eyes changed, and he looked ever so slightly sheepish. He said:

'The whole time that I had these experiences – the women and then the hand of a bear – I found I could no longer pray to God. All the prayers I had been taught at church disappeared, and I couldn't even remember one of them. I didn't like that, I didn't like to be the only one who was seeing things, and be different to my friends. I read Sunday prayers, but however hard I tried I couldn't remember the prayers. I wanted to get away from the visions; I didn't like them any more, and all my young friends were so happy and having a good time! And so I went to church every Sunday and I read the prayers so much that eventually I started to remember them again, and I started to forget all the visions that I had had. There was an old woman called Lucia who I used to go and talk to a lot, she knew so much about the Bible and she used to tell me many stories. She helped me to pray too. The spirits left, and I don't have them any more; it feels good to be away from them.'

I was surprised at this turn in the conversation. I had heard from friends that Qaviunnguak used to heckle the congregation on their way to church, bellowing abuse at them for forgetting their roots and for being hypocrites: for their souls with no direction and their piety only on a Sunday. I found myself disappointed that the old man had meekly joined the flock himself.

I wondered whether perhaps the willingness of the Polar Eskimos to accept Christianity in the beginning was because it offered a set of beliefs that were simpler than the ones they had followed until then: before Christianity their every footstep was bound with taboos and superstitions. The Eskimo was imprisoned by his own beliefs, and fear was omnipresent. Perhaps Christianity provided a spiritual sanctuary away from the meddling forces of the natural spirit world – or an escape route from the suffocating laws of the supernatural – and in God and Jesus they envisioned protectors who would give them great peace of mind in return for their allegiance.

We both drank our tea, lost in thought. Qaviunnguak broke the silence: 'Here in Thule these days they are not interested in the Bible and the hymns, and they don't really know about what happened in the Bible – when we were young and we went to school, we were taught all the stories of the Bible by the catechist, who came to the school.'

'But didn't you find it difficult to relate to parts of the Bible if all you have ever known is the Arctic?'

'It is not difficult to understand,' he answered, 'because some of the things that happen in the Bible could happen here too; we have seen strange things happen here. But now everyone has so much that they don't care so much about the Bible, and there are some of us who want to teach it to people again. We have video machines and writing machines, so we can teach that way, and maybe we will talk on the radio too. There was a time when I so wanted to talk to people and give them the teachings, but then some young people in my family killed themselves, and it was a long time before I wanted to talk to anybody.' Qaviunnguak's face clouded as he spoke of the suicide, but like most Inughuit, he was resigned not to show his grief.

'I think now I am ready again,' he said quietly. 'I think I should go and teach the young people about the Bible.'

I left Qaviunnguak wishing that Aata was still alive so that he could enchant me with his stories of his black polar bear spirit guide, and so that he could stand alongside Qaviunnguak with his tales of the Bible, and teach the young people about *Inua* and the spirits of their ancestors, before the last of the angákoqs forgot the value of his unique spiritual heritage.

7. A Woman's Place

The sky was brooding, and a flag flew at half-mast outside the church. A hunter had died, Louisa told me, but before she could go on the door opened and Baali and Edo filed solemnly through the door. A small crowd of people were gathering in front of the church, standing in silent groups, waiting. The girls stood beside me at the window and watched, immobile, as a small procession wound down from the hillside behind the house. Four men carried a corpse, coffinless, swathed in a white sheet on a red plastic stretcher. The immediate family surrounded the body, weeping quietly. A line of supporters trickled behind.

Without much ceremony the procession came to a stop at the tiny shed that served as a morgue behind the church, the body was unloaded and the mourners promptly dispersed. I was confused. Wasn't there going to be a service? I tried to ask the girls, but my lack of language wouldn't permit it, and we stood in confusion until I finally understood that we were all going to the graveyard.

Hans disappeared around the side of the house as we gathered outside and reappeared a moment later with a whitewashed wooden frame, six feet long and three feet wide. We made our way slowly towards the cemetery and to my surprise the family was in high spirits. It seemed strange to be so light-hearted in the midst of funereal proceedings, but I joined in with their cheery banter until we were all helpless with giggles as they performed vignettes of our childhood together. All the girls linked together in a chain, arms squeezing one another with rough love. And behind us the only man, Hans, carrying the frame as if he were shouldering his crucifix.

The group became subdued as we reached the boundary of

the cemetery, and I found myself being guided directly to Maria's grave. The girls gathered around Hans and lifted the frame from him; it was not for the fresh grave as I had suspected, but for Maria's. Together we cleared away the area around the grave and used the rocks and sharp dark pebbles to secure the frame so that it wouldn't stray in the high winds that strip the hillside of any loose objects. It was deeply moving to watch the sisters work the grave, rearranging the silk and plastic blooms in silent communion, tugging out the few stray grasses. Baali turned to me and produced an imitation long-stemmed pink rose from a plastic bag. I was touched by the gesture and knelt down, pressing the stem into the sandy topsoil. Louisa handed me a small grey stone to weight it in place amongst the other flowers, then Baali and Magda did the same. We stood back, tears slipping unhindered down our cheeks and onto each other's shoulders.

We moved among the graves, Baali and I with our arms around each other. Magda moved away from us to stand at a beautifully kept grave, brimming with colourful wreaths and floral tributes and surrounded by a white picket fence. A glass jar protected a stump of a once-lit candle. She gripped a stave of the fence and swayed ever so slightly, lost in another world. Edo tugged at my sleeve. 'Her son,' she said, stabbing a finger at her sister. 'Dead.' The sound was so final, so devoid of life on her tongue. I nodded, not taking my eyes off Magda in case she keeled over. Edo persisted. 'Dead!' she reiterated, and I turned to look at her. In tragic comedy she wound an imaginary noose around her neck, stood on tiptoe, and tugged the air upwards, rolling her eyes and opening her mouth in a hideous gape, with her tongue lolling to one side. I stared at her, astonished. Finished with her mime she opened her eyes wide and with great solemnity said in English, 'He dead himself.' A whisper of emptiness scuttled through me.

With one mind we carried on, this time towards Avatak's grave, pausing briefly at a tiny grave that coincidentally I had filmed a few days before – it had looked so tiny, so perfect and I had been irresistibly drawn to it. I hadn't looked at the plaque, but as Baali and I stopped there I realized that the name was familiar. 'My daughter,' Baali whispered hoarsely, her face streaked with tears. The baby had lived for only one month.

By the time we reached Avatak's grave I was numb from the intensity of the emotions flowing through the group. Baali produced another rose for me, and I placed the flower carefully on the grave, but I felt as though I was not in my body when I did it.

We turned back towards the town, and no sooner had we crossed the threshold of the cemetery, than the mood lifted again. The girls skipped and danced their way home as if the last couple of hours had never happened, pulling Edo's little daughter onto Magda's shoulders and answering the excited barks of the dogs with calls and songs.

We filled our lungs with light.

Sunday is not a day of rest in the summer. Men who have been working as carpenters, amenity workers or office clerks during the week escape to the waters to fish or join the full-time hunters in their kayaks further down the fjord; the women not on summer camp or fishing with their husbands bustle to finish their chores so that they can go for long walks – in late summer they collect berries from the mountainside – or visit friends.

Visiting is a fundamental part of life for the Inughuit. The bond between the inhabitants of such remote hunting communities has to be strong, for it is only through the combined efforts of each individual that a community in this harsh environment can survive. But visiting for the Inughuit is more than just a re-establishment of a communal bond, it is a means through which to avoid the threat of utter boredom and loneliness. When we were first in the Arctic, there was a constant flow of visitors going from house to house, with often the same faces visiting again and again; but even if there is no real desire to be with other people, visits still took place, because company, however dull – with no new news or stories to impart – was still infinitely better than being left alone. As Jean Malaurie said in *The Last Kings of Thule*:

There is often dramatic contradiction between the Eskimo's basically individualistic temperament and his conscious belief that solitude is synonymous with unhappiness. He knows that an igloo which is seldom or never visited will be engulfed in the cold of the earth, wrapped in the shroud of death. Even though he may have the security of a family, if the Eskimo is abandoned by his fellow men, he is overcome by the depression that always lies in wait for him.

Loneliness for the Inughuit is a condition to be avoided. The men may crave temporary isolation while they are hunting, but they cannot be without company for very long, and will seek out other hunters if they are out on the ice to share tea, tobacco and warmth. Traditionally the need to be with others was more than just a lust for companionship, it was a prerequisite for survival. An individual in such an environment was both vulnerable and inefficient.

Nowadays in big towns or villages such as Qaanaaq, there is not so much emphasis on visiting, and the people have a more relaxed attitude to the necessity of being with other people. But Louisa was adamant that visiting, albeit for a short time only, had to be a daily occurrence.

Qaanaaq rustled with quiet activity: the disjointed sound of a hammer striking metal carried on the breeze as someone worked on their house; those men that did not have their own boats gathered at the shoreline helping to repair a boat or enviously eying their companions as they skidded out over the slick waters of the fjord. As Louisa and I headed towards Inudliah's house figures swung in and out of doorways ahead of us, some staggering from the night before clutching sore heads, others squatting on their front steps waving cheerily, clutching a cup of coffee or a cigarette.

Inudliah was a childhood friend from Herbert Island, and had always been a somewhat shy girl who had become an honorary member of the Qaerngâq family by virtue of the fact that she practically lived in our neighbour's house. Inudliah's home was very different to that of the sisters. Outside the ground was strewn with dog shit, greasy piles of discarded blubber, boxes of tools and once-useful junk. The house was raised, like all the houses in Qaanaaq, but Inudliah's house seemed taller than the rest, and stood with an arthritic gait, like a long-legged beauty queen gone to seed.

The steep stairs protested beneath us as Louisa and I clambered up to the entrance, which gave us a grim welcome. The walls, floor and low ceiling were dark with layers of dried blood. A pair of petrified rubber gloves linked fingers in a corner, cocooned by hardened fat and blubber, and skins in various stages of forgotten preparation hung from hooks on the wall. Inudliah beckoned us in and chirruped in urgent conversation, her voice high and shrill like the call of a surprised bird.

Inside, the place was spartan and shabby. Lines of washing sagged across one corner of the living room above an old black-ened stove and a piece of meat that was bloodying a plastic bucket. There was no running water like the more modern houses, and the place had a faint dank and musty air to it. But I liked her place, it was closer to what I had been expecting than any of the other houses; there was a familiarity about its simplicity and grime.

Another woman sat in an armchair by the window, dreamily plucking at a loose thread on the worn upholstery. She looked up and smiled warmly; she remembered me, she said, from when we played together as children. She had a look in her eyes as if she knew my most intimate secrets.

Inudliah fretted, apologetically handing us stained cups, and putting a few slices of white bread, butter and lurid red strawberry jam on the table, urging us to help ourselves. Inudliah was not comfortable as a hostess; she was acutely aware that her house wasn't as smart as the other girls' and that her meagre wages from cleaning at the school were not enough to provide expensive treats for her guests.

'My husband is away,' she said, searching the southern horizon through a grubby window as if she was Isolde waiting for the wind-filled sails of a ship to bring back Tristan, her true love. Now she lived alone with her children. She smiled weakly, denying me the rest of the story. Her hands fluttered about her, not knowing where to rest. The women looked down politely, and quickly changed the subject.

Even in modern Qaanaaq it is unusual for women to live alone, and often women who no longer have husbands live together, partly because living expenses are crippling if one is alone, but more for the company; some of the older generation of women I spoke to have never experienced being alone in a bed.

It is not that long ago that there was a stigma attached to being a single woman: the (mostly unfair) opinion was that there must be a reason why the woman had not been taken under the care of a man — perhaps it was because she was lazy or had other troublesome personal traits. For men too it would be embarrassing to be without a wife. Any fine hunter would have the pick of female partners; the man may be single as a consequence of being a poor hunter, and would therefore have to swallow his pride and live with a married family member so that the host's wife could prepare his food, flense and stretch the skins from his hunt and make or mend his clothes. For this privilege the single hunter would have to sacrifice his quarry to the family with whom he stayed. Although there is no longer such a stigma about being alone, many women still feel uncomfortable if it is noted that they do not have a partner.

Throughout the world, many believe that finding a lifetime partner completes an aspect of ourselves; in the High Arctic such a partnership was not just a fantasy, it was a necessity. Throughout their lives, boys and girls were taught gender-specific skills, and to establish the separation between the sexes taboos were enforced corralling each to their own realm of experience. In this way a successful partnership was ensured, and survival more likely. But without a partner life was intolerable, and almost impossible. The union or marriage between a man and a woman not only ensured that the couple could form a viable unit and work together for a common purpose – survival – but would also by association create an extended circle of kinship on which they could depend in times of need; for the ancestors at least finding a partner was as a consequence more practical in purpose than romantic. As Frances C. Smith points out in *The World of the Arctic*, the function of the woman in the economic unit was uniquely demanding: 'Very long ago, Eskimos did not have dogs, and women often served as the beasts of burden on the trail, pulling the sledges, while the men hunted.' But things have evolved dramatically since those days. Women want to find husbands and partners for love as much as security, but partners they want even though they can now support themselves financially.

As modernization blurs the boundaries between gender prerogatives and makes life generally much easier, perhaps the younger generations will evolve to be more independent of one another, but at present at least the young people of Thule do not aspire to having their own space in the way that they do in other neoteric societies. Young bachelors may yearn for some freedom and find accommodation outside the family home, but the accommodation is likely to be a boarding house with communal facilities. Young women still live with their family until such time that they find a long-term partner.

We made light conversation, the girls laughing and reminiscing about the old days when we were children: 'Ah the innocence of youth and now look at us, all women with responsibilities!' The happy banter was abruptly interrupted by a shriek from Inudliah, and we watched in amazement as she bolted from her chair and ran around the room possessed with either excitement or terror.

'What is it?' we cried in unison.

'Look, look there!' she shrieked again and started delving panic-stricken into cupboards, under piles of clothes, desperately searching for something.

'Urgh!' Louisa joined her almost leaping into my lap. I couldn't work out what the fuss was about and wondered if they had lost their minds.

'Ah-ha!' Inudliah shouted, producing a newspaper, which she quickly rolled up into a baton and brandished in the air. She flew across the room in a fury. It was like watching amateur dramatics. With unnatural force she pounded at something at the window, and then leapt away cowering as if she had pulled the tail of a lion in jest, and had just realized the possible consequences of her actions: 'Is it dead?' she asked quietly.

We all walked closer and peered at the prey, the girls leaping behind me in terror as the object wiggled its legs and limped on the blistered window sill.

'What is it?' Inudliah asked me, whispering, clinging to my jumper.

'A fly.'

'A fliee,' the women repeated in wonderment.

'Urgh. It's so *big* . . .' Inudliah shuddered, watching the blue-bottle expire in the sunlight.

'We have never seen one like this before,' the other woman said in stilted English. 'Is it dangerous?'

'No,' I replied, suppressing laughter, 'no they are quite harm-less. Horrible though,' I added, to which they all nodded in agreement. Louisa steered us back to the table.

'Maybe they come from the big ship,' Inudliah volunteered, still spooked, but stabbing an accusing finger at the tourist ship that had appeared overnight and anchored offshore. The girls talked urgently about the threat of disease from the ships, and that many illnesses and strange creatures had come to their land from the ships, from as far back as when the big white men came to hunt whales. They had heard the stories from their grandparents.

Like any remote tribe that has been visited by people from 'The Outside', the Thule people have had to contend with more than just the benefits of trade that brought them metal tools, rifles and ammunition; the whalers and early explorers also brought with them influenza, diphtheria, smallpox, tuberculosis and a colourful blossoming of venereal diseases.

The Polar Eskimos first came into contact with *kadlunas* in 1818 when John Ross journeyed to the area. The 'Arctic Highlanders' he came in contact with were what he described as being a primitive Stone Age people. The Eskimos thought the white men strange too. The Eskimos had marvelled at Ross's ship, which they described to their descendants as 'a whole island of wood which moved along the sea on wings, and in its depths had many houses and rooms full of noisy people. Little boats hung along the rail, and these, filled with men, were lowered on the water, and as they surrounded the ship it looked as if the monster gave birth to living young.'

Hot on his trail the whalers ventured into the wild waters to satisfy the demands of their civilized society – whale bone for the corsets of the ladies at court, grease for wheel axles, oil for lamps, soap and perfume, and even bristle shavings for stuffing early train carriages – and started a trend of trading things of little consequence to them, such as wood, tobacco and needles, in return for the valuable ivory of the single-tusked narwhal and walrus and the prized furs of fox, seal and bear. Some crews wintered in the area, enjoying the warm hospitality of the Eskimo women. The Eskimos were fascinated by the white people and their possessions; in particular they were intrigued by glass which they recognized as ice that never melted. The women brought back tales of the living quarters below decks where the men slept in their hammocks like the *appaliarhuk*, the little auks on the bird cliffs. The Inughuit called them '*Upernaallit*' – those who arrive in Spring. And in the wake of the *Upernaallit* came more explorers: Elisha Kent Kane, Hayes, Hall and later the two that made the most impact on the area, Robert E. Peary and Knud Rasmussen.

The conversation faltered as we all thought of the influences the outside world had pressed upon this community of hunters.

Inudliah brightened with a change of subject. 'One of my dogs has had some babies,' she said beaming; 'do you want to see?' She disappeared before I had a chance to answer. Louisa smiled with what seemed to be a tinge of pity. Moments later our hostess returned grinning with pride, holding up a tiny smelly ball of fluff.

I sat with the puppy on my lap in the sitting room, with Louisa regarding the scene with astonishment, wholly affronted that an animal should have been brought into the house. The girls laughed together watching me, and the other woman translated: 'They think it's funny that you like the puppy,' she said. 'When you were little you used to pick them up like this,' and she grabbed the puppy by the scruff of its neck and pretended to carry it around like a handbag. We laughed again, and then the mood suddenly changed for no apparent reason. The show was over. Inudliah retrieved the puppy from my lap and with faint embarrassment hefted it out of the door. Our time was up, and we had to go. Louisa insisted that I scrub my hands thoroughly as we left the house, using some water that Inudliah had obviously had to carry for some distance to her house. Inudliah pulled on her kamiks and coat as we waved goodbye. '*Namupilergait*, where are you going?' Louisa called out to her and pointed at the tourist ship, teasing mischievously, 'Going to find a new husband?' Inudliah blushed deeply, adjusted her glasses and giggled.

'*Umiassuaq!*' The tourist boat floats silently in the fjord and the town is awaiting an invasion of red-parka'd tourists toting cameras like guns. But the town is unbothered, even the children don't seem to be the least interested in the ship's arrival. There was never apathy like this at the prospect of visitors when we were living in Thule, quite the opposite in fact. Any kind of new arrival – by ship or helicopter – was treated as a great event.

Louisa and I made our way to a cousin's birthday party, communicating with the few words that we had in common. We started on the subject of food: 'At the party,' she told me, 'we will be eating mattak and cat.'

'Cat?' I repeated in astonishment. She exploded into giggles.

The party was for a little girl who was celebrating her third birthday, and she greeted us shyly in traditional dress: high creamy white kamiks with a fur ruff, perfect tiny fox fur pants and a bright ornate anorak. We both gave the modern customary present of Danish kroner and she staggered off in her unwieldy footwear to put it in her piggy bank.

A large trestle table groaned with the weight of food outside the house; it was a celebratory feast, and the family were making sure that no one would go hungry. It was more than an act of generosity, it was tradition, and not only that, it was an indication of the status of the hunter, and generosity is one of the most respected traits in any person. A small knot of people had gathered around the food, amicably chatting and eating. Slabs of fresh mattak – whale blubber – slick with oil, shone in the sunlight next to withered pieces of dried narwhal meat, which looked suspiciously like fibrous tree bark, and a selection of dried fish.

'Hello.' A high nasal voice greeted me at my shoulder; it was Navarana, who had worked as an interpreter with my father on a film several years ago, and she looked lovely. She was elegantly dressed, and it was clear that she had developed a taste for style in her years of living in Canada and Copenhagen. Today she was wearing a long slim tailored jacket with a delicate flower brooch made from silk. Her hair softly framed her fine-boned face. Dark steely eyes surveyed me and then flicked to the food on the table.

'This is dried halibut. Eat! It's good for your heart.' It was delicious too. The oily white fish had a light texture, and melted in one's mouth. We tasted everything as a matter of courtesy – everything tasted pungently of fish – and turned into the house to congratulate the mother and to warm our greasy hands.

A clamour of women filled the main room with their ample bosoms and twittering chatter. The tables inside were also laden with food: sweet currant buns, biscuits, homemade cakes and gallons of tea and coffee, and the hostess was still cooking. She glanced up at us in a hurried welcome, a smudge of flour highlighting her hot flat cheeks. Again, the house was another clone of Qaanaaq's basic architectural style, and even the furniture looked identical to Baali and Kristian's, complete with the obligatory image of Christ, except this image had him holding a rose with his red heart exposed and glowing.

I sat with a group of women at the kitchen table and chatted to Navarana and Louisa while we watched the little girl charming her audience with baby chatter and demanding their attention. Navarana had given the birthday girl a small bottle of nail varnish, and the little girl was obsessed with it, insisting that every person that came through the door had to paint her nails. By the time I had arrived the polish on her tiny nails was several layers thick. A sturdy hunter came through the door and she proffered her hand as if waiting for him to kiss it, and produced the nail varnish with the other. The hunter looked bewildered and the women hooted with laughter, teasing him. He would have to learn how to apply the polish or be held responsible for the squalling. He blushed deeply, his temples glowing crimson as he quickly put another slick of 'cosmic blue' on a miniature nail, looking behind him to make sure there weren't any men watching. The women tormented him and gave him a round of applause as he turned and bolted for the door, but the little girl was unimpressed and promptly burst into tears holding up her hand in dismay that it hadn't been finished. She turned to me and held up her arms and I scooped her up into my lap; she looked at me coyly and stopped crying as quickly as she started, grabbing a biscuit with a teary hand and leaning into my shoulder. The women clucked with appreciation, and then laughed again as they imitated the bashful hunter.

It was just as we were leaving that I met Pauline Peary. A dignified and elegant woman, the same age as my father, she is one of the most respected women in the community, and was a close friend of the family. She was the granddaughter of the explorer Robert E. Peary and his Eskimo mistress Aleqasina, and sister of Peter Peary, who travelled with my father on several of his training expeditions. Of all the women I met in Qaanaaq she had the most regal bearing. Her smooth face shone with grace and was framed with perfect silver plaits secured in a coil at the nape of her neck. I remember being in awe of her when I was little.

Pauline seemed shaped by the very best of the Arctic. She was a woman both of land and sea; she was the only woman Dad had ever known from the district to be a mistress of the kayak, and she had an affinity with her homeland that many would envy. We still have family archive footage of Pauline teaching my mother how to catch little auks in early summer – a skill involving much dexterity and keen observance.

Pauline Peary was unusual in the district; she was not only beautiful, but could also rival almost any hunter's skill, and she had inherited her great-grandfather's strength of character. Pauline was elected the first mayor of Thule in 1976, and was the first and only woman to occupy the role. As a representative of the area she spent many years in the capital Nuuk, until she felt it was time to hand over the responsibility to someone younger so that she could return home.

She looked at me softly, time seeming to slow its heartbeat for a moment as she cupped my face in her hands – 'Kaari?' she whispered, and the town seemed to go silent for a moment to watch the exchange. 'Eie, yes,' I replied, and in a childlike moment I wished that time had stood still and that she had never aged.

There are several women in Qaanaaq who are endeavouring

to bridge the gap between their traditional role as wife and mother, and the modern necessity to find paid work to support the family, and perhaps to find their own identity. Pauline was one of the first who not only embraced openly the role of all the women before her, but who also looked to the future pragmatically and decided that she had something to offer to the community as a whole.

'Once we were only hunters' wives, but today things are very different,' she said later, her voice low and warm. 'Living here is expensive and if you live just trying to be a hunter it is very hard because you have to pay for everything, pay your bills . . . Being a hunter is not like having a normal job, so a wife's economy is very important to have now. So it is a good thing that the wives can have a job besides just looking after the home and her husband.' She smiled, her eyes shining. 'My granddaughter wants to go out with her father hunting every time. Like my grand-sons, she just wants to be out there, she loves to live in nature that way; it is a part of her life. So maybe she likes to become a hunter too!'

It is almost impossible these days for a family to live by subsistence hunting alone, particularly if there are children to look after, and as the Inughuit become more reliant on imported foodstuffs and develop a keen desire for material goods, the drain on the family income is unsustainable. Many families have already steered away from a hunting way of life and either find what work they can within the community or succumb to living on benefit. The men generally find manual labour – as carpenters, builders or plumbers as well as working for the store or the fisheries; few work in the community offices – whereas the women work as nurses, teachers, childcare workers or in clerical positions for the *Kommunea*, the municipal authority.

I was curious how women could manage juggling both their traditional and modern roles at home, and Navarana had suggested that I talk to Manomina Eipe. 'She is my heroine!' Navarana had enthused. 'She holds down a full-time job as well as being a hunter's wife, as well as looking after seven children. You have to meet her.'

Manomina looked up shyly as she came to join me at the top of her stairs, stamping the snow off her boots with such force that we bounced on the wooden boards. Lines of drying fish swung like bunting outside the door. 'Come into my dirty house,' she said grimacing as she took off her coat and stood awkwardly beside two plastic buckets filled with pots of gristle and yellowing blubber. A piece of cardboard lay by the doorway stained with blood and the comings and goings of the household. The prefabricated house looked older than most of the houses I had visited so far, and was clearly the house of a hunting family: an old oil burner squatted to one side, growling away to itself with a familiar rough melody that took me straight back to my childhood; beside it two sealskins on stretchers were propped against each other to dry. On the small dining table lay an assortment of children's toys and a few leftover remnants of fur. Four patched red-leather chairs surrounded the table – the legs on two of the chairs looked as if they could not support a child – and instead of the expensive-looking entertainment systems that many people in Qaanaaq had (if they worked for the community) Manomina's home had a battered television and old video player.

She gestured for me to take a seat, and sat next to me on a sofa that was caving in from the exhaustion of supporting so many people. She had seven children aged between five and nineteen, and all still lived in the house, with everyone sleeping in one bedroom, except for the eldest girl who had escaped to a relative's house to give the others more space.

Manomina looked tired and distracted. As well as working a nine-to-five clerical job at the municipal office, she had to look after her large family, and was also a hunter's wife, which was a full-time job in itself as her husband was one of the best hunters in the district. I wondered how she managed to get everything done, but she just answered simply that she had learnt that she had to schedule everything carefully. Mostly she prepared the skins just at the weekends, and used the evenings to care for the children and make and repair hunting clothes for her husband, and kamiks and mittens for the children. She smiled wearily when I asked her if she ever had time to do the things that she wanted. 'If I have a little free time then I go for long walks out of Qaanaaq. I love to walk. Then sometimes my husband takes me and the children out down the fjord, if he isn't hunting. We always look forward to those times' – her eyes brightened at the thought, but instantly they clouded again – 'but often my husband is away. Life is harder when he is away; at least when he is here he can watch the children while I work.'

I asked what her husband thought of her working as well as having to do all this work at home. She shrugged. 'I had a job before I met my husband, so it wasn't something we decided, it was just the way it was.' With so many children she needed to have a paid job to be able to feed and clothe them all. It was simply impossible to stay alive with just the income from her husband's hunting trips, even if he was a fine hunter. One of the youngest boys came in dressed in a small army camouflage jacket and stood close by, curious at the visitor. His long glossy hair was tied into a long ponytail at the back, unlike most of the boys in Qaanaaq that either have very short hair, or the men's Thule hairstyle – short all over save for a long soft quiff at the front. 'I don't know if my boys will become hunters,' she said, wiping mucus from his nose with the pad of her fleshy thumb; 'the eldest ones are finding out if their application for further education is being accepted.' A tall youth sprang through the door, quickly changed his boots and smiled brilliantly before disappearing again.

'Life is definitely easier now,' Manomina continued. 'It was so much harder for women when I was a child; so many rules! Now men and women are more equal. Men have to listen to women now.'

She got up, poured some water from a jerry can into the kettle

– there was no running water – and put it on the stove to boil and then pulled out some stiff sealskins from behind the sofa to show me. They were perfectly prepared – flensed, dried and stretched with the fur removed – and ready to cut and sew into women's traditional long kamiks ready for the confirmations of two of her children in early summer. The skins had been dried and bleached in the Arctic sun, and were creamy-white and tough but with a slightly springy texture when squeezed between your fingers. The same skins dried inside would be used for hunter's kamiks; they are tougher and the wife has to work them hard to make them pliable, but they dry translucent instead of white and are more waterproof than the women's version.

As she moved her hands over the tough skins I noticed a long scar across the palm of her hand. She smiled for the first time as I complimented her on the quality of the skins. She delicately brushed a strand of hair off her wide comely face. A graze was healing over her eyebrow.

I asked her if she had learnt how to prepare skins as a child. 'No, I didn't come from a hunting family; my father died when I was a baby, so I was brought up in Siorapaluk with my mother and grandmother. We didn't have a man hunting in the family, so I never learnt how to prepare skins. When I married my husband I had to start to learn about skins from my grandmother.' Her mind seemed to drift before she continued: 'My grand-mother had not one grey hair when she died. That's because they didn't have so much to think about then.'

Some early travellers to the Arctic brought with them what to the Polar Eskimo seemed the inexplicable mysteries of 'white man's medicine' and techniques of healing. The anthropologist Peter Freuchan tells this story, related to him by the Eskimo Samik:

The only white man who showed ability and good sense went by the name of 'Doctor'. In many cases he knew how to exorcize the spirits.

When one of us got sick he knew how to chase the disease away. When someone was wounded he used long rolls of beautiful thin skin to wind around the wound and when a leg was broken he knew how to put it together again the right way. As a rule, a broken arm or leg would be twisted and shorter once it was healed. The reason is plain enough; the bone heals in such a manner that it will keep alive the memory of the event. When a leg or an arm was healed by 'Doctor' there was nothing to show for it afterwards.

Once he took care of me when a bullet had accidentally lodged in my thigh. He had such ingenious tools that he was able to remove the bullet and make the wound heal as if there had never been an injury. Thus he cheated death and since that time he should by rights have been responsible for me and taken care of my food and shelter, for he had given me a new life.

Today the 'healing' takes place in modern hospitals using techniques familiar in most European countries.

Louisa insisted that I visit Qaanaaq's hospital. I hate hospitals, but allowed myself to be led across the shiny linoleum of the various wards, shaking hands with people who greeted me dreamily. A voice called my name from one of the wards, and a woman sat on a narrow hospital bed, her foot in plaster holding her arms out to me and pleading as if only I could save her from some torment. I had no idea who she was, although she repeated my name over and over again, and looked to Louisa for help but she was looking as confused as I was. A couple of orderlies and nurses ambled up and down the main corridor. I stopped at a picture frame filled with snapshots of the patients over the years and pointed to one that I thought was hilarious – two middle-aged Inughuit women in gaping hospital robes sitting by a window smoking cigarettes. 'Anaana, my mother,' Louisa said. On closer inspection I realized that Maria was one of the women, staring at the camera with a rebellious smirk on her face.

I was curious how the hospital operated and who the doctor was that dealt with the whole of the Thule municipality.

Navarana's sister was working in the office and came out to greet me in her starched white overalls. She gave me a coarse hug and tugged on my hair. 'When she was little she had such curly hair!' she exclaimed loudly to an old woman sitting nearby. Louisa scurried off as I waited to speak to the doctor.

Dr Klaus Jacobsen appeared a few moments later, filling the doorway. 'You wanted to talk to me?' he said in perfect Danish-accented English. He was an imposing character and I had to quell the immediate urge to compliment him on his extraordinary beard. He guided me into one of his treatment rooms and we talked under an ominous looking surgical light, surrounded by precisely ordered ranks of modern sterilized equipment. The hospital in Qaanaaq rivalled many that I knew of in the UK for cleanliness and atmosphere, and was bright and airy with friendly and helpful staff. The building itself was relatively new, although there had been a hospital in Qaanaaq since I was here as a child. The new hospital was built about eight years before, on the foundations of the old one.

Klaus first came to Greenland in 1967 on a frigate as an inspector of health facilities in Greenland, and returned several times in the following years, but he had only ever come as far north as Upernavik. He had for years worked in Denmark as a highly qualified surgeon, but often wondered what it would be like to work in Greenland, and so decided that in his 'old age' he would like to have an adventure and work in Qaanaaq. He arrived in 1997. I asked him if he felt he had made the right decision. 'Oh yes!' he said emphatically. 'It is wonderful here.' His thick silver eyebrows looked as if they were just about to go into flight.

I asked what happened if there was a sick person out in one of the smaller settlements, as sometimes the weather was so unpredictable that it is difficult to get back to Qaanaaq. Each settlement, he told me, had an unqualified but reasonably trained person who could administer first aid and basic medical procedures, and all were well stocked with a variety of medicines, but for any proper treatment they would have to come to Qaanaaq; the only reason he would fly out was if there had been some kind of accident. Occasionally they could also be flown to the airbase for treatment. 'The airbase has a couple of doctors and a large medical staff, but I am actually a better surgeon so sometimes I am flown over there to do operations, or people from the airbase come over to Qaanaaq and I operate here.' He waved a hand to encompass the entire hospital. 'But we do everything here, people come to us for any kind of problem, big or small. We offer primary care here, and often secondary too.'

As I listened to his tenor voice I had visions of how the hospital used to operate before it was modernized, and had to suppress a smile as I remembered a story Mum had once told me about a check-up she had had at the hospital in Qaanaaq. The amiable doctor had given her a thorough examination, during the course of which he had put on a crash helmet. Mum was astonished by the head protection and immediately enquired why the doctor felt it necessary. He, somewhat bashfully, replied that he had been examining a local woman the previous week and that she had kicked him viciously in the head, and from then on he had decided to take precautions. Just before our arrival in Thule there was such a national problem with sexually transmitted diseases that every visitor had to be given an obligatory examination to ensure that they were not infected before they entered the area. The doctor had told her that two days before a hunter had come to the hospital complaining of an STD, and that he had been asked to name all the lovers he had recently been acquainted with. The van was still picking up all the people he had had associations with. Dr Klaus Jacobsen assured me that although STDs are still a common complaint they are not as rife as they once were.

Louisa's condition had made me curious about midwifery in Qaanaaq, and whether it had become usual practice for expectant mothers to be sent to Nuuk or Ilulissat for treatment, when the hospital in Qaanaaq, however small, seemed to be perfectly equipped to handle childbirth. Were there local women trained as midwives in Qaanaaq? He told me that there were five women on the staff who worked as midwives, but they had had some basic training to be nurses as well.

'The system up to now has worked very well,' he said enthusiastically, 'the women have had years of experience and they know exactly what they are doing, but things are changing. These five women are getting old now, with one of them close to death, and the methods of training nurses and midwives is not the same as it once was. And now the people in Nuuk want to have the women flown down to the capital to give birth as they believe that it reduces the risk of the children dying in childbirth, but really we don't have a problem with that here at all. We have around twenty births a year here in Qaanaaq and that is enough to keep the population going. Besides, the women don't want to fly to Nuuk, they prefer to stay here.' As for home births, that doesn't happen any more unless it happens too quickly for the mother to get to hospital. 'I have delivered only one baby at someone's home in all the years I have been here!' he said laughing heartily.

Inughuit women have always been strong-willed, and besides, their men never easily tolerated complaints about their discomfort. Giving birth was no exception, and was regarded by many as being a somewhat bothersome experience, particularly given that many women gave birth while on long hunting trips.

Generally, in rememberable history, the woman would give birth sitting on her knees, and often a belt was tightened around her belly, or her husband encircled his arms around her while supporting her from behind to produce the same effect. According to Jean Malaurie, once the baby was born and the umbilical cord cut with a mussel shell or a piece of ice, it was licked clean by its mother and swaddled in rabbit skins before being cleaned more thoroughly with dampened feathers. In earlier times the poor mother would then be burdened with taboos and duties. The clothes she wore during her pregnancy had to be destroyed;

she could only eat while barefoot and for a year after giving birth was not permitted to eat young seals, animals' entrails or eggs, nor was she allowed to have sex for three months following delivery.

Living with taboos, up until just seventy years ago – by which time the persistence of the suffragettes had gained women the right to vote in the UK – was simply something that women had to accept. Women in those days were considered vastly inferior to the hunters of the community, and were supposedly incapable of having an original or useful thought; if a wife ever did happen to suggest something that might be of benefit to her husband, her husband would naturally proclaim the idea to be of his own creation. But the woman's 'impurity' was her greatest downfall, and she had to constantly be reminded of this, particularly during menstruation, mourning or miscarriage. The menstruating or mourning woman was forbidden to urinate on the icefield (because the ice belonged to the sea where all the animals the men hunted were to be found), but she could urinate on icebergs (they came from the land); she must wear her hood outside of the house, and not walk near other houses and was forbidden to walk between any houses and the icefield, or come near any animals that had been brought in from the hunt. She was not allowed to utter the name of the polar bear or the walrus, and was not allowed to eat certain foods.

The taboos were even stricter for a woman who had had a miscarriage or a stillbirth. Until as recently as 1930 either case was supposed to be a direct result of the woman insulting the spirits; she was to be kept under strict observance, for she had scared off the spirit of her unborn child and was likely to drive all the animals away from the hunting grounds. Not only had she to abide by the taboos that other young mothers lived by, but on top of those for a year she was forbidden to cut meat herself, or drink from the same pot as other people, or turn her meat on her plate in case she aborted again and caused some great natural catastrophe – this could be avoided if another woman held her hand while she turned her meat – and any of her leftovers were given straight to the dogs; she could not name the animals she ate, and anyone talking to her had to use different words to describe the animals they had been hunting. There is reportedly one incident where a woman who had miscarried a child and had not reported it was blamed for the community having no game and was sealed in an igloo and left to die. However, there was one consolation for grieving mothers: the Inughuit believed that the aurora borealis was made up of the souls of stillborn children who were dancing and playing football with their umbilical cords.

Only a century ago baby girls were considered more of a burden than a boon, whereas boys would become hunters and were regarded as an insurance policy for old age. A son had a duty to look after his parents once they could no longer hunt and provide for themselves; in contrast a daughter's skills and contribution would be lost to her parents as soon as she was married. The result was that in the days of hardship girls were often strangled at birth or left out on the ice to die of exposure.

Infanticide was not necessarily always purely the fate of girl babies; boys too could be killed, in times of great famine. Anyone, in fact, who could not contribute to the community – babies, children, old people, the disabled and, in particular, orphans – in such desperate times were left behind or killed. But women were always the preferable loss.

The consequences of having such a scarcity of women was that polyandry became quite common. For survival it was essential that a hunter had a wife to prepare and sew the skins of the animals he hunted for his clothing, look after his children (which in turn would look after him in old age, if they were boys) and keep him well fed and warm. Women in the dark times of Eskimo history therefore often had two husbands. Although her workload was increased in one way – there would be more clothes to take care of and more skins to flense and prepare – she would have the benefit of her husbands vying for attention and trying to prove that they were not only the better hunter of the two but the better husband. In their eagerness to please, it appears that some hunters in this position actually began to take on some of the woman's chores – such as collecting ice for water – and both tried to rival the other for bringing home particular delicacies to please their wife; this rivalry between the two husbands, however, often seemed to strengthen the bond between the hunters, and generally they remained the closest of friends.

I returned to the house after leaving the hospital and sat near Louisa who was sleeping lightly on the sofa, her belly round and firm under her jersey, and found myself overwhelmed with gratitude that she and her baby had such a progressive hospital to look after them. Without the attention she had been given it was possible that she would have lost her baby by now. Perhaps she too would have been in danger. She gently opened her eyes and smiled, beckoning me towards her. Gently she took my hand and placed it on one side of her motherhood; inside the baby pummelled her gently as if she were a drum. 'I think maybe it is an angákoq,' I whispered.

'Yes!' she chuckled softly. 'I think so too.'

8. Twilight Years

Savfak's face crinkled into itself as she smiled and announced, 'Tee!' and put a battered kettle on the oil-burning stove before putting away her carving tools. That done she cleared away the last pieces of her work off the coffee table and carefully rearranged crocheted coasters on the plastic tablecloth, and lit a candle – a modern equivalent to the blubber lamp. In the days before hurricane lamps and oil burners the only source of heat and light for the Polar Eskimos was the blubber lamp; the warmth it provided was a symbol of the community spirit, and still the modern Inughuit always light a candle when guests arrive at their home as an unconscious nod to the ancient tradition that bound them together over the centuries.

The blubber lamp was usually fashioned out of soapstone, with a deep bowl carved from its centre. Lumps of blubber were placed in the bowl, with a wick of slow-burning moss at one end. As the moss burned the blubber melted, and was sucked up by the moss, keeping the moss alight. The flow of blubber to the wick was regulated by gently tilting the lamp, and the flame controlled with a small bone implement; it was a skill mastered by the women over many years, and a well-maintained lamp – or lamps if the wife was particularly skilful – was a source of pride for the entire household.

It was into Savfak's arms that I had been first thrust when we arrived at Herbert Island: where I had first felt the buoyant warmth of the tribe. She was one of the elders of the community, whom I called 'Aana' – grandmother; I called everyone that looked older than forty grandma or grandpa.

'*Aana, mammak*,' Savfak growled, wheezing as she stuck her head in a cupboard and scrabbled around for something. She laughed triumphantly as she produced a dusty packet of hard-tack biscuits that could have passed as a museum exhibit.

'*Illit*,' she said prodding me, 'when you were little you would say "Grandma, I'm hungry" and go in my cupboard.' She imitated me as a child waddling to the double cupboard that served as an entire kitchen – there was no sink or running water – and happily brandished the hard-tack biscuits, before sucking on them contentedly. She chuckled to herself, and repeated the whole scenario all over again to make sure that we understood what she was saying.

Savfak pointed to the plastic tablecloth saying that she had to put it there because sometimes visitors came in drunk and they tended to spill their beer everywhere. She suddenly exclaimed and clapped her hands remembering a story of the time that I was taken to Thule Airbase with Mum and Dad when I was little. My mother had told Savfak that at dinner in the Officers' Mess I suddenly threw a tantrum and pulled the tablecloth sharply, fully laden, off the table. She nodded her head at the thought and cackled an old woman's laugh. 'One minute you would be really loving and sweet, and the next you would be a little whirlwind stamping your feet!'

'Look,' she said, pointing at the table. She had found some old Polaroids of when Louisa and I were children. In among the eclectic collection were some faded yellowing pictures of my parents; one of Dad looking fit and glowing with happy youth leading his dogs with his whip snaking in one hand, and one of Mum sitting on a sledge sewing skins, her copper hair falling like molten metal over her shoulders. 'Ahhh,' said Savfak, tapping on the Polaroid, 'Marie.' She imitated how Mum had found the skins tough to sew. She took one of my hands and studied it briefly before dropping it again in my lap. '*Eie*, yes,' she mused, 'you have the same soft hands as your mother.' I studied the picture carefully with the dawning realization that I was exactly the same age as my mother when she came up to the Arctic.

Savfak prepared tea and swung with a pronounced limp over to the low table to pour the weak brew into our cups. Her eyes danced as she slumped heavily on her small sofa, and insisted that I should move closer to her. I produced my small collection of pictures to amuse her. Her hands moved delicately over the images: tiny, blackened and gnarled hands from years of sewing, skinning and carving.

You could get lost in the folds of Savfak's face, and in them see echoes of the rugged landscape she had survived in for perhaps seventy years – she could never be specific about her age and like many of the older generation, giggled at the absurdity that her age should even be a subject worth discussing. Savfak's body was bowed and partly crippled by life but the fragility of age had bypassed her somehow, for she was not a delicate woman, and instead had the gritty air of a woman who has had to be self-sufficient for many years.

Savfak moved to Qaanaaq before the rest of the community as her husband had been diagnosed with cancer and he needed hospital treatment. Savfak's face creased as she told the story: 'It was a very sad and difficult time.' Savfak stayed in Qaanaaq when her husband died; there were too many memories in their old house on Herbert Island, and life there was hard if you didn't have a husband who could hunt. She missed Herbert Island so much in the beginning, she said wistfully, she was homesick and lonely, and the people in Qaanaaq were not so friendly but, she insisted, she was OK living there now, she had got used to it.

The last time she had been to Herbert Island was 1998. 'I would cry all the time if I went back,' she added. I told her that I had been there two or three weeks ago and told her about the wind damage to Migishoo's and Avatak and Maria's house. '*Ajor . . .*' she said, wide-eyed, she hadn't heard. I thought it was probably best for her not to see it the way it now was; it was so very different to the way it was in the 1970s.

As we left Savfak's neighbour banged loudly on his window-pane, and we waited for him to arthritically come out to greet us. He waved vigorously, although we were but two feet from him. 'Minik,' said Louisa, introducing him to me, '*Qeqertassua-mit*, from Herbert Island.' Minik leant happily on his walking stick. His skin was the colour of burnt toffee, and his rheumy eyes glistened with the ready childlike emotions of old age. His face seemed too smooth for his years and I could see the round-faced boy he had once been as he smiled. '*Ajor!*' he exclaimed slowly, and time slowed respectfully for him so that we could appreciate each treasured breath in the old man. '*Angiho* . . . how big you've become . . .' His voice trailed off and he chewed his gums thoughtfully before detailing his ailments. He held up a trembling hand to his face; his right side didn't work too well, since he had his stroke. Louisa said a loud goodbye to his cupped ear and he waved, patting the air affectionately as we walked away.

Even as recently as seventy years ago the old people of the High Arctic used to give themselves up to the ice if they felt that they were becoming a burden on their family. This act of selflessness was almost expected in times of great hardship or famine if an elder could no longer contribute. They had, after all, had a good and full life, and it was more important for the young to go on living; survival of the community rather than the individual was always the priority. An elder would sometimes sit towards the back of the sledge on long journeys with their family, and would finally slip silently off the sledge with no histrionics, not even a cry of farewell, and would succumb alone to the icy embrace of death. The family would respectfully keep looking ahead.

Nature gives no memorial to the dead, but occasionally a feature in the landscape can remind one of those days of self-sacrifice. Along the steep banks of the Ice Fjord in West Greenland is such a place.

About a mile or two inland from the mouth the cliffs of the Ice Fjord become steep and rough-hewn, rising and falling like irregular breaths. In one of the outcrops of black basalt rock is an angled split, just wide enough for a small human figure to pass through; on the other side is a sheer drop. Over the centuries many elders who felt that 'life was heavier than death' have come here to leave behind their decrepit bodies before going on to their next life, and one can easily understand why they would pick such a spot. Beyond the rock crevice the cliff drops approximately one hundred feet to a jagged assembly of rocks beneath. A brittle body could not withstand the impact and death should be mercifully quick. But, beyond the bone-thirsty rocks is a landscape of extraordinary beauty. At this part of the Ice Fjord, the freshly calved icebergs cluster together as great temples of iridescent ice rising out of rolling crystal icescapes and lakes of azure blue. On the day that I visited this site an iceberg lay directly in front of this gateway of souls and, magically, echoed precisely the shape of the cliff with its distinctive cleft.

In other areas where there were no such appropriate geographical features, the elderly who believed that their time was drawing to a close, would simply walk out onto the ice field, or occasionally to a small cave away from the settlement to wait for death. But, as more influences came from Europe, and with them the arrival of the annual supply ships, famine and hardship became less of a daily threat for the hunting communities, and as life was no longer at such a premium the elderly had less need to give up their lives so readily. These days those that are too old or sick to look after themselves are cared for in a modern nursing home and suicide or euthanasia is pretty much unheard of.

The new nursing home was built in Qaanaaq several years ago, and as far as nursing homes go it is light and well equipped, manned by a handful of starched care-attendants who give the place an atmosphere of well-oiled efficiency.

Hans Jensen's mother Thericie was sitting by the window overlooking the fjord as Louisa and I arrived, playing a board game with a young girl. The girl looked up and smiled and relinquished the game quickly, hovering for just a moment to be polite before disappearing, her duty over. The old woman had such a regal air that I felt quite awed in her presence. She looked at us with intelligent young eyes and politely asked us to take a seat while she carefully packed away the game – she was not to be hurried – and then laced her fingers together on the white crocheted tablecloth; the small slender fingers did not belong to a hunter's wife. Cool flickers of sunlight bounced off the long window ledge and a few strands of her hair shivered free from her tight bun.

Thericie had been polite but distant when we first entered her room, but the moment she heard who I was her cool demeanour vanished and she pulled me into a light embrace. It was like hugging a fairy. Her willowy body pressed into mine, her head barely reaching my shoulder. Unlike the clinical feel of the other rooms in the nursing home, Thericie had transformed the sterile canvas into a cosy grotto. The hospital bed was disguised with a colourful crocheted throw and a tumble of cushions, one wall glittered with an array of traditional beadwork, and opposite a photomontage covered the white wall with posters of Greenland interspersed with family portraits. In the centre was a compelling black and white photograph of Thericie when she was younger; she was strikingly beautiful. 'It is me!' she exclaimed laughing vivaciously. 'But now I am very old!' Yet, I thought, it would be many years before the sparkle would dim in her eyes.

The other residents were not so cognizant. In the next room a ghost of a woman lay unmoving except for some shallow painful breathing and the occasional spasm of coughing that would throw open her terrified eyes. She seemed not to hear Louisa's words. Her room was bare and was filled with the acrid fumes of disinfectant and the elusive smell of near-death. Incontinence pads lined the windowsill next to a solitary plant that seemed to be sickening in sympathy with its room-mate. The room had no life, and neither did she. Next door the story wasn't much different. Her neighbour stared at the time card on the television, immobile but dressed smartly in a pair of beige trousers and a blue cotton shirt. A pair of red braces lay beside him on the hard sofa, and his old sealskin kamiks lay on his bed. He was quietly mouthing the *Ajaja* of a drum song, his body stiff and unmoving. As the song took on its own life I closed my eyes and could visualize him swinging his hips in polar bear skins and a soft worn anorak, hitting the side of the drum and calling upon the ancestors. But the strange melody was broken by a hacking cough and a noisy spit into an enamel mug that held a stiff paper Greenland flag.

Baali and Edo came out of the shop and waved vigorously when they saw me pass by. Baali was carrying another rose and beaming as usual. 'The church,' she said simply. 'One p.m.'

It had been a week since I had first seen the corpse being carried to the church, and finally it was the day of the funeral. Usually at least a week's grace has to be given so that family members from other settlements have time to travel to the funeral and for the grave to be dug. Before the missionaries came, the dead were buried in stone cairns above the ground, with the stones secured well enough so that roaming polar bears or foxes couldn't get at the bodies: iron-hard permafrost lies just a few inches beneath the surface of the ground, and so digging a grave by hand was impossible. These days there are more modern methods: graves are often dug by pneumatic drill. Over the last couple of days the distinctive clunks of a small yellow digger could be heard on the breeze as more tundra was cleared away to extend the graveyard.

At 12.30 sharp a crowd started to assemble outside the church and I quickly left the house to join them, but as I neared the chapel I felt shamed by my curiosity and came to an awkward standstill, bobbing up and down on the periphery of the gathering. Someone nudged me roughly. It was the woman I had met at Inudliah's house. She looked at me with compassion, and she seemed to sense my uncertainty at being there.

'You knew him,' she said, with a tone of sympathy reserved for the recently bereaved, 'on Herbert Island.'

'I did?' I replied hesitantly.

'Go, go!' she insisted, pushing me towards the people clustered around the chapel shed. She propelled me forwards through the crowd, ignoring my whispered protests and the startled looks from those shoved out of the way, until I bumped up against the open coffin. It was a bit closer than I had intended to get. An old couple opposite nodded at me in solemn approval. Flies buzzed in a thick veil over the body, their vulgar drone almost drowning out the sound of the woman weeping behind me. Waves of people jostled towards the boxed corpse, taking turns to lean into the coffin, pressing the dead man's face as if they were trying to wake him from a deep sleep. When they received no flicker of response they sniffed and pressed their noses to his face in affection. Before me one solitary dead hand, stiff as a statue and dark indigo blue, half-heartedly grasped a plastic flower. I couldn't bring myself to look at the hunter's face, which no doubt had an expression of horror frozen on it: the man had drowned after a walrus had attacked his kayak.

The walrus is a notoriously unpredictable and quarrelsome beast, and is by far the most dangerous to hunt by kayak. The kayak-borne hunter only has one shot at killing the walrus, which he must do by harpooning the creature near the head, but avoiding the solid bone skull which would be nigh impossible to penetrate. If the hunter misses he can be in big trouble. It is wrong to assume that the walrus is sedate because of its size: contrary to its appearance the walrus can move at astonishing speed once provoked. Every year there are incidents of walrus attacking and crushing kayaks, or even dragging the hunter under the water until he runs out of breath. Hunting walrus takes great skill, and they are considered to be the most dangerous animals to hunt, due not only to the fact that they are unpredictable and easily enraged, but also because it was once believed that the walrus could understand human language. Walruses are regarded as being mysteriously intelligent, and are particularly hostile to man, therefore the Eskimo hunter had to be fastidiously observant of the ritual of prayer when killing a walrus. 'Walruses are like people,' the Eskimos used to say. 'They hear you when you talk and if you brag they might get you for it. If you never hunted them before, I'll tell you something now. Remember when you hunt walrus you must not act like a man. Do not be arrogant; be humble. Always respect the walruses and watch them closely when you hunt them.'

I managed to extricate myself from the throng and stood a few feet away. The crowd moved in a respectful murmur. Then a woman started keening at the foot of the coffin. The wailing started softly, melodically, and then grew in passion to tear at the hearts of us all. It was a primeval, ancient call of grief that emanated from the depths of her belly and filled her tiny frame and the air around us. The town seemed frozen, and I wondered how far that haunting cry could be heard. Much of the crowd held hands, and simply stood gazing at where the coffin lay, in disbelief that another one of them was gone.

I later discovered that the dead man had had a very significant role in the life of this community. It was rumoured that he had been one of the residents of Uummannaq when the American airbase was built. As a hunter, the man knew the whole of the Thule district well, and although young was respected by the Danes of the area. As he was so well regarded the hunter was asked to accompany some important guests of the government – American military men on a tour of the area around the site of the proposed airbase and further north to Inglefield fjord. 'If you were to live in this area,' one of the Americans asked him, 'where would you bring your family?' They were passing between Herbert Island and the mainland at the time. The man thought quietly for a moment of where all his relatives lived; he would want to be close to them all and pointed at where he thought would be the middle point. It was a fairly barren piece of land, but it would suit him well enough and although Uummannaq had richer reserves of game there was good enough walrus and narwhal hunting to be had nearby. It was where the community of Uummannaq would shortly be moved to, and where Qaanaaq stands today.

After all the main family members had paid their last respects to the old man and bathed his tired old body with their tears, the minister nodded to his assistant, and the young man jogged to the back door of the church and pulled out a small toolbox and an electric screwdriver. The lid of the coffin was sealed tight with the finality of screws splintering wood. The twelve-year-old granddaughter of the dead man was handed the enormous white crucifix that would head the grave, and in mournful procession she led the party around the church and through the entrance. It was a scene that in its colour and melancholy was faintly reminiscent of early religious paintings, apart from the red-leather jacket of the crucifix-bearing girl.

The church was small and sparsely decorated. Tall candlesticks guarded the pews, with a tall pink candle burning in each. Above the altar was a naive painting of a benevolent Christ cradling an Eskimo girl in traditional dress in his lap, and extending his right hand to an Eskimo boy who knelt at his feet. Baali and Magda appeared in the row in front, looking every bit the mischievous twins as they turned round and grinned at me in unison. A beaming rose-cheeked woman joined them and whispered my name as she offered her hand. It was Tekumeq Peary. I had known her from childhood too.

The catechist hovered uncomfortably beside the altar, watching with mild terror as the congregation filled the church. He lifted a trembling hand and smoothed his broad sweeping fringe over his right temple. His hair was perfect: glossy and immobilized with layers of hairspray. Heavy side-burns hid the dark skin of his cheeks. The service was short and moving, the catechist's voice breaking as he quietly muttered the sermon. Three hymns gave him some relief, of which the last was 'Silent Night' sung of course in Greenlandic. The hymn sounded so much more melodic in Greenlandic. Avatak's sister Benina gripped my arm and watched me curiously as I quietly sang the English version, her one blind eye wobbling in a milky film behind thick glasses. By the end of the service the entire church was in tears.

The new head of the family solemnly picked up the crucifix, rested it carefully on his new white canvas anorak, and led the way out of the church with the other members of the family, both men and women, carrying the coffin in his wake. The crowd dispersed quietly but quickly outside the church, with around thirty or forty people keeping procession towards the cemetery. Baali, Magda, Edo, Tekumeq Peary and I all walked arm in arm to the first junction on the edge of the village, whereupon the coffin was unceremoniously shunted onto the back of a small red pickup truck. The procession became light-hearted, most people chatting and behaving as if they were going for a stroll in a park. A child in a pushchair squealed as it saw a husky, '*Awawa!* Doggy!' The girls laughed and teased me saying that I still used baby language.

We hadn't walked far when the sisters briefly hugged Tekumeq Peary and me, and turned back, giving us a chance to bond alone.

'I have your house,' Tekumeq Peary said proudly, adding, 'but I stay in Moriussaq now.' I smiled weakly, and wished that we were all staying together on Herbert Island instead of these modern towns.

The two of us walked together most of the way, following the truck that by now had most of the children piled inside the cab and all over the coffin itself. All the boys of the family wore new traditional white anoraks, and baseball caps. Outside the entrance to the graveyard the little truck stopped and the procession halted while the coffin was manoeuvred between the pall-bearers who were all of different height and build. The children ran ahead squealing, all eager to get a ringside seat.

The catechist stuttered his way through his final reading with no one paying him the slightest attention. Beside the open grave the young children played with stones and the pile of dirt while the older children, looking more solemn than the rest of the congregation, held up long-stemmed plastic roses or wrung their baseball caps into tight knots; an old man squatted against the grave next door grinding his toothless jaws and hawking up blood.

The catechist took a small ceremonial shovel and tossed in a little dirt at a time, chanting almost inaudibly as he worked. Then, as the catechist's last shovel of topsoil hit the plywood coffin a boom filled the air as if from a cannon salute, and a distant iceberg crumbled into the sea. The soul had departed. Immediately the prayers had finished the men set to work filling in the grave, while the mourners stood patiently by, waiting to offer up their flowers and small wreaths. Some walked to other graves, attending to flowers that were in danger of being blown away or neatening up rows of stones.

In the days when the first white visitors came to the area, the Polar Eskimos were still bound with traditions and taboos, and the rules that surrounded death were particularly respected, for the spirits of the recently dead were not to be angered. The Polar Eskimos feared malevolent spirits more, it seems, than they feared death itself. Knud Rasmussen described in his book *People of the Polar North* that when a person died all the members of his or her family would plug up their left nostrils and then the closest relatives would remove the corpse feet first from the igloo through a specially made hole, which was quickly filled in so that the spirit of the dead could not re-enter. All those who were present then plugged both nostrils with grass or fur and the children wore their hoods up and mittens on their hands. The body, sewn into skins with its eyes closed, was placed on its back with its head turned to the sun, and buried beneath a cairn of stones. In some ancient graves hunters have been found buried with the tip of their harpoon and a miniature sledge so the spirit could continue hunting in the spirit world until its next incarnation.

For a period of five days following the burial, the immediate family were obliged to continue wearing mittens and hoods and were not supposed to speak, lie down or prepare food, and were forbidden to hunt. Furthermore, all sledges were upturned so that Nature and The Dead could see that no one was breaking the taboo of hunting. Women during this time were not supposed to sew, but if they must, they first had to blacken their eyes with soot. For a full year the son of a dead father was not permitted to cut ice or snow, fetch water or build an igloo. And the period of mourning always lasted longer for women than it did for men. The taboos were so restrictive that some families would leave the community so that they were not duty-bound to fulfil the demands of mourning.

Once the initial period of mourning was over, another set of rules was enforced: the name of the deceased could not be spoken out loud until the spirit – and the name – was reborn in an infant later that year. This could cause havoc in a society where so many people had the same name, so it was imperative that the spirit was reincarnated as soon as possible.

By the time that we lived on Herbert Island these taboos were no longer adhered to and the Christian methods of burial were much favoured. Still, however, there seems to be a hesitancy to speak the name of the recently dead, and mourning is expected only to consume the closest family members for a week or two at the most. After that grief should be nurtured no longer.

A fine mist hung low over Herbert Island, and I walked over to join Benina at her brother Avatak's grave. Slowly she smoothed the dirt around a long-since faded wreath, and indicated that it was the one that we had put there when I was nine years old. She hugged me tightly and we walked together back to the fresh grave.

By the time we returned all the flowers had been laid out on the fresh thin soil and a long line of people were shuffling up to the family to shake hands and touch cheeks in commiseration. The keening was now taken up by other women too, albeit quietly, and men were openly weeping as they embraced the family. The crowd fell into a thick-flowing torrent of grief, as dark and clinging as molasses. Loss found its voice through this ebb and flow of primeval sound.

Not wanting to go back indoors, I took a long walk down the beach, picking my way through the sodden sand and relics from life in Qaanaaq – wellies with soles half torn off, rusted cans of beer, plastic bags and food packaging. In between them delicate ice sculptures that had washed up on the beach were melting out of existence, their last few hours lit by spectrums of light. Small waves pulled at the shingle, and sandpipers plucked at the shallows.

Ahead of me a large stranded berg shimmered in the sand, with a long slender neck stretching into the sky. I was walking transfixed towards it when I was stopped in my tracks. A dead dog was lying rigidly at its base, his harness still partially intact. I had seen so much death in the last few days that I shouldn't have been shocked, but it took me by surprise. It said so much about life here: beauty and death constantly sharing the same ground.

9. Wolf Dog

The sun broke through the clouds and the fjord gradually settled into a slick of dark glass. The air was filled with the sound of mechanical insects as people buzzed around Qaanaaq on quad bikes; a blue-overalled Inughuit worker moving a fridge waved to a rugged Danish office clerk collecting bags of fresh mattak for his breakfast.

By lunchtime the house reeked of both the seal meat that Louisa was boiling on the hob and a large salmon skin that covered the veneered sideboard. She was indulging her pregnant appetite and stood engrossed in her meal, sucking at every last shred of raw flesh. Louisa finished her 'Eskimo sushi' and went back to sit in front of the television, licking her fingers absent-mindedly and gazing at the Tour de France cyclists speeding across the screen. It was the end of the Tour, and for the last few days the whole of Qaanaaq had been watching the race avidly on their single TV channel, riveted by the alien scenery and culture. I could almost taste the dust from the wide Parisian boulevards as I perched beside Louisa on the arm of the couch. Crowds of onlookers in bright summer clothes rippled with applause as the athletes bobbed past in a haze of heat and sweat, and my body prickled as it remembered the sensation of summer warmth on my skin.

After a day of lethargy Louisa and I quietly prepared dinner together. I loved spending time with Louisa in this way; we could stand together in easy silence shoulder to shoulder, and somehow communicate in the subtlety of the smallest action. I sensed that something was unsettling her, and before long she disappeared to her room. Soon after I could hear a faint sobbing trickling down the stairs. I was torn whether I should go to her, but Hans shook his head when I started up the stairs to comfort her. It seemed appropriate to give them some time alone, so I walked to my usual refuge from town and made myself comfortable on a large lump of granite to call my partner Laurence, who was filming on a beach in Thailand. We laughed together at the absurdity of our situations, with me sitting swathed in polar gear in minus 5°C, and him in shorts with his toes in hot sand.

I was mid-conversation when I suddenly noticed a dark shape heading towards me on the abandoned dirt track; it was a large stray husky. In a flash it bolted towards me and I jumped up with a sudden rush of adrenalin. I was in the middle of nowhere with a wild dog at least half my body weight tearing towards me baring its fangs. It could be rabid. I lunged at the nearest rock I could find and hurled it as hard as I could just in front of it to try and stop it. The dog slowed down momentarily, spinning on his feet, but kept coming, although a little slower now. Shouting '*Awawa Ayapok!*' ('Bad doggy') didn't really fit the bill. It snarled silently. I decided to use a softer approach, although I still held another rock in my hand, and talked to him in a soothing voice to calm him down. Laurence's voice called at me down the earpiece of my headset: 'Kari, are you there? What the hell is going on?' I had to ignore him. My calming tone seemed to work and as the dog came closer he slung his head down lower and lower until he was nearly crawling along the ground. He finally reached my feet and rolled on his back, legs akimbo. I stared at him in astonishment.

I sank back on the rock in relief, my knees suddenly feeling as though they couldn't support my weight, although I was still wary of my new companion who stayed at my heels and sat beside me. It was only then that I realized quite how big this dog was: his head was level with mine as he sat on his haunches, and I was sitting on a boulder. He looked at me with neurotic devotion, one eye coloured blue-grey and the other dark mottled brown. He was a war-torn outcast with a snout lacerated with old scars and a shredded left ear. His coarse fur stood in matted clumps crawling with fleas. He was most definitely more wolf than dog.

Huskies are not generally vicious animals, but like their feral cousins, they are unpredictable, and it is a common sight to see packs of dogs ripping each other to shreds in terrifying fights, which unless they are stopped quickly by the hunter, often result in a gruesome death. I had seen several mauled corpses around town in the last few days. Throughout my life I have often heard stories of children who had been badly injured by dogs, either by mistakenly walking through a restless pack, or being attacked by hungry runaways. Even on my last trip I had heard that some dogs had carried off a toddler. As a matter of necessity the children are taught from a young age how to protect themselves with whips and stones.

I returned to the house, still slightly shaken from the fear that the dog could have been rabid. It was the first time I had felt truly vulnerable and it had brought back a strong memory of another frightening experience I had had when I was a child: I was about nine years old and for some reason I had been walking alone down the main dirt road of Qaanaaq. My memory of it was somewhat washed out, in monotone. Suddenly, from nowhere, three huskies broke free from their traces and came for me. The dogs were enormous. I screamed at them, but everything I screamed in English just seemed to excite them more. They were practically on top of me when a hunter appeared from nowhere and with great precision picked off each dog with a well-placed stone in quick succession, making them cower and run away whimpering. More than anything else I remember the hunter laughing at my terror, in a typically Inughuit way. Later I discovered that my cries were reminiscent of a hunter encouraging the dogs to chase a polar bear, not to bugger off and leave me alone.

The following evening Ilannguak called to say that he was leaving for Herbert Island immediately and wanted to know if

I wanted to join him. He had to see to his dogs and he wanted to make good use of the weather as it looked as though yet another dark front was heading our way. I agreed to meet Ilannguak at the beach and quickly put on some warm travelling clothes; it was late in the evening and we would not be back until around 4 a.m. so I had to make sure I was prepared. Already I could see the weather changing and the clouds closing in.

Magda was on the beach as Ilannguak was preparing the boat and she ran towards me as soon as she saw me, calling out 'Hello Darling!' in theatrical English. She and the rest of the children had picked up the expression from my parents when we lived on Herbert Island. I laughed in delight. I hadn't seen her for two weeks and we hugged each other tightly comparing where we had been. The water was really rough she said, did I really want to go to Herbert Island? She looked at me with concern. I was in a dilemma; I knew how far it was to the island and it was grim when it was rough, but it could be my last chance before re-turning to England. Ilannguak overheard our conversation and came over. It was rough, he said, but we would roll with the waves, not slam into them; he imitated the movements of the boat with his ever-expressive hands. The family looked at me expectantly and I jumped into the boat making Ilannguak smile with glee, with Magda beside him pretending to be sick over the side of the boat. I waited for Ilannguak's wife Arnarulunaguaq to come on board but she shook her head and laughed, and said she was not crazy enough to go in this weather. I grimaced and they all laughed as Ilannguak again told me not to worry and made gentle rolling motions with his hands at me, telling me to ignore the others.

Herbert Island looked dark and withdrawn and had a heavy grey blanket of cloud pulled in around its shoulders as we motored slowly towards it. For hour after hour Ilannguak rolled us gently over the swollen waves and I let thoughts ebb and flow with the motion of the boat and gazed at the elephantine icebergs, marvelling at how quickly they disappeared into the low cloud that engulfed our path from Qaanaaq.

Qeqertassuaq was utterly deserted and every sound eerily became dulled with the thick cloud hanging over us. Impenetrable veils of mist clung to the mountain and hung over the storm-damaged settlement. Bones and boulders tricked the step and for a moment I felt as though invisible hands were pulling my feet from under me. The filtered light played tricks on the eyes and strange spectres seemed to shift and hide among the strange dark formations of rock and tundra.

Ilannguak immediately set to his chores of tending to his stunning team of huskies. The excited baying of the dogs rang out harshly through the ghost village, setting my nerves on edge and sending thrills of excitement up my spine. I wandered over to help, but realized that I was going to be more of a hindrance than a help, so went to visit our old hut again. I sat among the discarded clothes and boots that still bore the footprint of their owners in the sole, and finally it occurred to me that however fond my memories of this place were, I was never going to relive them fully. I had to look forward and make something new out of my return to Thule.

The dogs were frenzied as Ilannguak hauled supplies of meat off a nearby rack towards the team, which strained and leapt against their chains, almost garrotting themselves in the process. Feeding a semi-wild pack of huskies takes both skill and fearlessness. The dogs almost looked rabid from hunger, in particular one bristling beast who threw himself so violently towards his master that his chains broke. The escapee belted towards Ilannguak, and I cried out to warn him, but he continued, unflinching, to divide up the seal carcass and merely growled deeply under his breath. The sound stopped the dog in his tracks and he meekly sat down on his haunches and waited, only occasionally reminding Ilannguak of his presence with a throaty whine.

Some visitors to the region are shocked at the apparent abuse that the dogs endure at the hands of the hunters. They believe the Inughuit to be cruel and heartless towards their huskies, but it is an opinion based on ignorance of the way of the polar hunter. Huskies are semi-wild, and as such are prone to being both vicious and uncontrollable and the hunter has to find a way of gaining their respect, and to command leadership, much as dogs in packs do to enforce their superiority. It is not unusual to see a hunter belting a disobedient dog, but this shouldn't always be interpreted as a brutish act: the hunter will never beat a dog to break its spirit, only to teach it a lesson. Besides, an injured or broken dog is no good to a hunter. True, there is the odd exception, and there was one hunter that I saw in Siorapaluk who openly abused his dogs, and it was a terrible sight. He was not respected in the community for it. Every hunter is aware that a good team of dogs can be his most valuable asset, and on a hunting trip the hunter will often feed his dogs before himself. The better the dog team, often the more successful the hunt, and both dog and man – as well as his family and even the community as a whole – benefit. Hunter and dog have an understanding based not just on mutual dependency, but also on a deeper mutual affinity with the world that they both inhabit. Independently they can just about survive in this environment, but as a team they make powerful allies.

The routine of feeding the dogs not only strengthens this bond between a man and his dogs, but also clarifies the hierarchies within a team, which is essential in order for the pack to be at its most content. A hunter also has to ensure that every dog is fed well; if left to their own devices, only the strongest dogs would eat in the inevitable fracas, and the weaker dogs would be severely injured.

The dogs followed Ilannguak's every move, every muscle taut with expectancy. With great precision Ilannguak threw the brick-sized chunks of meat to the dogs in quick succession, each catching his or her quota mid-air, swallowing with a single gulp to be immediately ready for another. The prize pieces were awarded to the lead dog that stood distinct from the rest: keen-eyed, proud and with an unmistakable commanding air. The lead dog is the hunter's greatest asset, and his best friend. He is an extension of the hunter himself. The best lead dogs possess an exceptional intelligence and an almost heightened sensory perception, which makes them able to track down seal, walrus and bear from a great distance, and also ensures the safety of both team and hunter on the ice. There are many stories of hunters being saved by the internal compass of the dogs in blizzards, and as a child I remember my father talking of his one-eyed lead dog that had an uncanny ability to sense danger and avert it.

I was starting to feel the cold seep into my muscles and I took refuge in Aata's house to try and warm up before the long ride back to Qaanaaq, and as soon as I stepped into the old hut I felt myself absorbed again into a familiar golden-honey warmth of happy memories.

Again, I sat next to Aata's old armchair and put my hand gently on the arm and squeezed it in a sort of communion with the old man, to let him know that I finally came back. This was where the old man always used to sit, and it was a special privilege to be allowed to sit in the dog-eared chair; I could not bring myself to sit in it even now without having his permission somehow. I remembered so clearly the times that he would sit there quietly smoking his pipe, his face impassive with thought or smiling at the antics or conversation of people in his home. I remembered him listening with glowing eyes, his mouth soft and proud as I chattered to him excitedly about my antics with my Eskimo friends.

I vividly remembered his wife Aana working with a white fox that Aata had just caught in a trap. With the deft precision of a good hunter's wife, she had carefully removed the inside of the animal through the mouth of the fox without a single puncture to the skin or fur, and with great skill turned the fox entirely inside out before then stretching the whole skin and starting the lengthy process of meticulously flensing it.

Ilannguak came in and sat heavily on Aata's chair, cleaning his knife of blood. He smiled broadly and crossed the room quickly to see if there was any water in the kettle – none – then went to the enormous water pot with its wooden lid where for years chunks of icebergs were melted for the household's water needs; that too was empty. I looked out the window; there were no grounded icebergs to be seen, and it would involve a hike to the nearest stream that came down from the ice-encrusted mountain.

Ilannguak interrupted my thoughts, asking if we could go back to Qaanaaq, pointing at the darkening sky. I nodded, bleary-eyed, and he led the way back to the boat. The water had turned steel-grey during our short time on the island, and immediately out of the small sheltered harbour we were cast bucking and reeling on the waves as if we were riding wild mustangs. The sharp breeze caught the white crests of the waves, sending plumes of fine spray over the bow and into our raw faces. We rode the boat with exhilarated eyes; light was breaking on the crests of the mountains and in the distance the soft golden hues of an almost sunset rippled through the bruised clouds. Kittiwakes and guillemots wheeled and dived around us as if urging us to hurry home.

I went to bed that night listening to the sound of the rain pounding on the windowpane, and relishing the near dark, the first I had encountered for over two weeks. I pulled the thin summer duvet under my chin and folded my legs into a flat lotus position, the only way that I could have my whole body under the child's duvet at once. Then Karen and her friend had all the lights blazing as they came into the bedroom at 3 a.m. As soon as they settled down I turned all the lights off again and succumbed to a restless sleep that whirled with the storm outside.

Two days later the wind finally died and left us with solid, unrelenting rain. I stared out of the window and thought of

Arquenguak and Tukúmek and their young son who had gone
out on their boat; I hadn't heard anything about them coming
back and wondered if they were still out on the fjord. The
weather was miserable. The temperature was bitter, with the
rain lashing the ground so that the dirt tracks ran fast with
terracotta rivers. We could barely see the fjord from the house,
but with the occasional moment of clarity we could make out
the dark peaks and troughs of the water capped with pale foam.
Many other hunters were also still out in the fjord, and there was
obvious concern in the community. Eyes were constantly pressed
up against binoculars, dozens at a time, in case someone tried to
make it home.

I struggled against the rain to the store simply to get a change
of scenery, and found that half of Qaanaaq had had the same
idea; groups of people stood chatting in the doorway, some with
concern, asking about their friends and if they had returned from
hunting. Although it was freezing and wet I took a walk down
to the beach. Waves broke furiously over a band of low rocks
thirty yards from the breakwater. A great cathedral of an iceberg,
ten times the size of an English village church, was moving
with perceptible speed at the whim of the strong currents. You
wouldn't have lasted more than thirty seconds if you fell in this
water. The flagpoles in the town swung in loops in the wind like
upside-down pendulums, the flags starched and flying straight
out at half-mast. Another old member of the Qujaukitsoq family
had died the day before.

The following day the dogs were going crazy, howling for hours
on end and whimpering as if they were souls lost and crying on
the wind. The unearthly sound, high-pitched and wavering on
the wind, blew in through the fine pale-pink curtains that sifted
neither light nor the sounds of the Arctic. Sometimes, with all
the modern comforts crowding in on us – duvets, films, music,
and rationed hot running water – it was easy to forget that we
were surrounded by wilderness. But on those days when the

storms hold you hostage and your eyes gaze upon anything but the solid grey wall of Nature, one can sink into a lethargy of spirit and mind. It was such a day, and the whole house felt withdrawn.

A momentary break in the weather saw the town leap into an orgy of activity. I had never seen so many people moving around, all escaping cabin fever and desperate for air and a change of company. Children swarmed over the playground, people gathered in the street and talked urgently to one another and then moved on. It lasted barely forty minutes before everyone took refuge again. The waters of the fjord still looked challenging. I shuddered and wondered again about Arquenguak and his family. I walked through town alone, feeling the sting of the rain on my skin, and headed towards Baali's house.

I could still feel the restlessness of the dogs, and wondered if it was full moon. I was missing my lunar pivot. I imagined myself lying on the spare bed at my parents' house in Scotland, with my head resting on the pillow, looking up through the small rectangular skylight at the Milky Way, and seeing a shaft of moonlight playing on one of my father's watercolours that hangs over the bed – a team of huskies, panting on the ice, ready for adventure. The moonlight always seems to bring them to life.

No sooner had I got to Baali and Kristian's house than Baali spotted Arquenguak's boat limping into shore. In a flash we scrambled into our coats and ran towards the beach. Maria was already there waiting for her parents, looking anxious and pale; Magda had her arms around her niece. Arquenguak easily negotiated his way into shore and Kristian and Gideon waded into the water and quickly pulled Tukúmek and little Erich out onto the sand. It was an emotional reunion for Tukúmek. She grasped her daughter tightly and gently sobbed into her shoulder. Soon almost all of the women were teary eyed. I stood to one side as Tukúmek went round all the women, hugging and crying; I wanted to show my concerns of the past few days, but I was still feeling slightly bruised from our last meeting, and I was unsure of the reception I would receive this time.

Tukúmek came to me at last and I gave her a long hug before telling her that I had been worried for their safety. She nodded; mute. They had been stuck on the tiny boat for three days, unable to come into land because of the waves crashing on the beach, and she had been particularly scared for the safety of her young son.

The crowd soon disbanded; Arquenguak and his family were exhausted from their ordeal and needed sleep. Tukúmek turned and called to me as the family walked away: '*Kaari-gna*, maybe you will come and visit us?' I smiled with relief. 'I would love to!' I replied. She flashed a smile, took Erich by the hand and slowly headed home.

Downstairs the family was banging and crashing their way into the day. I could hear hard-boiled eggs being smacked on the dining table and shelled, and the vigorous carving of a crusty loaf. The radio was blaring out the polka, played badly on an electric keyboard. I descended the stairs to find Hans checking out the births and obituaries in a West Greenlandic newspaper. The rain and sleet came and went in flat grey sheets, but there was fresh snow on the peaks of the surrounding mountains, breaking up the monotony of the dark rock embrace.

Desperate to get out of the confines of the house I pulled on my waterproofs and headed back down towards the beach. It was completely deserted, save for one old hunter tending to his beached boat. He waved enthusiastically at me, as if we were two like-minded travellers on a big adventure. I kept him company for a short time and then left him to his repairs and walked across the sodden beach. The downpour of the last few days had etched causeways into the sand. By the time I had rounded on myself and returned to the old man's boat he had given up and gone home.

A group of children ate ice creams in the freezing rain, leaning against the railings of the store, and a hesitant tourist followed me into the shop. He had the air of a new arrival, and was not dressed appropriately for the weather, wearing thick tweed trousers and a matching blazer.

An inebriated couple were weaving their way down the hill as I headed home. From a distance I saw the woman slump on the bench outside Louisa's house and take a swig from a plastic bottle, before swinging uncertainly to her feet and joining her partner, weaving slowly, comically, sadly down towards me. As I neared them I recognized her as one of my childhood friends with a man I hadn't met, who was not her husband. The man greeted me darkly, trying to focus on my face. My friend gripped his arm and tried to take another swig of whatever they had been drinking. She was in her own world, and I am not sure if she even noticed that they had stopped and that there was someone in front of her. I felt my heart drop into the pit of my stomach.

I quietly let myself into the house and leant against the door, feeling winded from distress. Louisa poked her head around the door and grinned, gripping a handful of hair in one hand and a pair of scissors in the other. She was naked except for a pair of curtains that she had swathed around her growing midriff. She laughed, disappeared and reappeared a few minutes later still in the soft-furnishing ensemble, doing a fashion parade for me with her new homegrown haircut. I looked at her and felt my heart swell and gave her a big kiss on the cheek.

Hans was standing at the window in his favourite position, laughing at something in the street. Just missing the scene of amusement I asked him what had happened and he started staggering around the room, pretending to be drunk and laughing, before grabbing my language book and poring over it. I leant over as he pointed with a rough finger at the religion section. 'The catechist,' Hans said with some help, 'drunk!'

Baali and Kristian arrived shortly after for a light lunch of raw frozen salmon and dried figs that Louisa had brought back from Nuuk. Louisa turned to me and said that Baali and Kristian were going on summer camp to find narwhal and go kayaking; would I like to go with them? 'Yes!' I said emphatically, jumping out of my seat. Kristian raised his eyebrows and laughed; Baali grinned happily. I was thrilled, although secretly hoping that the weather would improve before we left. I had only been outside for fifteen minutes earlier and had returned almost as frozen as the salmon we had just eaten. I immediately began to work out what equipment I should take with me, how much in the way of provisions – would I even be able to get enough now that the shop was so low on stocks? We would be leaving in two days, just as the supply ship arrived.

The store was buzzing with life. Although it was early, customers had already been queuing outside, impatient to stock up on essentials – it was the first clear day after a week of stormy weather and everyone was desperate to get out to summer camp or on the boats to fish. There was a constant hum of speculation about when the supply ship was likely to arrive. Throughout town curtains had been twitching for several days as binoculars were trained on the horizon to see when the *umiassuaq* might come. It was inevitable that the ship would be delayed because of the bad weather, but already the merchandise in the shop had dwindled down to absolute basics and the town hadn't seen any fresh food, apart from narwhal and seal meat, for some time.

I quickly made my way around the shop, grabbing what supplies I could find, but almost all of the food left on the shelves was beyond its best-before date by several months, including the 'longlife' milk and tinned foods. There seemed to be an air of mild panic as the shoppers filled their baskets with the last few boxes of tea, and seized the precious loaves; daily less and less bread was appearing from the small bakery. Turning a corner blindly I ran headlong into Baali and Kristian, who were grinning with wind-chapped lips from their early-morning journey on the fjord. They had gone to recce the camp the day before and had returned to collect supplies and ferry more passengers out for the kayak-rolling course that was to take place at the camp.

I could hardly contain my excitement. I have never felt that Qaanaaq is my hometown – I have known it only as a stopping-off and resupply place – and have never wished to spend any considerable amount of time there. It has none of the spirit of the 'real' hunting villages. Going out into the wilds to join summer camp held a familiar excitement for me, and called up the happy dreams of the freedom felt by the hunting families when they left their dark winter houses to live out on the tundra. Summer camp was cherished as being a place for communal outdoor meals of fresh meat, entertaining gossip, energizing walks, and lovemaking.

Louisa, Edo and Magda came to see us off and join in with what was becoming quite a festive occasion. Boats were being pulled up to the beach, children, women and hunters piled into boats and wasted no time in skimming off in different directions laughing and calling farewells to those left on the shore and leaving a cross-hatch of ripples on the water's surface. There were going to be five of us crammed into Kristian's small boat along with all the provisions and camping gear and it felt like a real expedition. Baali's two girls Naduk and Little Tekummeq were already at the camp, but a couple of teenage boys had secured a lift with us so they could join the workshop. The two of them couldn't have looked more different. Both in their early teens, one had the swaggering confidence of a young hunter, and although barely fourteen had already learnt to smirk at the apparent inferiority of women. The other had the thickset look of a clumsy rugby player, whose apologetic air didn't fit his physique. He kept his eyes lowered at all times, and with the briefest eye contact would blush into his already ruddy cheeks.

The boat was already desperately low in the water and we packed it carefully, stacking the heavier provisions, fuel and heaters all in the bow to try and push the weight forward. The sun glittered off the water and I felt a surge of happiness to be on the move and to be getting out of the oppressive feel of Qaanaaq.

The journey was long with a biting wind that had us huddling together for warmth, although the boys had to practically hang off the front of the boat to keep the bow down to make any progress at all. Baali and Kristian were glowing with excitement, cracking jokes and trying to make the straight-faced boys laugh by pulling silly faces. The water was like a bolt of rippling blue-silver silk that had been thrown to the foot of the dark grey mountains, which had been recently dusted lightly with fresh snow. Guillemots dived and skimmed the water and tiny black-backed, white-breasted auklets bobbed daintily on the small waves. A small pod of seal broke the surface of the water in front of us, somehow aware that we were too overloaded to be interested in them. The sun glinted off their sleek backs as they tumbled playfully in the waters – I felt my spirits soar higher and higher. A single seagull flew directly overhead, all of us watching its low languid path, and the quiver of its tail feathers as it shat twice, perfectly, just either side of the boat.

Baali squeezed next to me on the hard plank of wood I was sitting on and pointed to the dark mountains in front of us, her finger following a line of a valley down to the water's edge, saying that there were two huts there, and that was where we were to make camp. Steeped in the shadow of the surrounding mountains our destination looked bleak, inhospitable and hostile. She bumped into me jovially. '*Nuanneq?* You like it?' she asked, laughing.

I laughed with her. '*Eie!*' I replied truthfully. 'I love it.'

10. Arrival at Summer Camp

Provisions: Rice, tins of tuna, sardines and corned beef, noodles/macaroni, dried fruit, bread, jam, water, tea, sugar, dried narwhal, frozen meat . . .

I was greeted at the summer camp by the smell of death and the gruesome aftermath of a massacre. The scent of the hunt hung heavy and warm on the bitter wind. Two narwhal had been caught and were semi-dissected on the beach. The air was shattered with the shrieks of birds fighting over floating chunks of blubber and fat, and sculptures of meat-clothed vertebrae created a macabre outdoor exhibition. Streams of blood seeped into the crimson-stained waters of the fjord.

Beyond the gore, a couple of tiny boxes no bigger than garden sheds stood apologetically on the beach, with the smaller of the two pinioned to the ground with guy ropes to prevent it from scurrying away. This was to be our home.

The camp was steadily coming to life as we pulled into shore. Maria, Arquenguak's daughter, had already spent a night with some of her friends in the larger of the two huts and crawled out sleepily in a thin T-shirt and shorts onto the beach, waving at us as she brushed her teeth and spat toothpaste onto the pebbles, oblivious to the freezing temperature.

A couple of hunters who had been busily filling their boat with meat from their kill paused to help us unload the boat and advise Kristian where the narwhal were in the fjord. They were happy men, they had killed two sizeable narwhal in one morning, which would feed their families and dogs for some time, and they would have extra meat to sell to the community. They pointed to the meat left on the beach; they knew that there would be more people arriving so they had graciously left a contribution for us all. Baali went up to the oldest man, who was bent almost double from seventy-odd years of waiting for seals at holes in the ice, and handed him some kroner and a bag containing a jar of instant coffee and two packets of cheap cigarettes.

We relayed the supplies and equipment to the first hut, stepping over the dark rivulets of blood that ran in gullies down the beach, and piled our bags in a heap at the entrance. On first impressions it was a gruesome resting place: ancient blackened joints of meat hung forgotten from the roof next to a bleached skull of a seal; piles of fresh mattak lay on the beach like fleshy slabs of carpet, and two dead seagulls lay with limp necks on rocks directly in front of the door. I dreaded the thought that one of my tasks would be to pluck them, but swallowed hard and reminded myself that this was not the place to succumb to squeamishness.

Baali called to me from inside the hut to help bring in some of the bags. The doorway was barely four feet high, and was reached through a short entranceway that would help keep snowdrifts from covering the door itself, and where visitors should take off their snow-encrusted clothing, allowing more elbowroom inside, and minimizing condensation.

The hut was tiny, only nine feet by eight, with the ceiling skimming my head at 5 ft 8 in and a sleeping platform running across the length of the space, with just enough room at its foot to set up a Primus stove to heat the space and cook over. The interior was dark and stained with grease from years of boiled seal and walrus stews; in places bored residents held ransom by the weather had carved their names and Greenlandic graffiti into the soft wood. Under the platform was a bundle of forgotten clothes that looked disturbingly like a shrivelled corpse. I immediately felt at home. Two small grubby windows filtered light into the gloom above the entrance. Naduk fingered a crack in one of the windows and grinned at me, wiggling her fingers

through the hole. In the past, windows were made of the intestines of the bearded seal, which were split, dried and stretched
across the window frame, with a small hole made through it so
that the occupants could see outside; a plug of tundra grass or fur
used to block out uncomfortable draughts, although the houses
as a matter of necessity were always kept well ventilated. Even
when glass was first brought to the area the Inughuit mostly
preferred to use the seal-gut pane as it was less prone to cracking
in the extreme cold.

Within minutes we were all crammed into the hut trying to
sort out the bedding and stack our gear so that there would be
space enough for all of us to sleep together. I wondered how we
were all going to fit on the platform, and wondered whom I
would be sleeping next to. I stopped just short of laying out my
sleeping bag as I remembered the stories of wife-swapping.

The attitude of the Inughuit to sex is very different to the
average European's. Traditionally from an early age the children
of the High Arctic were educated as a matter of course in
the natural functions of the body; in the days when the entire
family slept on a single sleeping platform there simply had to be
an open attitude to relationships, and nudity in the home was
commonplace. As a result it was only to be expected that youngsters would experiment with one another, and in some communities an empty house was given over to teenagers so that they
could have some private time together. It was not unusual for
girls to fall pregnant in their early teens, although it was not
necessarily as a result of the covert fumbles in the teenage house
but more because the girls were often 'married' long before their
twenties – the boys usually married later as they would only be
considered suitable partners if they could support a wife. As a
result girls would sometimes partner a man old enough to be
their father.

Keeping the gene pool strong was vital for the future of the
people, and as a consequence partners would be shared across
communities, particularly at trading meets, where some ethnol-

ogists have recorded that the women were 'traded' just as often as the furs, ivory, meat and knives. Having said that, the wife-swapping arrangements were only usually with the husband's trading partners or friends, with the open agreement of both parties. In the past there was never any stigma attached to illegitimate children; if a wife fell pregnant with another man's child, the baby would be brought up as if he or she were biologically part of the family.

It is said that sexual fidelity has never been a virtue in Thule, but this shouldn't be taken the wrong way. Sex, and thereby procreation, is of course as much a part of community life as the need to eat and breathe. And although Christianity has changed the way the modern Inughuit think about sexual relations, they do not have the centuries of inherited guilt upon their consciences that we do, and as a result are much more liberated in their interpretation of faithfulness.

The Inughuit were quick to insist that devotion to a partner was deeper than a sexual act, but also that sexual fulfilment was essential to the happiness of their partner and the community as a whole; when hunters were away for long stretches of time it was expected that their wives would be 'kept warm' by friends staying in the community. Likewise, if a hunter was going on a long journey and his wife was needed at home – perhaps she was heavily pregnant or needed to look after the children – another hunter who was staying in the settlement would often be more than happy to 'lend' his wife to his friend, and in return the wife left behind would act as the wife to the village-bound hunter.

Although in the old days – just a few decades ago – partners were regularly exchanged, it was unthinkable for a wife or husband to run off permanently with another lover. The humiliation caused by such a situation could provoke the cuckold to exact revenge, which at times could be as violent as murder. A marriage was an agreed contract for both parties to look after one another; if a husband ran away with another woman to another community, his abandoned partner would have no one to bring home the meat and she would have to throw herself at the mercy of the community. Quite often a young bride would be taken far away from her childhood home, so her own family would not be nearby to support her. If a wife ran away from her husband the insult would be compounded; not only would the man have lost a wife and her skills – which was not only inconvenient, but also potentially hazardous, as a hunter relies heavily on well-maintained furs – but he would also be seen by the others in the community as being a weak man for not keeping his wife happy and well fed – why else would she run away? This sort of humiliation was intolerable for a proud hunter.

Paradoxically, for all that has been claimed about the Inughuit's carnal exploits over the centuries, they have never been openly sexual in manner – 'loose' women who were indiscriminate about whom they slept with were not highly regarded – and as a rule the Inughuit are almost painfully modest, unless their inhibitions are loosened by drink. Moments of intimacy are snatched in rare moments of privacy, and more often than not couples are resigned to silent fumbling in a room shared with an entire family. Even in these modern times many families still share a single bedroom, albeit with a couple of narrow beds.

By the time we arrived at Herbert Island in the early 1970s the old tradition of wife-swapping was joked about more than acted upon, although even then there were a couple of occasions when it seemed as though the locals were more than willing to extend their courtesy to the bedroom. Dad came up to Thule a few months in advance of our moving to Herbert Island in order to make essential arrangements, and while travelling around the area stayed a night in a small settlement further down the fjord where he was warmly welcomed by the villagers. After eating a communal meal with the hunters he tried to make conversation and, not knowing what else to say, said in Greenlandic, 'Ah, it is such a shame my wife is not here.' The men immediately scrambled to their feet and hollered for their wives, all of them offering their partners to Dad for the evening. 'It was bloody

Part One:
A Long Way Home

1. Avatak, Aata and Aana outside their skin tent in 1940.

2. The white whale is notoriously difficult to catch. Maria proudly holds me over the whale Avatak has caught, 1971.

3. Summer camp, 1972. Although many things have changed in Thule, still daily life at summer camp is little different to when I was a child.

4. With my mother on the ice during a long sledge journey in 1971. The sun has left the northern sky and will not be back for another six weeks.

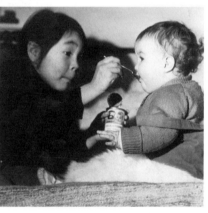

5. Najannuaq feeding me from one of the hundreds of tins donated by our sponsors.

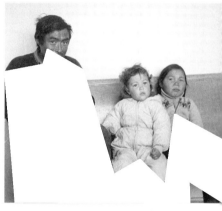

6. With Avatak and Edo, 1972.

7. The family home for two years. The store hut in the foreground was used for storing furs away from the heat of the small kitchen.

8. My father and me in our tiny hut surrounded by supplies and equipment.

9. The *Daily Mail* reports on our return to England.

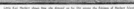

Daily Mail, Friday, December 15, 1972   PAGE 37

Kari the explorer's daughter comes home for Christmas with a taste for boiled seal

Words: LEO CLANCY
Pictures: PHILLIP JACKSON

TODDLER Kari Herbert returned home from the Arctic yesterday with her parents—and a penchant for boiled seal.

Her father, explorer Wally Herbert, was worried that two-year-old Kari might find it difficult to adjust to 'civilisation.'

Her mother, Marie, t h o u g h t her daughter might be frightened at seeing so many white people hurrying about.

No glamour at 15 below zero

ALL TOGETHER. The Herberts as the Polar Eskimos know them

Little Kari Herbert shows how she dressed up for life among the Eskimos of Herbert Island

No loneliness for hunters' wives

10. Posing in traditional costume on the steps of a friend's hut in Qaanaaq when we returned in 1979. Now the Inughuit rarely wear the traditional dress except at weddings and confirmations.

11. Doing my homework with Aata. Aata is sitting in his favourite green armchair.

12. With my father and baby sister Pascale, 1979.

13. Collecting ice to melt for drinking, cooking and washing.

14. Avatak and Peter Peary stalking walrus, 1972. Only the most experienced hunters would dare to get so close to these unpredictable animals.

Part two:
Return

15. The ice surrounding large icebergs can be treacherous, but the ancient glacial ice is still the only source of fresh water for the people of Thule.

16. In Qaanaaq in March 2002.

17. Midnight in Qaanaaq. Herbert Island is in the background.

18. Naduk in the hut I lived in as a child.

19. Uusaqqak at summer camp at 2 o'clock in the morning.

20. Summer camp, 2002.

21. Little Tekummeq and Naduk asleep in our tent at summer camp.

22. Sledging back to Qaanaaq from Herbert Island, 2003.

23. Funeral, Qaanaaq, 2002.

24. The church and playground in Qaanaaq. To the left are empty meat racks

25. *Far left*: Orle Kristiansen flaying a narwhal.

26. *Left*: Children playing around a hunted narwhal.

27. With the girls (from left to right) Baali, Najannuaq, Magda, Louisa and the children.

embarrassing,' Dad laughed as he told the story. 'It was not what I had implied I wanted at all, and besides, they were all a bunch of old crones!' My mother too had a few offers from the young hunters while Dad was travelling, who said solemnly that her husband was a bad man for leaving such a beautiful woman cold and alone. A couple of them were very bemused at her chastity.

In that little hut I couldn't help wondering what the situation was going to be with Baali and Kristian. It must have been obvious what I was thinking as Baali started giggling and Kristian hastily elbowed his way to the platform bed and looked back at me as he laid a reindeer skin on the left-hand side of the platform. '*Illit*, you,' he said seriously, 'will sleep here, and I will sleep . . .' pausing for a moment, '*ikani, there!*' pointing to the other side of the platform, hurriedly explaining that Baali, Naduk and Tekummeq would sleep in the middle. He looked sheepishly at me for a moment, gauging whether I had understood what he had said. Baali chuckled behind me. The girls thought this was hilarious and started teasing Kristian until he was overcome with embarrassment and stumbled outside muttering something about getting the rest of the gear indoors.

We shooed the giggling girls after him and Baali and I, still laughing, busied ourselves with sorting out the little hut. I swept the floor and unpacked what groceries I could in the space available and laid out a couple of reindeer skins and sleeping bags to make the platform more comfortable while Baali found the radio, lit the Primus and filled pots with water from a stream nearby to make tea. Baali and I fell into a natural rhythm as we worked to make the small hut a welcoming nest, and finally as the chores were finished we leant against each other for support and cradled steaming mugs in our tired hands.

Small boats arrived throughout the afternoon, and we spent the next few hours relaying supplies and children of various ages from the boats to the beach and helping to erect small homemade canvas tents. The camp grew steadily with shining faces, as hunters and their families settled into the sunny atmosphere;

children's chatter and laughter carried on the breeze as the women helped each other to make their temporary homes comfortable, and the men stood in twos and threes, gazing out across the fjord or helping each other to prepare their kayaks.

The Polar Eskimos of the Thule district had used the kayak since the first migration from Canada but they lost the art of the kayak around 1600 – mostly due to the englaciation of the water – and although the traditional craft was reintroduced into the area in 1863 by a second migration from Baffin Island, the knowledge of how to right a capsized kayak was never regained (unlike further south where the West Greenlanders retained their kayaking skills). John Ross testified that when he 'discovered' the Thule people in 1818, they didn't even know the name *kayak*, but it has since been discovered through archaeological research that kayaks were used in the area before. The modern result is that few Inughuit hunters know how to do the 'Eskimo roll' for which they are apparently famous, and the fatal consequence of which is that there are many deaths by drowning every year.

Uuli, the instructor for the 'Eskimo rolling' lessons, was a short stocky man with ratty features, bushy black eyebrows and a chunky moustache. He looked at me with beady eyes behind his thick glasses and called a cheery 'Welcome!' as he jogged up the first hill behind the camp with a rolled up Greenland flag. His disciples and the rest of us who had come along for the ride swarmed up the hill for an impromptu opening ceremony, which involved a grave speech from Uuli, the raising of the Greenland flag, a little polite clapping and a scrambling run for the teenagers over the mountain behind. By the time the youngsters had returned from their run the kayaks were ready on the beach and Uuli and Kristian were getting kitted out in the two bespoke wetsuits for the first demonstration.

Uuli had learnt how to 'roll' in West Greenland from a Canadian Inuit teacher who had come over specifically to teach the Greenlanders how to right themselves if they capsized. Uuli was already trained as a sports coach and had worked in both Denmark and Canada, so was well qualified to be leading the workshops. Kristian, Baali explained to me as we sat on the beach watching the men get into their kayaks, had learnt how to roll for another reason. Early in the previous summer he had been out on his kayak in the fjord hunting as usual, when a narwhal capsized his craft. Like all of the other hunters in the Thule district Kristian had never learnt how to swim despite the fact that he spent so much of his time working on the water. Unable to right himself and not able to release himself from the kayak, nor able to swim, he had almost drowned. He finally managed to struggle out of the capsized kayak and had desperately clung on to it in the frigid waters. Thankfully Arquenguak had spotted that Kristian was in trouble and sped into the fjord on his motorboat, rescuing Kristian just before hypothermia fatally set in. Kristian believes that it was the thought of his family that kept him alive. Baali brushed away a loose tear as she told the story. 'We heard what had happened on the short-wave radio,' she said softly, 'and when Kristian came home we were all crying at the thought that we could have lost him.'

It was a life-changing moment for Kristian. He had seen people roll kayaks on the television and had heard that Uuli was on a course. As soon as Uuli returned he pleaded with him to teach him immediately. Once he knew how to roll himself he convinced Uuli that he must teach other hunters and young people at summer camps so that there would be fewer deaths on the fjord.

Watching Kristian from the beach it was difficult to believe that he had ever had a problem with rolling. Placing the paddle along the length of the kayak, he leant forward and rolled fluidly into the water, reappearing a moment later with a twist of his back and a comical shudder at the freezing temperature. The children looked on with wide eyes, fascinated.

The demonstration was impressive. Uuli went through a range of techniques for righting the kayak, with or without a paddle, and even using the handle from his harpoon to right himself. And as soon as he saw that I had produced a little video camera he really put his back into it and spun himself through the water again and again to wild applause and cries of admiration from the onlookers. Just then someone cried out behind us and Baali ran down the beach calling urgently to some of the teenagers. Everyone had been so engrossed in the kayak rolling that no one had noticed that the tide was coming in, and some of the meat that had been left on the beach was starting to slip into the water. A couple of the bolder teenagers went to help, pulling huge chunks of meat out of the water between them and carrying them up to a dry part of the beach, trying not to get blood on their new Nike and Adidas gear.

Our hut was the pivot of the camp. The door was in constant use and water boiled ceaselessly over the stove as children came in to warm up after playing outside and hunters and their wives came to visit and share news. The heat in the cramped space was intense compared to the chill outside, and any visitor who stayed longer than five minutes was soon stripping off.

As more people arrived and descended on our warm little haven I began to wonder how many more people were thinking of sharing the hut; after all it was a place of refuge for any hunter who happened past. At least two or three newly arrived parties of people had yet to set up their tents, including Uuli and his young son. I thought perhaps we would have to take shifts in sleeping in the hut.

The atmosphere was light – the teenage girls came and went from our hut, even though they had their own to use, and rummaged in Baali's wash-bag, pulling out her mirror and brush and sitting together as they preened themselves, looking pristine and fashionable even though they had had their arms deep in bloody gore just a few moments before. Two of the five boys were just as self-conscious, and casually checked themselves in the reflected glass of the huts, running soft hands through their gelled hair, before prancing up the hilltop behind the camp to call their girlfriends in Qaanaaq or to see if they had any text messages.

Deciding to explore the local area I left the hub of camp activity and walked towards the fresh glacial stream that gurgled triumphantly out of the hillside. The site of the camp had obviously been a favourite for centuries, and at one time supported a permanent community of perhaps four or five families. Overgrown with moss, lichen and tundra grasses, the remains of ancient dwellings nestled closely together behind a protective hummock of rock. Ranging between six and ten feet in diameter, these igloo-type houses (*iglu* or *igdoo* means 'house' in Greenlandic) had been excavated into the gently sloping hillside and were built using rock and turf, with a short, low entranceway which would have been a desperate struggle for anyone over seven stone to get through.

It would have been dark and claustrophobic in these ancient dwellings, with virtually no room at all in which to manoeuvre. Still the rocky supports survived from each of the platform beds, which took up most of the room in the dwellings, but broken flat pieces of rock were all that remained of the platforms themselves – raised two feet off the ground – and the roofs had long since disappeared. Originally the roofs would have been constructed with spines of driftwood, if it were available, otherwise the jawbone and ribs of a whale were used to support a roof of sods. Often the inside of the home was lined with skins for additional warmth and comfort.

The traditional Polar Eskimo dwelling was a masterful construction, whether made of snow or stone and turf. They might at first give an impression of being primitive, but they are extraordinary when you ponder the materials available to them and the environment in which they had to survive: the perfect dome of the snow igloo and stone houses antedates both the Roman arch and the domes of the Muslim masons by four thousand years. Not only was the dome construction a piece of architectural mastery (particularly of the snow igloos, where the dome was constructed of a spiral, with each tier leaning in at a level greater than the tier below, until all that is required is the key block, perfectly shaved to fit the crown), but so was the early builders' understanding of thermo-dynamics. Quick-witted enough to realize that warm air rises, the Polar Eskimos had to devise a method of entering the dwelling without losing precious heat from the inside. No doubt this was perfected by trial and error: if a hole was made directly into the side of the construction the heat would escape immediately through the doorway. Building a long entrance passageway would partially solve the problem, as long as skins covered the entrance; but the most ingenious development was to tunnel *under* the igloo, surfacing in a pit or 'cold trap' in front of the sleeping platform. Thus constructed, the entranceway could be left open and the cold air would flow into the space (providing much needed ventilation) but would not rise above the sleeping platform, so long as the interior was heated. In addition a small vent was made to let foul air escape – of which there was plenty – and to allow the fresh air to circulate; finally a window was made in the wall above the tunnel with a piece of freshwater ice, or seal gut in the case of the more permanent stone and turf dwellings.

This structure of the snow igloo itself was fairly sturdy, but glazing the interior with ice increased the strength of the dome tremendously, so that it could even support the weight of a hunter or a polar bear. Glazing the dome required an increase in temperature in the new construction until the whole of the interior was wet, then turning off the heat – quelling the numerous 'wicks' of a blubber lamp – which caused the snow to freeze into a sheet of ice. The benefits were two-fold: the structure was greatly strengthened and the inhabitants could move around freely inside without bringing down a shower of snow crystals which would thaw and wet the caribou skins lining the sleeping platform.

Even so, controlling the thermostat of the snow igloo was

still a tricky business. The thickness of the snow determined the insulation levels of the home: if the igloo was too cold, the hunter would pile on more snow on the dome outside; if the heat inside was too intense and started melting the interior, the hunter would shave off a few inches of snow. Lining the interior with skins, which were suspended from string frozen into the igloo wall, was another trick, which enabled the family to increase the heat inside without fear of melting the structure.

The snow igloo, however, was never used as a permanent residence in this part of the Arctic. Stone, driftwood, turf and whalebone were in abundance, and it made little sense painstakingly to construct a house of snow when there were stronger materials available. The snow house in the Thule district has only ever been used as a protective structure on long hunting trips when the weather looks as though it is closing in, or when a base sturdier than a skin tent was required.

Like the snow house, its rocky counterpart had a low narrow tunnel that led into the heart of the tiny home, and the centre of the space was identical, with the home built in the round and a sleeping platform made of rock, which was then covered in thick layers of dry grass with musk ox and caribou skins on top. The inhabitants would sleep naked with their feet to the far wall under 'blankets' of fox, caribou, hare and eider duck skins. The walls of the stone house were built in two layers, with peat or turf packed in between them for more insulation. Fresh ice would be brought in by the women of the house and melted for drinking water, and would often be kept in a sealskin bag. Inside such a house the blubber lamp and the numerous bodies could generate some considerable heat, and usually the inhabitants, both male and female would sit only partially clothed – perhaps the women may still wear their fox skin knickers – or relax in the nude. The discarded clothes would often be tied in a bundle with a skin thong and hung from the ceiling to avoid them getting infested with lice. The Polar Eskimos were purported by

Peter Freuchan to have a saying that, 'We would rather be a little chilly and be the only ones in our clothes.'

Lice were a perennial problem for the Polar Eskimos; these hardy little pests seemed not to acknowledge the cold, and could survive a spell of temperatures lower than forty below, and still wriggle with abandon when the Polar Eskimo returned to the warmth of his or her tent or stone house; there seemed no way to control the spread of lice, and as a result the people simply had to tolerate their annoyances, and make the best of the situation. A wife would often delouse her husband, and the husband would often delouse his children, merrily feasting on the tiny creatures. Delousing sometimes even became a sign of courtship – the way a young woman deloused a young hunter was an indication of her feelings for him.

The more permanent stone and turf dwellings could be used throughout the entire year, but by the summer months most of the inhabitants preferred to travel to other camps and to sleep outside under skin tents. Thus relinquished, the house would automatically become public property, and any family could move into the house come the autumn. It must have been quite a relief to get out of the cramped and often squalid home quarters: the Polar Eskimos were never praised for their cleanliness and the potent mixture of sweat, rotten meat – such as kiviak – and the stale urine that they used for curing skins and washing their hair must have eventually been unbearable. Summer for the Polar Eskimo signalled a time of freedom, of light, and lungs filled with fresh air.

The tundra immediately around these ancient settlements was richly carpeted with purple saxifrage, Arctic cinquefoil and the ground-hugging Arctic willow, just starting to mellow into rich autumnal colours. Bones littered the ground all over the camp. Giant whale vertebrae, bleached by the unrelenting summer sun, lay close to a well-preserved cairn that could well have been the burial spot for the old community.

★

Laughter carried on the breeze over the sound of the energetic stream and I headed back to the others. A group sat in a long line on the washed-up log, the chores had been done, the camp was set up and everyone produced their own mugs as Baali brought out freshly brewed tea. Everyone on camp had their own signature mug, a vital custom that grew out of the need to avoid the spread of tuberculosis. It is still unthinkable to go on a journey or on summer camp without one's own utensils.

Naduk and Little Tekummeq stood at the shoreline with the freezing water lapping at their wellies, examining the oddities that they found in the shallows. With great delight they squished strange jellyfish-like creatures between their fingers before reaching for some more, shrieking with delight as the squelchy bodies burst at their touch. Mum told me that she had once seen Maria eating these strange morsels while they had stood chatting at the water's edge. Baali joined us with a tall thin hunter by the name of Niels who had lived with old Migishoo on Herbert Island in the early 1970s. His mouth gaped limply as he realized who I was, revealing a couple of teeth still clinging obstinately from rotten gums. Niels grinned toothlessly, and regaining his composure laughed hoarsely and rejoined the others on the log and lit a cigarette.

Another boat drew into shore and two weathered hunters scrambled out. They headed immediately to the small hut and installed themselves without a word, with only a subtle nod of the head to the others in greeting. They were mismatched companions; the first man was squat and stocky with piggish eyes and a puffy round face squeezed tightly into a stained woollen cap. In complete contrast his companion was tall and the most aristocratic looking Inughuit I had seen in the district. Unlike his livid-faced partner, his clothes were almost impeccably clean and his skin was smooth and swarthy, peaking in a high, proud forehead. Few Inughuit have much facial hair but this man had cultivated a perfectly coiffed goatee with a moustache Dali would have been proud of. I wondered how he prevented the ends snapping off in winter. Baali and I set to putting more water on to boil and again swept out the sand that was settling into drifts across the floor.

The men warmed their hands over the heat of the stove and spoke in gruff short sentences to one another, eyeing me greedily. The atmosphere chilled. Baali started acting strangely; her usual light humour was replaced by an awkward, almost subservient manner. She busied herself by putting out a bowl of water with a knob of soap for washing hands and hung a towel near to the stove so that it would be warm to use. The short man staggered over to where I sat on the platform sorting through the supplies and plumped himself heavily beside me, patting the platform with a fat and calloused hand. He said something insistently to me, breathing sourly on my face. Alarmed, I froze for a moment, and shot a look towards Baali who was looking darkly at the hunter. Sighing he gripped something under my left thigh and pulled sharply, throwing me off my balance. I was sitting on his thin and grotty mattress. I stood up quickly and allowed him to gather up the disintegrating foam and looked back down at the platform, which was now completely bare and showing large gaps between the old stained planks of wood. Someone had tried half-heartedly to cover some of the holes with a bloodstained piece of cardboard, but it barely covered even a fraction of the platform. A draught whistled through the cracks and I shivered, wondering how we were all going to keep warm. Thankfully I had brought a thin Thermo-Rest with me, which looked as if it was going to be a lifesaver. I prayed that the men were not going to be sharing the hut with us.

Kristian peered through the small doorway, looking thoughtful. A moment later he thrust a spare *tugto* (reindeer) skin into my hands, which would be a necessary extra layer to keep the draughts at bay, and would even out the bumps of the badly constructed platform. The men suddenly left, the round man grabbing another bag that he had just stowed under the bed, and made a great show of departing.

I was relieved that they had gone, and Baali also visibly relaxed and sat with me to take in the scene. The door was a perfect frame to the beach where the Aristocrat and Red Face were squatting next to the narwhal carcass, gorging themselves on the dark raw flesh. The hut smelled heavily of animal skins and the tinned fish paste that I had opened to share with the girls. Already clothes were drying on the washing lines that crosshatched the low ceiling. I was constantly astonished at how many pairs of socks the Inughuit seem to wear. The Aristocrat, having had his fill, returned to the hut to wash his hands and blow his nose loudly after his feast. '*Kiak*, it's hot!' he said loudly, smiling broadly. I returned his smile warily and he nodded and turned away, preoccupied with finding his pipe in his anorak. Red Face followed shortly after, blood smeared across his cheek and down his front. He looked cannibalistic. There are many stories of cannibalism in the Arctic. The stories are ancient enough to warrant the status of myths but, some of the elders insist, there were indeed times when famine and desperation forced some of the ancestors to become savages. Peter Freuchan tells a story related to him by old Mequsaq: in one of the toughest times for the Polar Eskimo people, Minik and Mattak became mad with hunger and attacked Mequsaq's family while his father was out hunting. Mequsaq, just a boy at the time, watched powerless, bleeding from his own wounds as his mother and sister were stabbed to death and carried away to be eaten. The cannibals returned some time later but, seeing that the small group of families were well prepared for them, instead found the fresh graves of those who had died of hunger, removed the bodies from under the rocks and disappeared with them on their sledges. The two men were never seen again, but Mequsaq remembered being fearful for years afterwards whenever he heard sledges come into the settlement in the darkness. I thought of old Mequsaq as I watched Red Face slump on the platform bed. He wiped his bloodied hands on the clean towel without washing them and started helping himself to biscuits, bread and fish paste from my supplies. I made a strong mental note not to use the towel myself, and left the hut to get some air.

The two hunters must have had a previous claim to the hut, and they wasted no time in making their feelings quite clear to Kristian. Immediately Baali and Kristian started removing our gear. Within just a few minutes all trace that we had been in the hut was gone and Kristian was already starting to set up a new nest. We were going to camp.

Kristian was on a mission to make his family comfortable and in no time found a site that was quite clearly an old favourite. I hadn't noticed before, but now it was obvious that the ground had already been prepared: large flat stones had been laid in a rough mosaic the size of an average hunter's tent, and a shallow pit had been excavated facing towards the fjord so that the 'bed' was slightly higher than the entrance, vaguely similar in design to the old dwellings. Tarpaulins went down first over the stones, and with practised hands the tent was up without delay. Once again I set to making the tiny space comfortable with Baali, although this time we had even less space to play with. Even with just Baali, Naduk and myself we were crammed in, elbowing and kicking each other by accident as we tried to move in the tiny space.

Alternately the teenagers returned from their lessons dripping and rigid with cold. Although only their small moon-like faces were uncovered by thick wetsuits, the water was cold enough to freeze the blood and they staggered up the beach with their teeth chattering violently. Several pairs of hands were always ready to help take the waxed wetsuits off and to rub their frozen limbs, Baali often being the first to leap to their aid. Frostbite at this time of the summer was thankfully not such an issue, but great care nonetheless had to be taken to warm and dry the body quickly. The two girls who were taking part amazingly didn't seem as affected by the cold as some of the men. Their bodies, although womanly, still had a healthy layer of puppy fat that helped to insulate them. The older, thinner men in particular shuddered long after everyone else.

It was the middle of the night – about 3 a.m. – although we were all oblivious to it. The sun shone ecstatically, never once bowing to the cradle of the mountains. The lessons finished for the day and two large stoves were set up outside, protected from the wind by upturned wooden boxes. The distinctive roar of the stoves was familiar to me and I fell into the warmth of their sound. At home we have old Ektachromes of the summer camps of 1972–3, and the scenes look almost identical, the only difference being the more modern clothes and the fibreglass kayaks that have replaced the traditional skin crafts. Even in the old pictures the Polar Eskimos wore western clothing, particularly in the summer months – of course once winter set in the furs, kept in cold storage during the summer, would be worn. The same Primus stoves were sheltered by the same stained boxes; handmade tents, worn and bleached by the sun, were pitched using large boulders to secure the guy ropes – digging into the permafrost was a backbreaking job – and our tent was still pitched in exactly the same way. Men and women mostly still sat in their own groups: the men smoking their pipes, preparing their harpoons or hunting equipment; the women tending to the children, preparing food and generally looking after the skins or doing chores. Nothing really had changed.

The only real exception was the sound of the portable electronic games that the children constantly played. The tinny, repetitive sound punctuated the chilling breeze of the camp, and gnawed at the peace that the rest of us were hankering for. In an attempt to encourage the children to do something other than stare inanely at the little bright yellow object, Uuli strung two thick taut ropes between one of the huts and a dark beam of wood that stood like a totem nearby, and then swung on the ropes like a gymnast, looping his legs in and out of the ropes so that he spun himself like a spindle. These antics drew the whole camp as an audience, everyone wanting to have a go, although the boys very nearly castrated themselves in the process.

Again the two hunters were on the scene, as they too had been drawn to the spectacle of the spinning ropes, but they stood a short distance away, smoking and quietly watching. I felt myself scrutinized again by the grubby gaze of Red Face. The two men followed, too, when we all went up the hill, and sat not too far away from me on one of the driftwood logs that was the universal 'sofa' for whale watching. Baali shot a protective look at me and quickly motioned me away, as if she was a mother hen and had just seen a fox near one of her chicks. I desperately hoped that there would be no drinking at the camp. I had my suspicions of how alcohol would amplify the strange mood of these men. Kristian looked put out that we had left the party and followed Baali and myself back down to the tent.

The three of us sat quietly in the strange orange cast of the tent. The light in the eyes of my friends danced and glowed, and they looked like children at a fairground. This was where they were happiest, out in the wilds, living simply and in nature. In the distance we could hear the children, still entranced by their new game, laughing and shrieking; we could hear the rasping undertones of the fires painstakingly warming great cauldrons of water for cooking, the incessant calling of the seagulls, and the sucking, gurgling sound of the glacial stream running alongside the hut, which at times sounded eerily like a strong wind blowing through a copse of trees.

The meal was light that evening; everyone was exhausted, and the general consensus seemed to be that pots of ready-made pasta snacks were the easiest option for dinner. Baali sleepily took my hand after we had washed out the plastic containers in the stream and called to the children that it was time to sleep. The tent was already cramped with just the four of us in there, and Kristian was yet to join us. I struggled out of my clothes, keeping a thermal layer on and scrambled into my sleeping bag, all under the watchful eye of the girls who were fascinated by my every move. The girls lay down fully clothed on top of their sleeping bags. I was to discover that they weren't going to change clothes or even take them off at all for the whole time that we were on camp.

The sleeping plan stayed the same; I was to sleep on the left-hand side of the tent, Baali next to me and then the girls, with Kristian on the other side. As we four girls lay down I looked over to see if there was going to be enough room for Kristian and saw all three pairs of eyes watching me; my look of surprise had them exploding with laughter. The tent had the air of a pyjama party; everyone was exhausted but too excited to get to sleep. Baali squeezed her eyes tightly shut and feigned light snoring with her face nuzzled into the crook of my neck, her warm breath tickled me and I squirmed giggling. 'Ahh . . .' she said softly, putting her arms around me and snuggling up close, 'Kristian . . .' The girls shrieked, and I laughed, Baali opened her eyes pretending nothing had happened, and once again repeated the performance until I was gasping for breath, pinned up against the side of the tent. 'Oh!' she said opening her eyes again as if she had just realized what she had done. Kristian's head appeared through the flap of the tent curious at the hilarity inside. Outside our giggles had been infectious and we could hear sniggering from other tents near by.

We were all lying on top of each other by the time Kristian had squeezed himself into the available space. One of us turning in our sleep affected everyone else. Naduk snored loudly and I woke more than once with my face being tickled by Baali's hair or by the fur of the caribou skin on my other side. I was pinned in, all I could move was my head, from side to side, and my feet which were resting on my camera bag that had to be kept inside to prevent the equipment from freezing. Outside the sun still shone brightly, casting burning shafts of light through thin patches in the tent fabric. At 4 a.m. the camp was still, and finally quiet.

11. Narwhal Song

I woke to the thunder of icebergs crumbling in the distance. My position hadn't changed all night and I was still pressed hard against the side of the tent by the bodies of the family, suffocating with the heat and my nose and mouth furred by moulting tugto skin. I scrambled out of the tent and down to the stream and bathed my face in the cold water to cool my skin, and quickly recoiled, gasping as the temperature change bolted through my body.

The camp was deserted. Soft snoring emanated from a couple of the tents and the place was steeped in the downy peace of slumber. I quietly boiled some water over the stove that still purred in the tent, filled my tin cup with sweet black tea and wandered down to the beach and stood gazing at the steady slate-coloured ripples of the fjord. The light was pale and liquid, the mountains dark and crusted with old snow, their heavy outlines dissected here and there by hungry glacial tongues. I felt my pulse quicken with the realization that I was standing alone almost on top of the world in the desolate vastness of the Arctic. I felt the spirit of the northern wilds catch at my lungs and I stood mesmerized.

A flicker of movement in the water caught my peripheral vision: dolphins. I stood motionless on the rocks, cupping my hot drink and feeling as though I had been let into a secret. Perhaps aware of the stillness of the camp, the pod swept gracefully through the fjord, teasing the shore, the light playing on their fins and noses as they paused and dived in front of me before moving on again. I stood for a while, straining to see if they were going to come back, but they were gone.

In the lethargy of the camp atmosphere I allowed my imagination its freedom, and in the space I gave it my sister Pascale appeared. I realized for a heart-stopping moment that I had hardly thought of her since I had arrived; of course she was always somewhere in my thoughts daily, but fearing that the emotions, still raw, would overpower me, I hadn't let myself think of her.

Pascale had been my closest friend, another aspect of myself. Although seven years apart in age, we looked extremely similar, only her eyes were a brighter shade of green than mine, and her hair was the colour of burnished copper. She had my mother's light complexion, while mine was dark like my father's. I felt as though there was a void where she used to be, even though ever since she had gone I had tried to fill it with memories. I pictured her beside me, wrinkling her nose at the hunters munching on the carcasses on the beach, giving me a knowing look and sticking her tongue out in theatrical distaste when no one was looking. I imagined her lying back on the spongy tundra, her hair the colour of flames in the midnight sun, her soft curls loose among the tiny, perfect cinquefoil and her gaze, eerily wise for her fifteen years, glinting at me with life. I imagined her delight at seeing the dolphins, the whales and the seals in the fjord that she loved passionately, and felt her heart-wrenching dilemma of watching the hunters on the kill, chasing the creatures she cared most about in the world, hoping beyond hope that there would be no successful catch that day, yet knowing too the importance of the hunt. She would never have eaten mattak.

I missed her dreadfully, and sometimes the loss consumed me, particularly if I had not thought about her for a few days. Always there was something that took me by surprise: a girl on a street corner whose smile was familiar, the thick smell of white roses from her funeral.

I wondered if she would have thought of this place as I did. Would she have felt the same desire, the same need to come back and reconnect? Pascale spent only a short while here, and she was very young, but with our shared family history I was sure that she would have wanted to come with me. Perhaps she would have wanted to tag the narwhal with an environmental agency. I took comfort in my thoughts, although sometimes they made the loss seem more acute. But picturing her there with me made the place seem somehow even more extraordinary.

Slowly I retired to one of the old logs that had been worn smooth by the decades of hunters' backsides that have sat in the same spot summer after summer waiting for the narwhal to come. Beside me lay a pipe waiting for its keeper, yellowing Sellotape binding it together. On the sand a smooth round stone had a cord bound tightly around it, with one end masterfully knotted into a looped handle – an ancient implement for killing birds. Six kayaks lay on the beach, a couple had *avataks* – sealskin bladders which are tied to a harpoon line – still attached and inflated. The rigid flippers looked like tiny hands waving.

Starting to feel the chill I turned back to the tent to put on more clothes. The others were still asleep, save for Baali who was reading a West Greenlandic newspaper, several days out of date. She left the tent and I fell into daydreaming. My bare feet rested on the tugto furs, and I gripped the soft hairs between my toes, luxuriating in the moment. Little Tekummeq wriggled, unconsciously aware of the extra bit of space left by Baali and flung herself into it. Naduk's arm flopped over her father's face; he barely flinched.

Bright blue flecks were starting to appear through the tent canvas, and the ventilation hole too was a soft O of cobalt blue. Baali was making tea and trying valiantly to move Little Tekummeq's stray limbs that were gripping my left leg. I had fallen asleep again. I went back to the stream and washed my face, and returned to the tent with a flushed face. Baali looked at me and laughed touching my cheek, telling me that the water was too cold to wash in, and then pointed to the yellow hut. 'The children in the hut were freezing!' she said; the stove had gone out in the night and she found one of the boys shivering and fiddling with it, not knowing how it worked. Baali had the

stove working in a matter of seconds much to the embarrassment
of the boy. She tut-tutted. 'He is thirteen!' she said shaking her
head; it was amazing that he didn't know what to do. Neither
did I, and I felt suitably ashamed, but for a thirteen-year-old son
of a hunter not knowing how to light a stove was unforgivable.
There are boys of the same age in the smaller settlements who
have their own dog teams and go seal- and walrus-hunting with
their fathers. By sixteen the boys are usually confident and
accomplished enough to go hunting alone.

Baali and I shared a rock and a couple of pieces of bread and
jam that we had managed to buy from the store before we left.
Our reverie was broken by Kristian yawning like a bear and
crawling out of his flimsy cave. He sleepily gave Baali a big kiss
on the cheek and rubbed her back, launching into an '*ayayaaaa*'
drum song to the dual cries of '*Ajor, Angakoq!*' from Baali and
myself.

'*Kaari-gna – Qilalugaq!*' Baali suddenly gasped and pointed at
the fjord. Narwhal. She ran to the tent and grabbed a paper bag
of ship's biscuits and the flask of tea and pulled me up towards
the lookout; 'your favourite,' she said, holding up the bag. I told
her that old Savfak had said the same thing, and she laughed and
nodded.

We scrambled up the slope, mouths full of the hard dry
biscuits, and joined the men who were struggling sleepily up the
lookout to the hoarse cries that there were narwhal in the fjord.
All eyes were clamped to binoculars, and although there was
space on the log to sit on I hung back, observing that Baali hadn't
sat down and was instead standing behind the hunters, pointing
out dark patches of water where the narwhal could possibly be.
In a flash Red Face and the Aristocrat took off to the beach.
It looked as if they were moving in slow motion; their movements were unhurried, practised, focused. As soon as the two
men had left Baali jumped onto the log and took their set of
binoculars, getting me to train them onto a spot in the distance.
The whales were large and majestic, glinting in the sun as they

moved gracefully through the water, but they were miles away.

The day passed quickly. Ilannguak and Arquenguak arrived, and promptly left again in their kayaks. Then the kayaking lessons started. The whales were not staying in the sound, so there was little point in waiting for them; there would be people on the lookout all day, and the hunters had their gear all ready prepared so that they could leave at a moment's notice if it looked as though the narwhal were returning. Red Face and the Aristocrat came back to camp looking disgruntled.

The atmosphere was relaxed. Baali showed me how to eat a small dried fish from their supplies. The fish was rock hard, and impossible to eat as it was. Taking it to one of the big boulders she picked up a smaller stone and started to pummel the fish to soften it. 'The skin should not be eaten,' she warned, but it was flaky and easy to take off once you had bashed it about a bit. The innards too had to be removed, although they had almost entirely disintegrated and were little more than grey powder. It took a great deal of exertion for such a small meal.

Hoots and squeals of excitement filled the air as one of the girls succeeded in righting the kayak. The women were ecstatic, the boys grim-faced and envious. Only one of the boys had managed to right the kayak and it was embarrassing that a girl managed to roll before the other boys. Women weren't even supposed to use kayaks. Needing to prove his manliness, one of the boys took a whip from a pile of equipment belonging to Niels, and playfully cracked the whip into the sand. His technique was amateurish for a young hunter and Niels wasn't going to allow it. Slowly walking up to the boy, he gently retrieved his whip and had the boy shrieking and dancing up the beach with cracks and flicks that stung his feet and his backside, every flick perfectly placed. I watched in awe. The 20ft whip takes great skill to handle, and even some of the best hunters have been known to blind themselves with a misjudged crack.

The sky was hard and clean. Deciding to get a better view of the surrounding landscape I started walking up the mountain behind the camp. The air was fresh and caught at my lungs, but it was invigorating. As I scrambled over a ridge of loose shingle I saw two figures ahead waving at me. It was Baali and Naduk. Together we continued climbing until we reached a natural dip in the flank of the hill with a small natural platform of boulders. Mostly barren, the grey hillside was occasionally broken with blooms of vivid yellow of tiny Arctic poppies and the dark burgundy of autumnal Arctic willow branches that hugged the earth. Baali and Naduk pointed out pods of *Dilfiniq*, dolphin or *Qilalugaq*, narwhal, or groups of *Aataaq*, harp seal. From that distance they all looked the same to me, but Baali could easily spot the difference. The Inughuit have developed keen senses, necessary for survival in the Arctic, and their long-range eyesight is extraordinary. They were bewildered by my fuzzy take on distant objects; they can spot a seal and know what breed and gender it is, when I would just see a speck on the horizon.

'The men like it here,' Baali mused as she lay back on the rocks. I nodded in agreement; it was a breathtaking spot to camp, and for the men I supposed that this was a good hunting area. I looked back at Baali to see her eyes glinting mischievously. She pointed at the hill behind her, and cried out: '*Iviangiq!*' I didn't understand what she meant, but as I looked at the hill it dawned on me what she was saying; the hillside was the shape of a perfect woman's breast, lying in repose. Baali cupped her breasts and pointed again at the hill and then collapsed into giggles beside her daughter.

Baali cooked something brown, unidentifiable and delicious for the girls and me, and started cooking another stew of old blackened walrus for the others. It was good to eat something hearty and hot after sitting outside for hours watching the hunters on the water. They were out on the fjord sometimes for well over four hours crammed into the tiny kayaks; no wonder most of the older hunters walk at right angles. Gradually the hunters came in off the fjord, cold, stiff and famished. Baali had ensured that food was waiting for them all. People started to gather around the enormous cooking pot, moving through the steam like heavy spectres. The women and teenagers held back as the hunters drew around the warmth of the stove, moving their hands stiffly over the heat before skewering large hunks of the fragrant meat into chipped enamel bowls or discarded plastic containers which they had half-heartedly swilled out with water from the stream. Stiff-legged they swaggered to one of the logs or settled onto their haunches near the pot to eat.

The camp was silent but for the excited cawing of the *nauja-vaarhuk* – seagulls – the gurgling stream and the hiss of the Primus. Families sat in loose groups, eyes flicking over the scene, wholly engrossed in their meal, both adults and children furnished with sharp knives, tearing the meat off the bones with their teeth as if they were at a medieval banquet; with tougher pieces they gripped the meat with their teeth and sliced it directly into their mouths. I was astonished that there weren't more casualties at dinnertime. As the stripped bones piled up on the sand, people sank into a satiated lethargy; fingers, faces and hair shining with fat and grease, contented smiles playing on their lips, still smacking from the taste. The camp murmured happily, the men slapped their rotund bellies and the women attended to the children or washed the pots and cutlery in the stream.

Two hours after the last of the hunters had returned and eaten, narwhal were spotted again, this time very close. Within an hour even those of us on shore could with the naked eye see the plumes of spray from the narwhal catching the light in a spectral play of colour. Two large pods of narwhal circled in the fjord, often looking as if they were going to merge, but always slowly, methodically passing each other by. Scrambling back up to the lookout I looked across the glittering kingdom in front of me and took a sharp intake of breath. The hunters were dotted all around the fjord. The evening light was turning butter-gold, glinting off man and whale and catching the soft billows of smoke from a lone hunter's pipe. From where we sat at the lookout it looked as though the hunters were close enough to touch the narwhal with their bare hands and yet they never moved. Distances are always deceptive in the Arctic, and I fell to wondering if the narwhal existed at all or were instead mischievous tricks of the shifting light. Looking through the binoculars I could see Arquenguak silhouetted in the distance, his wet kayak gleaming like a tiny beacon. Beside him a single plume of spray from the narwhal hung for a second in the air, showering incandescent flickers of light around the lone hunter. He was motionless. The narwhal have highly developed senses, and the slightest movement from a hunter can quite literally give the game away. But on those ethereal summer days when nature is still and silent, the hunter can fall into a void of sensory confusion. It is called kayak illness; the hunter, confused by reflected light and hypnotized by the expanse of air and water which no longer seem separate entities but instead a fluid mirage with no defined end, finds that his body – already so still from hours of patient waiting on the water – is paralysed. Panic-stricken, he may not be able to move or shake himself from the spell until something outside himself – perhaps the spray of a narwhal – brings him back to reality.

The narwhal rarely stray from High Arctic waters, escaping only to the slightly more temperate waters towards the Arctic Circle in the dead of winter, but never entering the warmer southern seas. In summer the hunters of Thule are fortunate to witness the annual return of the narwhal to the Inglefield Fjord, on the side of which we now sat.

The narwhal, which the Inughuit call *qilalugaq qirniqtaq* – and similarly its near cousin the white whale *qilalugaq qaqurtoq* – is an essential contributor to the survival of the hunters in the High Arctic. The mattak or blubber of the whale is rich in necessary minerals and vitamins, and in a place where the climate prohibits the growth of vegetables or fruit, this rich source of vitamin C was the one reason that the Eskimos have never suffered from scurvy; had some of the early explorers taken heed of their hosts' dietary habits, there would have been far fewer suffering such painful and needless deaths in the Arctic. For centuries the blubber of the whales was also the only source of light and heat, and the dark rich meat is still a valuable part of the diet for both man and dogs (a single narwhal can feed a team of dogs for an entire month). Its single ivory tusk, which can grow up to six feet in length, was used for harpoon tips and handles for other hunting implements (although the ivory was found to be brittle and not hugely satisfactory as a weapon), for carving protective tupilaks, and even as a central beam for their small ancient dwellings. Strangely, the tusk seems to have little use for the narwhal itself; they do not use the tusk to break through ice as a breathing hole, nor will they use it to catch or attack prey, but rather the primary use seems to be to disturb the top of the sea bed in order to catch Arctic halibut for which they have a particular predilection. Often the ends of their tusks are worn down or even broken from such usage.

The women clustered on the knoll of the lookout, binoculars pointing in every direction, each woman focusing on her husband or family member, occasionally spinning round at a small gasp or jump as one of the women saw a hunter near a narwhal. I sat in the middle of the log, pressed tightly between two large round bottoms, the owners of which politely took it in turns to fart, sending uncomfortable vibrations down the length of the log. I couldn't decipher who was who even through the binoculars as the hunters were too far away, but each wife knew her husband instinctively and watched their progress intently; it was crucial to her that her husband catch a narwhal – it was part of their staple diet, and some of the mattak and meat could be sold to other hunters who hadn't been so lucky, bringing in some much-needed extra income. Every hunter was on the water. It was like watching a vast, waterborne game with the hunters spread like a net around the sound.

The narwhal, Baali whispered quietly, are intelligent creatures, their senses are keen and they talk to one another under the water. Their hearing is particularly developed and they can hear the sound of a paddling kayak from a great distance. That, Baali said, was why the hunters had to sit so very still in the water.

One hunter was almost on top of a pair of narwhal, and they were huge. He gently picked up his harpoon and aimed – in that split second my heart leapt for both hunter and narwhal. I urged the man on in my head; he was so close, and so brave to attempt what he was about to do – he was miles from land in a flimsy kayak, and could easily be capsized and drowned. The hunter had no rifle, only one harpoon with two heads and one bladder. It was a foolhardy exercise and one that could only inspire respect. And yet at the same time my heart also urged the narwhal to dive, to leave, to survive.

This dilemma stayed with me the whole time that I was in Greenland. I understand the harshness of life in the Arctic and the needs of the hunters and their families to hunt and live on animals and sea mammals that we demand to be protected because of their beauty. And I know that one cannot afford to be sentimental in the Arctic. 'How can you possibly eat seal?' I have been asked over and over again. True, the images that bombarded us several years ago of men battering seals for their fur hasn't helped the issue of polar hunting, but the Inughuit do not kill seals using this method, nor do they kill for sport. They use every part of the animals they kill, and most of the food in Thule is still brought in by the hunter-gatherers and fishermen. Imported goods can only ever account for part of the food supply; there is still only one annual supply ship that makes it through the ice to Qaanaaq, and the small twice-weekly plane from West Green-land can only carry a certain amount of goods. Hunting is still an absolute necessity in Thule.

A flurry of excitement sent me scooting down the hill to the water's edge – the narwhal were heading our way! Although spread out right across the fjord, the hunters were nowhere near the camp and the narwhal sensed it. In the evening stillness we heard them. Great pressurized bursts of water with a hollow tenor note bounced off our chests. The children as always followed me as if I were the pied piper, and watched me expectantly to see my reaction so that they could copy me. But I was not the only one to feel the presence of the whales – the women too looked awestruck. Light danced with the narwhal, their weight and size betrayed only by their slow sensuous movement through the water. Their single tusks were not immediately obvious as the narwhal rarely rear their heads above the water; it was only once that I caught sight of the glistening ivory that makes these creatures so unique.

The women were hopping with excitement and agitation. The water was rich with narwhal; both large pods of whales were heading our way, and there were no hunters to take advantage of the situation. The women desperately willed their husbands to paddle back, and some of the telepathy seemed to work as a couple of hunters skimmed across the water in our direction. Nature was in her element, and the narwhal were showing off. Coming close into shore they blew greetings at the audience, the women shaking their heads and laughing silently; then seals appeared. Suddenly this was like the first day of spring and all the animals had just come out of hibernation; the fjord heaved with the smooth groans of the narwhal and the playful frolicking of the seals. The seals tumbled over one another and scooted through their larger counterparts, almost somersaulting as they left. Their exuberance was a complete contrast to the meditative pace of the narwhal. It was as if they knew that the hunters were after larger game, and so they danced and danced. I was thrilled, and wanted to join them. I felt so trapped and rooted to the grey rock and tundra, bulked out with my layers of clothing and borrowed oversized mukluks.

Baali called the children back who were running across the rocks shrieking with excitement, and reprimanded them severely for making too much noise. It was the first time I had ever seen any Inughuit children being told off. Their fun spoiled they sulkily dragged their feet in the sand, kicking a rock back towards the huts.

It didn't take long for the hunters to regroup and try to get in on the action. Closing in, they appeared to be about to drive the narwhal up the beach. But the pod was one step ahead and were suddenly gone. It seemed an eternity before they surfaced again, a long way down the fjord. The mood dropped. A couple of the hunters, tired and cold, returned to camp to warm up and reposition. Others, proud and desperate for meat, carried on.

It was about 2 a.m. and still Kristian was on the water. Baali sat rooted to the lookout, now the only wife there, anxiously biting her lip whenever he paddled after the narwhal, letting out frustrated cries when thrice he missed his prey. Sitting out all day had taken its toll and people retired to their tents to warm up or to put on more layers of clothing. The wind was picking up and the camp was resigned to the fact that it was unlikely anything would be caught that day. Finally Baali, the girls and I took refuge in the tent, with the flap open and binoculars still on hand to check how Kristian was getting on. Baali called out theatrically to Kristian, who was several miles out of earshot, 'Husband, come to bed. I need to sleep now!' It seemed as though he had heard it. By the time I had brushed my teeth in the stream he had returned, and was walking stiffly up the beach.

He collapsed on the platform bed and smiled wearily with not an ounce of strength left in his arms which hung limply at his side. Baali helped him stretch his cramped legs and we all tumbled into bed, passing out with exhaustion as our heads touched the sleeping bags.

The light woke me – the tent flap was open and the light was blinding, unfiltered and calling me to get up. Baali and Kristian were already up, although I hadn't heard them even stirring. It was surprisingly late, about 11 a.m., but then time was irrelevant here. Baali grinned as she saw me; already she had sorted out all the fires and was busily sweeping out the hut where the teenagers had been sleeping. Our faces and hands were all getting darker: Kristian now had brilliant white lines on either side of his face from his glasses, and Baali had white crow's feet from where she perpetually smiled. Baali was my mirror, and she traced my tan lines sweetly. 'Now you look like one of us!' she said beaming.

Like the other girls, I was desperate to get into the kayak. Apart from the thrill of being on the elegant craft in such an environment, it was, I am not ashamed to admit, a novelty to be doing something that was once the bastion of the male members of the community. However, I decided not to join the classes themselves; it would take up the precious time of those who would only get this one chance to learn how to save themselves, whereas I have plenty of opportunities to learn at home.

The afternoon arrived with a sharp wind: a skin-stripping north-easterly. The water went from tranquil blue to a moody, choppy indigo. Nevertheless I was determined to get in a kayak. The girls gathered in an encouraging semi-circle, supporting their own as they always have done, the men close by, pretending to pay no attention. In the past it was unheard of to take any notice of what the women were getting up to – it was beneath a hunter's dignity even to listen to his wife. But this was slightly different, times have changed and Arquenguak, Kristian and Ilannguak wanted to see how I would fare, and besides, a white woman trying to do anything Inughuit style was always worth watching.

Kristian carefully laid a sealskin in the kayak to make it a little more comfortable and I was launched into the water with playful coos of admiration from the girls. The paddle felt smooth in my hands, polished by years of use, and I broke the membrane of the water on one side and then the other, marvelling at the liquid feeling sweeping through my body. It felt so natural. But my first experimental dips of the paddle had me scooting precariously close to one of the motorboats – my audience was far too polite to laugh at me although a cautious 'Be careful Kari!' from Baali had me giggling along with the others. I just about mastered a quick turn averting a collision with the boat and did a couple of strong strokes into open water to the *'Ajor Kaari-gnaa!'* from Ilannguak who was already back in his boat preparing to break camp. I flashed him an enigmatic smile and he laughed heartily, banging congratulations on the side of the boat and looking back at the others on the shore pointing wildly in my direction.

The water was getting rougher by the minute, and the waves slapped the side of the kayak playfully, gently tossing me in a dance over the water. Alas my adventure didn't last long. Concerned calls about the weather brought me back into land, whereupon I caused much amusement trying to wriggle free of the tiny craft; although I am only 5 ft 4 in (and a half), my legs are longer than the average Inughuit's and they had got firmly wedged inside. The rest of the kayaks were hastily brought up high on the beach and secured in case the wind increased.

I was sinking easily into the simplicity of camp life and the exquisite sense of family. I was beginning to understand the motion of the sun's spiral too and I buried my clock in the bottom of my bag, judging the start and close of each day by the direction of the shadows and the colours of the mountains.

It must have been 3 a.m. when I retreated to the tent – I had had my fill of light. I was just starting to strip off some of my layers when Kristian and Baali came in talking quietly together; they smiled happily at me and lay down together on the bed, Baali lying in the crook of Kristian's shoulder. They talked soft lovers' whispers. I suddenly felt terribly self-conscious, aware that I was invading a private moment, and quietly left the tent to give them some time to themselves. It was a strange predicament. From the years that I spent in Greenland I knew that privacy was not regarded in the same way as it is in our culture, but Baali and Kristian had the chemistry of young lovers, and they must have longed for some time alone.

Although dog-tired I sat squinting at the light that was painting the mountains in a russet blush and making the stones in the stream gleam like precious stones. The camp by now looked well lived-in. Wet clothes and inside layers of kamiks hung from lines around the huts and guy ropes on the tents, with the sealskin outer layers of the boots lying on rocks, drying into misshapen forms. Wisps of light cloud passed by the crests of mountains imitating the smoke from the hunters on the water.

After a time Kristian re-emerged from the tent grinning a satiated smile and climbed slowly back up to the lookout smoothing his chest as though he had just eaten a delicious meal. I continued to sit in my little exiled spot for a while longer, giving Baali some time to herself and then poked my head through the tent flap to see if it was OK to return. Baali was asleep in a contented heap, a wistful smile playing on her lips.

Baali shifted as she came to, and her restlessness spread like a fever through us all until we were all rubbing our eyes and yawning with disgruntlement at our early rise. Qaanaaq was on the day's agenda; the supply ship had been spotted anchored offshore and we needed to get more fuel and stock up on supplies that were rapidly dwindling after almost a week at camp. Bathed in watery light we sleepily brushed our teeth lined up along the bank of the glacial stream and swallowed cups of weak tea before saddling up the boat towards town.

The huge supply ship lay in enigmatic silence outside Qaanaaq, the four-foot waves slapping its sides affectionately. The vessel was completely deserted and much of the cargo had already been unloaded but a few mammoth metal containers remained on board, with a motorboat strapped on top, the prize for an eager hunter.

I headed straight for the shop, even though my whole body was screaming for a shower, but the temptation of fresh food was too much to resist. The shop was crowded both inside and out, people cramming their baskets with bananas and kiwi fruit, two different varieties of Danish mayonnaise-drowned salads and strawberry yoghurts. But that was all the fresh food there was even though the ship had arrived a day or two ago. The others were already loading the boat by the time I returned to the beach, but there was no sign of Baali – for some reason she was going to stay at home this time.

The camp felt different when we returned. Baali had stayed behind in Qaanaaq, Ilannguak and Arnarulunaguaq had gone hunting further down the fjord and Arquenguak, Tukúmek and Erich had also gone to get more supplies. The camp was suddenly quite devoid of my immediate family. Baali's girls seemed to sense how I was feeling and Little Tekummeq quietly sat next to me on the platform bed and gave me a fierce hug. 'You are our mother now,' she said softly. Naduk, not to be left out lay in my lap, hugged my knees and called me '*Anaana*' before they both gave me 'Eskimo kisses' and went out to play. I felt a wave of protectiveness sweep over me, and realized all of a sudden that it was going to be entirely up to me to try and fill Baali's shoes now that she wasn't there. It was the greatest compliment. Baali's decision to entrust me with the safety and well-being of her children and husband was her sign to me that once again I was part of the family. But it was a weighty responsibility. In this environment caring for a family was a full-time job, and for the first time I understood what it must have been like for my parents when we first came to Greenland.

I immediately hung all the sleeping bags and rugs outside to air, organized all our fresh supplies and set to collecting a large jerry can of fresh water from the stream and put some on to boil. Thankfully as we had not been gone long the stove was still alight and on a low heat so that the tent would be warm for our return. My date with learning how to light that contraption would be delayed, for the moment at least.

Later in the day another older couple arrived. There was something strangely familiar about them; perhaps it was the *joie de vivre* in the old man's face and the excited expectancy in the eyes of his wife as they came into shore. The woman leapt gamely off the boat before it grounded in the shallows and swung up the beach, swaddled in layers of woollen clothing. The old man had a kindly face and wore a stained hunting anorak and gold-rimmed sunglasses. He called enthusiastic hellos to those of us on the beach. Hopping out of the boat he threw his equipment to a line of us who helped them unload a comprehensive if old-fashioned camping kit.

I helped the wife carry their gear up to the high, flat part of the beach and laid their reindeer skins out to dry. The old man looked quizzically at me as he slowly made his way up the beach: 'Who is your father?' he asked directly in lisping English. I had barely spoken the first syllable of 'Wally' before he slapped me heavily on the back and threw his head back in a bellow. '*Ajor!*' he exclaimed, shaking me vigorously by the hand until I could feel my fingers smarting. 'I know your father *very* well,' he said slowly, and introduced himself as Uusaqqak Qujaukitsoq. 'You have come very far!' he said laughing again flashing a smile that was missing the front few teeth. 'Maybe you like it here like your father, and you stay long time!' I laughed with him, agreeing that it was a beautiful place. He beckoned me towards the log and sat down, the motion sending a whistle through his missing teeth.

'A long time ago I spoke Great Britain Engleeesh, *ammaqa*... forty-five years ago — ajor! Now I don't remember...' His words trailed off as he dug in his anorak for his pipe. He now lives in Qaanaaq with his family, he told me, but had spent the last week camping across the sound from where we were. He squinted out to the horizon and without looking down pressed some soft tobacco into the bowl of his pipe. 'I tell all my children they must learn your language. It is the language of the whole world!' He chuckled to himself and lit a match and sucked lengthily on his pipe.

It was a happy time. The hunters exchanged tales about the hunting that season, with their arms tracing the routes they thought the narwhal might take, while the women warmed themselves over the fires and helped themselves to the slabs of mattak still on the beach that were starting to get a bit tough around the edges; they too talked of the hunting, as well as other more interesting gossip.

The Inughuit have never been a territorial people; tradition-ally, a hunter will never keep secret a good hunting spot – the entire community survives because people help each other, and support each other. If one family has no food, another will freely offer theirs, for they never know when it may be their turn to be hungry. I wondered whether things were changing in the modern Arctic, if the people were learning to become selfish. If privacy is a modern concept in the Arctic, so is isolationism. As their world becomes increasingly influenced by the values of materialism that they are fed with daily on the television, and as the people become less hunting oriented and grow complacent about living on welfare benefit, perhaps too the fundamental principle of the community being the priority, not the individual, will change.

I began to wonder how I was going to feed the brood; originally I had brought with me two large chickens and lots of tinned food so that I could cook a few meals to give Baali a rest and do my bit. But now she had gone it was a completely different prospect. I had enough to cook for two or three days; beyond that and I would have to try and tackle the darkening bloody beast slowly shrivelling grotesquely on the beach, but I had no idea which bits one could eat and which one shouldn't. I had watched a few people eating the raw meat off the carcass and they were all quite particular about the pieces they chose. I didn't even know if you could cook narwhal. Some animals are best eaten raw or dried and aren't good cooked; others *had* to be cooked to prevent trichinosis. We had already eaten a couple of stews made with a dark meat but I hadn't noticed Baali carving the meat for the stew off the carcass, and I presumed that she had used walrus meat that they had brought with them. It was all very confusing.

I still had no idea even how to light the cooking stove, which was temperamental at the best of times, and I wished I had paid more attention to how Baali had done it. I didn't want to be seen to be the useless *kadluna*, but had to ask someone for help. With great difficulty I tried to tell Kristian that I was going to make the dinner, but however hard I tried to get the message across with brandishing a large pot and doing comical motions of stirring imaginary food, he simply could not comprehend what I was trying to say and looked at me as if I had gone slightly mad. However, in a moment of inspiration, and to my great relief, he offered to light the large Primus while I set about cutting up the chickens on a plastic bag – the most hygienic surface that I could find – with my small Swiss Army knife. All the big knives had disappeared and the process was agonizingly laborious. Deep in concentration, hands slimy with grease and innards, I didn't notice that Tukúmek was back at camp and had noiselessly come to observe, waiting quietly behind me so it didn't look as though she was interfering. She was so quiet that I nearly sliced a finger when she asked if I needed help; I thanked her and said no, I was determined to do it myself, but wondered if she had a bigger knife. She giggled at my pathetic blade and tried to find another one but the hunters crouching at the narwhal carcasses were using them all. I soon had a small audience, all sitting at a polite distance, smiling encouragingly at me every time I looked up; the women were obviously itching to take over. But by the second chicken I had mastered the art of butchering using a nail file. The crowd dispersed as soon as it looked as if I knew what I was doing as there was little entertain-ment value, but Tukúmek and Kristian still hovered, giving me the thumbs up as I finished.

The next challenge was how to cook the chicken and make it taste good, when I only had one pot, glacial water, no herbs and just a little salt and pepper and dry goods. I put the dismembered chicken into the pot of boiling water and hunted in the carrier bags I had brought from the store for some inspiration. I mixed up some powdered soup with water to a smooth paste and poured the mixture into the pot and then threw several handfuls of rice after it with great aplomb, until the stew curdled. It looked as if I were cooking brains, and my pride, after having the camp as my audience earlier, couldn't take another humiliating blow. I would never live it down if I couldn't cook a *kadluna* chicken.

Miraculously, I finally created a rich chicken stew. It definitely could have done with some white wine and some fresh garlic, but it was hot and surprisingly tasty. Tired but happy I called the family to eat and they devoured the food with relish, with Naduk cooing '*Mammaktoq*, delicious!' over and over again, and Little Tekummeq and Kristian helping themselves to more three or four times as they satisfied their enormous appetites. The women gathered round pretending to do chores around the tent until I offered them some food, whereupon they immediately took a few spoonfuls, nodding appreciatively at each other and smiling briefly at me before going off to prepare food for their own families. The pot of food which I had hoped would keep us fed for two days was soon completely empty, save for a thick layer of caramelized rice at the bottom. I sat back, content. Kristian smiled. '*Qujanak*, thank you,' he said, then cleared his throat and instructed me that the pot had to be cleaned immediately as the other women would need to use it too. My heart fell. I had to do it, and straight away; there were other hungry people in the camp. Still bloated from eating I struggled down to the icy water of the stream and filled the pot with water to heat on the stove, but it had already been hijacked by one of the other cooks. With numb hands I scrubbed the pot under the beady gaze of a group of strangers who had just arrived at camp, cursing the freezing water that just made the rice seem to stick more tenaciously to the pot.

A tempestuous wind blew through the camp in the early hours of the morning, threatening to blow the tents away, and anything not fixed securely to the ground. It was as though we had been caught in a small tornado; pots, pans and bags hurtled about, the huts creaked and moaned and the tent billowed and strained.

Half asleep I saw Kristian leap out of bed and heard him rescue the closest items before disappearing down the beach to lash down the kayaks. I struggled out of my sleeping bag and pulled on a fleece inside out in my hurry to help. Various belongings flew past as I fell out of the tent, narrowly missing my head. Bending double in the wind I rescued everything I could and stashed it all under the flaps of the tent. The wind quickly died to a murmur and I fell heavily back into bed.

The Sun and Moon, so it was told, once lived here on Earth as brother and sister a long time ago. Like all young people they were passionate and carefree and regularly enjoyed the game known as 'dousing the lights'. In the endless winter nights villagers would join together in a large igloo, and their oil lamps would be put out. In the darkness, those in the igloo would grope their way through the sensuous press of flesh until they found a partner with whom they would silently make love. In that mask of darkness identities would never be revealed, and there would be no shame when the lamps relit the satiated group, who were sitting once again independently of each other.

After several months Sun became suspicious that one man managed repeatedly to seek her out in the darkness and, she feared, that man was her brother. Keeping her suspicions to herself, she one night surreptitiously blackened her fingers with soot and when her lover came to her she pressed her fingers to his cheeks. To her horror, when the lamps were relit she saw the mark of disgrace upon her brother Moon's face. In fury and shame, Sun snatched up a torch of moss dipped in burning blubber and ran from the igloo. Moon chased her, hurriedly lighting his moss as he ran out of the igloo. They ran faster and faster until they ran up into the sky, Moon pursuing Sun for eternity, his torch burning weaker than his sister's; the light of her shame burning so brightly that in summer she warms the world. 'Look,' the Polar Eskimos used to say, 'in winter you can still see the mark of soot on Moon's face.' Some Eskimos believed that Sun and Moon shared a single house in the sky and that the Sun stayed outdoors in the summer, warming the land day and night; in winter she retired into the house, and Moon was locked outside. He only disappeared, they said, when he was looking for animals for the men to hunt.

In summer the moon is barely visible in the High Arctic. In its place the sun wheels in a languorous spiral, never submitting to the horizon. Below her, for all but two or three months of the year, the land is sealed with snow and ice but then, miraculously, as the permafrost recedes just a few centimetres, Nature sweeps a hand of colour over the land. The flora in Greenland has evolved, like the people, to cope with the uncompromising climate. Hardy flowers, lichens, and even dwarf trees – their growth retarded by the intense struggle for existence – hug the ground for some semblance of warmth and come out of their hibernation once every few years. Their parade of colour dazzles the eyes and confounds the feet – for where should one walk when the ground is carpeted with flowers that appear so rarely?

In these precious months between the close of spring and the first snowfall of autumn, the vegetation of the High Arctic has to complete an entire cycle of reproduction – growth, flowering and the production of seeds – that would take an entire year for most plants in the temperate zone. The plants have evolved so that they surge into activity as soon as the temperatures nudge a degree above freezing, and in the continuous sunlight these extraordinary specimens are active for twenty-four hours a day. As Peter Freuchan points out in *The Arctic Year*: 'The plants are capable, therefore, of growing at an amazing rate, the rapidity of their development being unsurpassed anywhere among flowering plants throughout the world.'

I rested in the chill of the morning among the purple saxifrage, white heather, Arctic poppies and spongy grasses of the tundra, feeling the velvet of green moss between my fingers and watching transfixed as a tiny diaphanous spider spun its silk between the golden leaves of a dwarf birch, unbothered by the sharp breeze.

Toffee-coloured butterflies cast delicate shadows over the lichens. A bumblebee swam lazily through the scene. There was another world at ground level. I marvelled at how wrong my first impressions had been of this place when Baali had pointed it out to me from the boat. At that moment – a lifetime ago it seemed – this wild spot had appeared so bleak that it looked as though nothing could survive on it. But as I lay back, kittiwakes, guillemots and seagulls rode the skies above me, and the ground that from a distance had looked grey and barren was bristling with life.

Tukúmek walked past, and with a wry smile held up a plastic bag full of dead birds, sticking out her tongue in mock distaste as she sat nearby to prepare them. It was a gruesome job. She was quick and deft with the birds, making firm incisions around the neck with a sharp knife before slipping her fingers between the meat and the skin, rolling off the skin and feathers all in one piece. I asked what the birds were and her smooth brow furrowed with concentration: 'Like *kiviak* birds but bigger,' she finally replied, and looked up to ask Niels what they were. 'Auk!' he said eventually, looking extremely pleased with himself that he had been of some help. I had heard through the grapevine that the Inughuit are not supposed to catch little auk anymore, and I asked her if this was true. '*Ammaqa* . . . maybe,' she said with a shrug and looked back at me, 'but there are many thousands of them, and we are hungry.' They certainly hadn't caught a surplus; the few birds she was preparing were going to feed almost everyone at the camp.

As the sun swung mid-heavens to face us, a clattering of spoons on heavy tin pots sounded the signal for dinner. It was a disconcerting sight. The auks were sitting upright in the stew of their own juices, heads buoyantly nodding as the thin gravy rolled in a steady simmer; eyes peering out beadily from the top of the pan. They looked disturbingly alive. Eagerly people came and helped themselves, spooning the soup into recycled plastic pasta-snack bowls, stripping the meat off the birds with teeth and knives. By the time I got to the pot all that was left was the scrawny wings and heads, but the soup was delicious, rich, gamey and peppery.

Fuelled by the good meal, the hunters suddenly became restless. There had been no sightings of narwhal all day and there was a sense of time running out for some of them for whom this time was their holiday – soon they would have to go back to their paid jobs. Tukúmek stood with me at the water's edge after we had cleared up the debris of the meal. She stared at the mottled blue water willing the narwhal to come: 'Please,' she whispered imploringly.

I longed for a hot, deep bath and undisturbed sleep on a soft mattress. I crawled into my sleeping bag, blinking at the sunlight and wishing someone would turn off the light. In this place the forces of light and darkness easily upset the natural balance of the body, and even the Inughuit are prone to periods of insanity at the onset of winter, or during the unrelenting light of summer. These short-lived episodes are known as *perlerorneq* (also known as *piblockto*) or polar hysteria, and are mostly experienced by women, although Knud Rasmussen encountered one particularly frightening episode when a hunter from the community became a victim of perlerorneq.

In Rasmussen and Freuchan's time cases of perlerorneq were fairly common. Without warning, a woman could suddenly leap up and become frenzied, foaming at the mouth and tearing at her clothes, her skin burning. Her strength would be increased tenfold, and she would become violent and uncontrollable. Often she would run, sometimes naked or only partially clothed out onto the ice field. Her community would race after her in concern, restraining her only when she tried to hurt herself, which invariably she would. The community could do little until the woman's strength started to fail, then quickly they would gather her up, wrap furs around her and carry her carefully, unconscious, back to the village.

Even though the Polar Eskimos believed in other spiritual

forces, they did not believe that someone suffering from per-lerorneq was possessed by an evil spirit, rather that the hysteria was brought on by the 'weight of life'. Jean Malaurie relates how the hysteria was explained to him by an Inughuit hunter: 'The Perlerorneq tries to get out at any price into the open, to breathe, to shout at the top of his lungs, to unburden his heart – but without being judged by the village, which is watching him, for being perlerorneq, beside himself, he cannot be judged. Perlerorneq is to be sick of life.'

Before we left I had heard that there was a teenage girl at the school who suffered from polar hysteria. The community were remarkably forgiving of the destruction she caused when she was having an episode. It was unusual in these modern times, they said, to have one of their community feeling this way, but then the young were always more prone to perlerorneq when the future seemed so uncertain.

Little Tekummeq gently stroked my arm and buried herself in my shoulder as I lay back on the tugto fur. My eyes closed as I watched Kristian gently feeding a sleepy Naduk with pot noodle, his glasses steaming up underneath his white golfing cap.

12. Leaving Camp

Departure was imminent, and suddenly the clean-up operation was on. Black binliners materialized over the camp as if our little population had had a single simultaneous thought, and almost everyone except the older male hunters set to clearing up the rubbish littering the beach.

Summer is a time when items long since lost in the snows finally reveal themselves and any settlement or campsite in Greenland tends to have a scruffy outlook, and this camp was no exception. Generally Greenlanders have a non-committal attitude to claiming responsibility for cleaning up other people's mess, so often the rubbish lies unattended until the winter claims it again and lends the place its pristine appearance. As with the rest of the world, plastic here is a boon, but also the bane of the environment. True, the Inughuit are extremely resourceful and a plastic container will often be used time and time again, but there is a surplus of modern debris in the Arctic these days such as discarded batteries and non-biodegradable nappies, which even at this remote narwhal camp filled an old rusted oil drum. Nappies were never used in the old days: babies and toddlers were carried around in an *amout*, a kangaroo-type pouch on the back of the mother's furs – the baby would be naked against the mother's skin, giving a sense of comfort and contact, as well as giving the mother quick access to the baby when it needed feeding without the baby ever being exposed to the cold. The *amout* would be filled with moss and soft skins to keep the child warm, and in an emergency to soak up as much waste as possible.

With its cold, dry climate and minimal precipitation, the Arctic is classified as a desert, and dealing with rubbish in such a climate is particularly difficult. Materials that would quickly disintegrate in our warm and wet climate will stay intact for decades, sometimes centuries, in the Arctic – remains of skin plates and even the remains of the meal that was eaten off them have been found in some archaeological sites in the Arctic that date back as far as 800 years ago. In 1977 the Canadian archaeologist Peter Schledermann discovered Viking remains from between AD 1100 and 1200 on Skraeling Island off the west coast of Greenland. He unearthed carvings, nails and tools, and even parts of Viking clothing. I had the luck to visit Skraeling Island with Peter many years later, and his passion for this place was infectious; the Vikings, he enthused, had travelled much further afield than people had previously thought. In fact there was evidence that a Viking longboat had over-wintered at Bache Peninsula on the east coast of Ellesmere Island, north-west of Thule. It was not Christopher Columbus who discovered the New World; it was the Scandinavians.

Decomposition in the Arctic is a lengthy process: organisms that can be found in all of the temperate zones that break down matter, be it flora or fauna, cannot operate in such an inhospitable climate, where not only do they have to contend with the frigid climate, but also the interminable darkness of the winter. This was never a problem in the past in this area; everything the Polar Eskimos used was organic, and there was very little waste as they utilized everything that they could; in addition, the cold dry atmosphere preserved the freshness of their meat, which was essential when there were long spells of poor hunting and they had to make do with the old meat stores. But this arid climate preserved more than just their foodstuffs.

The Qilakitsoq Mummies were discovered in the cliffs opposite the West Greenland town of Uummannaq by two young brothers, Hans and Jokum Grønvold, as they were hunting ptarmigan in 1972. At first the claims of the young men that they had found preserved human remains were ignored, but when the police finally investigated they were confronted by an extraordinary sight: eight mummified bodies, fully clothed in fur and skin garments that had barely perished in the five hundred years since their burial. The grave dated AD 1475 contained the bodies of six women and two children, preserved by the cold dry atmosphere alone.

The scientists called to investigate were baffled by the burial. Women and children in Greenland were never traditionally buried separately to men, and initially they believed that the mummies were killed as a result of a tragic accident in an umiaq, a large skin boat used by only women and children, but further tests complicated the theory: one of the women had a malignant tumour at the base of her skull which would have been the cause of death, the older child had contracted Calvé-Perthes disease, which affects the hip joints and makes one vulnerable to other diseases; but most poignant was the discovery that the youngest child, a boy of six months, had been buried alive with his mother. Custom dictated at the time that if a mother had died and there was no one to nurse her child, the father or guardian would bury the child alive or suffocate it. It was believed that mother and child would journey together to the land of the dead.

I had visited the gravesite of the mummies with my parents while on the icebreaker journeying down the west coast of Greenland several years before, and the place had had an eerie feel about it. I couldn't be sure at the time whether it was because I knew the story of the mummies or whether the cliffs themselves remembered their intimate connection with the women and children whose bodies had lain in their cold embrace, undisturbed for over half a millennium.

Exhumed with the greatest delicacy in 1978, the bodies of three of the women and the youngest child are now displayed in the National Museum in Nuuk. I had been unsettled at the cliff-top burial chamber, but was positively awestruck by the presence of the mummies themselves in their modern temperature-controlled tomb in Nuuk. They lay in the yawning silence of death preserved, their delicate hands placed over their chests, knees slightly raised, their legs still clothed in fur-lined kamiks. I felt like a voyeur, unable to tear my eyes from the recumbent figures. Most haunting of all was the six-month-old child with his perfect face embalmed by Nature, the round empty sockets of his eyes following me round the room as he lay next to his eternally sleeping mother.

The mood was solemn as we picked up the last few pieces of rubbish; it felt like the end of a holiday, the party was over and it was time to go back to town life. The wind was picking up again, and the water of the fjord was running fast and dark. It was going to be a rough ride home. I wondered if I was ever going to experience a smooth boat ride in Thule. A strange restlessness hung in the air, dampened only by the unwillingness of the camp to break up and leave this glorious wilderness for central heating, double-glazing and Friday boozing.

With the camp cleared of rubbish I took refuge in the warmth of the tent, daydreaming in the trembling orange glow, feeling as if I was nestled in the belly of a small animal frozen in fright. The fjord was by now a mass of frothing peaks, and I was starting to get concerned that it was too rough to attempt the boat journey with the precious cargo of the children. I wandered round to one of the huts for some company and found it crammed with quiet and despondent women and children. There was barely enough room to stand in the tiny hut and the air was heavy with the smell of unwashed bodies, but whenever anyone left for a change of scene they soon retreated, buffeted by the wind. One of the women had started cooking, crammed in one corner, with those around her desperately trying to escape ignition. The dark rich smell filled the small space, and we watched hypnotized by the stew bubbling and rolling. A single claw gently bobbed against the side of the pot as if making a dispirited last attempt to get out. The woman had already made one batch of stew and sat gnawing the last vestiges of fat off a bone; two children pressed against her on either side, one half-asleep in her lap, the other leaning against her shoulder rereading a dog-eared comic over and over again.

Through a crack in the doorway I could see Arquenguak carving some bloody meat for the communal pot, occasionally throwing a small raw morsel into his mouth and smacking his lips with satisfaction, before carrying the pot awkwardly back towards us in the crooks of his arms so as not to bloody the handles. Tukúmek was waiting for him and threw in half a rotting onion and a packet of mixed herbs. The weather was getting worse and I suspected that we would have to stay another night, although a couple of people in the camp were looking ready to go. The children sensed the strange mood and were restless and whining, frustrated with being confined in such a small and airless place.

The waves rose to meet the wind and were soon crashing over the rocks, angrily sending plumes of salt spray into the camp. Those that felt restless braved the elements wrapped up in thick clothing, wandering aimlessly from hut to tent and back again. I myself was suffering from cabin fever, and Tukúmek was complaining of the same agony and so we decided to have some exercise and take a short walk up the mountain.

It was invigorating to be out on the mountain, and our sights aimed higher the steeper we climbed as we felt the strength of the wind against our cheeks and shrugged off the lethargy of camp life. We thought about climbing the Breast mountain, but over an hour later we had barely reached its base and we were not prepared for such an adventure with no food or protection should the weather close in. Leaping between mammoth boulders and skidding up and down over scree slopes, we talked non-stop about our futures, her children and life in the community.

The wind tore at our faces and clothes and we stopped to catch our breath, sheltering in a crevice in the rocks that nonetheless gave us a panoramic view of the fjord. Tukúmek swung her hand delicately over the distant water and pointed at two steep-sided valleys: 'That's where we collect berries in late August. They are only there for a very short period, but the children and the women love it there. We eat berries until our tongues and teeth are stained red and blue. Sometimes the children eat so many they get so sick – I was the same when I was a little girl. I couldn't stop eating them!'

I asked her which was her favourite time of year and she sat thoughtfully for a moment. 'The summer is fun. The children sleep strange hours but we let them do it because summer time is holiday time too, and they should enjoy themselves.' I nodded and thought of the change that had come over Baali's daughters since being given the freedom of summer camp. Tukúmek continued: 'I prefer autumn though, when the sun is low in the sky and everything turns red. Oh, but then spring is my favourite too! But sometimes in winter, when the stars are shining bright and everything is lit by the moon, that is the most beautiful time: you can see for miles, right across to Herbert Island!' She sighed at the thought.

'I think we are very strong people, because the weather is so strong,' she said decisively, clambering up on a pile of boulders higher than herself, shouting out over the wind that was tugging at her voice. 'Sometimes we have storms so strong that we can't see our neighbour's house!' I joined her and we jumped from stone to stone. 'Then it is good to be inside my home, warm and safe. And I *hate* it in the mornings when there is a storm and it is dark, and I have to go to work like this –' she imitated a pose struggling through a blizzard – 'I really *hate* it!' She cried out laughing.

Tukúmek had a long and easy stride, placing her feet confi-dently on the edges of towering rocks or skidding over rubble. She had spent summers at camps like this with her parents when she was a child, and our walk reminded her vividly of her mother who used to take her on long walks up the mountain. 'I found them so exciting,' she breathed, her face flushed as pink as her headband and anorak. We scrambled over ridge after ridge, always aiming for the next one, but there was always another just a little further away. Frozen rivers of ice probed the dark silhouettes of the mountains, ending in blue-grey rubble that was being pounded by waves.

Finally we reached a cairn on a heavy rock promontory, and there we stopped, feeling as though we had reached a destination of sorts even though it wasn't the nipple of the Breast. I took a few photographs and then rested. Tukúmek pulled down her trousers to pee. 'Don't take pictures of me peeing!' she said gleefully. We sat together on a rock, pressed up together against the freezing wind.

'I really would love a cup of tea,' I said, feeling the chill of the wind whistle through me.

'And cake, hmm, something really sweet . . .' Tukúmek mused.

We didn't stay long; the wind was rushing at us with force, and looking down we suddenly realized how far we had come: from our vantage point the people on the beach moved like ants and the kayaks were mere slivers of colour.

The scramble back to camp seemed to get harder the further we went, and we found ourselves faced with a giant assault course of boulders and deep crevices, that we were sure we hadn't climbed over on our way up, and soon we were quite disoriented, finding ourselves time and again having to climb down into steep fissures and valleys and then up again to the same altitude we were at before. We had been concentrating so hard on finding the safest route through the rocks we hadn't noticed how far we were getting from the coastal edge. 'I think these rocks like each other too much,' Tukúmek announced flatly as we looked up at a tumble of rock the size of a three-storey house that was blocking our path. Our main bearing on our climb had been the Breast and we constantly looked to her, judging her shape to indicate where we were, sharing bizarre conversations about the relation of the nipple to where we were, with Tukúmek trying to work out our position by pointing at different parts of her own breast.

We rested for a few moments in a miniature valley, catching our breath that had been whipped from us as we climbed down, and luxuriating in the respite from the chill with our feet sinking into thick carpets of silver-grey moss that had grown lush in the protected spot. Swathes of Arctic willow clung to the ground, the leaves just starting to turn the colour of burnished copper. It felt as though Tukúmek and I had been friends for ever, and I could hardly believe that relations had seemed so strained between us when I first arrived.

We were clearly not utterly lost as the fjord was still nearby, but wave after enormous wave of gargantuan boulders made the going tough. We must have fallen behind a ridge without realizing it. Gradually we came upon a wide flat area with a large circular formation of small groups of rock. 'They are left over from when people lived in the stone houses,' Tukúmek explained. 'The old people would come up here and string traps between the rocks to catch Arctic hare.' We weaved across the space, and looked back at the Breast, laughing at our foolishness, and finally reached the side of the cliff from where we could see the camp, a few degrees off where we thought it was. 'Next time,' Tukúmek said with authority, 'we bring compasses, tea and a tent!'

'And a couple of men to carry it all,' I added, to which she agreed loudly.

Developing an accurate sense of direction in Thule is difficult for one who doesn't live there. In Thule a compass that looks as though it is pointing north, will in reality point a few degrees south-west towards the North Magnetic Pole – which in itself is not an absolute, stationary point (it is currently wandering listlessly around the Canadian Arctic), and although one can make appropriate corrections to the compass bearing, there are places in the Arctic where a compass is so affected by the proximity of the electromagnetic field that the needle will swing back and forth in confusion. However, the hunters of Thule have an uncanny inner navigational system, which intuitively uses the language of Nature to guide them: cloud movements, the depth of colour of the sky, the lie and species of vegetation, the type of ice and the formation of its crystals. For instance when travelling in winter or early spring, *sastrugi* is a reliable direction finder: these ice crystals are arranged in directional stripes by the dominant south-westerly winds.

The hunter uses his entire body as a navigational device, relying on each of his heightened senses to guide him home. The scent of the air, for example, can advise him of weather conditions and how close he is to land, while his eyes can find purchase on a distant landmark or can distinguish whether cloud is over land or water or even what type of ice lies in the distance by looking at the patterns of light or darkness in the sky – ice lying on the horizon often casts a subtle reflection in the sky above it called an 'ice blink': sea ice reflects a grey white in the sky; field ice reflects white tinged with yellow, marginally different is snow-covered land which is slightly more yellow, and pack ice is pure white. The bend of the ice beneath his feet will tell him its depth, age and density, he can taste snow on the air and hear telltale snippets of birdsong or even hear the vibration of the land itself.

A hunter's senses are his most infallible guide in an environment where the weather is famed for its unpredictability: blizzards and thick fog often obscure landmarks and reference points that one would usually cross-reference with a topographical map. Therefore a hunter has no need for maps, but they can certainly read them, and if asked to draw one they will do so happily, and accurately. But their map will not just be the outlines of the land; it will also be peppered with landmarks and experiences that have served to embed the subtle nuances of the landscape into his subconscious. The more experiences a hunter has had in one particular area, the more vibrant the map is likely to be, for the hunter cannot resist telling the story of where he saw many polar bears, where his trapping of foxes has been most successful, and which cliffs are the best for catching little auks for kiviak.

In his book *The Last Kings of Thule*, Jean Malaurie relates a story of a Canadian Inuit who in 1955 was taken on his first flight in an airplane over his home territory. Caught in thick fog and with limited fuel, the pilot of the plane had great difficulty locating where they were and asked the Inuit if he could help:

The hunter had been silently noting the speed of the plane and the distance they had already covered, getting his bearings from reference points he could glimpse through rents in the clouds and the curtain of mist. Calmly and with no great difficulty, the Eskimo reoriented the pilot, who brought his plane down fifteen minutes later at the airport he had been unable to locate.

Finally, to our relief, we rounded a corner and could see everyone crowded around the flagpole at the closing ceremony of the rolling classes. But by the time we had reached camp everyone was back inside the tents or huts rubbing their hands and arms from the cold. We were full of life, although our muscles were tight from the cold and punishing exercise, and were momentarily disappointed that no one had noticed our absence even though we had been gone for well over three hours. 'Even my son didn't miss me!' Tukúmek said pouting with mock dismay.

The general decision was that we should stay another night and leave early the next morning and, famished, I started throwing together some food for the brood – a strange mixture of tinned meat, rice and various other bits and pieces. The result looked remarkably like dog food, but the girls squealed with thanks and disappeared through the tent flap cradling steaming bowls of gloop. For once Kristian looked truly comfortable in my presence and made a great show of falling over on the platform bed after his meal, stroking his belly and sighing happily, pretending to snore loudly. He even disappeared to put water in the pan and heated it up so that it could be cleaned easily, looking at me sheepishly as if it was women's work – but this was an exception.

A heavy sleepiness crept over me with the comfort of a freshly laundered duvet. Even the smell of old socks didn't really register with me. I had a vague longing to boil a large pan of water, strip off and scrub myself clean and crawl into my sleeping bag, but my legs wouldn't permit me, and I was never sure who would be coming into the tent next.

I mulled over an earlier conversation with Uusaqqak. The old man had sat beside me as I had been writing and, waiting for me to look up and put my pencil to one side (the ink in my pens had long since frozen), started talking amiably about his role in the community, the relations between the Thule people and the Canadian Inuit, and the land-rights issue with the American airbase south of Qaanaaq.

Traditionally the Polar Eskimos did not believe that they owned their land; originally they were a nomadic people and did not even believe they owned their own houses; when a family vacated their winter houses of stone and turf for summer camp the family lost their right to the house and anyone who needed shelter could move in and take over the property. Even today no one in Qaanaaq owns the land on which their houses are built; one buys the right to build on the land from the state (which costs 500 Danish kroner – approximately £46 in pounds sterling), and then the pre-packed ready-to-build house (14,000 Danish kroner – approximately £1,275), but the state still owns the property for thirty years, after which time the building belongs to the person who bought the materials and built it. However, the land beneath the house – as far as I understand it – is still officially owned by the state. But, as some Inughuit members of the community become wise to the fate of other tribes throughout the world via the Internet and the world's media, so they are starting to warm to the philosophy that they have a right of ownership to the land of their ancients.

Uusaqqak was only four years old when he and his family were told to leave their ancient village under the protective shadow of the table-shaped Dundas Mountain. 'They [the US military] came to our land in 1951 and 1952, and in 1953 American people started making a rocket base in our village area, so they told us we must leave our village. We have houses but . . .' Uusaqqak couldn't go on, and raised his arms up in frustration, his eyes brimming with emotion. They were given three days to leave; if they refused, they were told, their houses would be bulldozed down. The whole community had no choice; this was a powerful enemy they couldn't fight.

Uusaqqak looked at me helplessly for a moment and then carried on. 'The Danish people made this special, what do you call it . . . ?'

'Agreement?' I offered. 'With the American military?'

'Yes, without speaking to my family or with our friends at Uummannaq, they do not discuss it but they give us an order that we have to get out, with three days' time to come out from our territory.' Uusaqqak stabbed three dark fingers in the air, and started speaking faster and with more passion; it was a long way to come from Uummannaq with the whole family on one sledge, with one team of dogs. 'We were the biggest family. We were maybe seven or eight children at that time.'

The journey was tough. Uusaqqak's entire family were piled upon a single sledge, with one team of dogs to take them and as many possessions as they could carry over the arduous trek across the Politiken Glacier to a new home. When they arrived, the accommodation they had been promised was not there. They arrived at the new settlement of Qaanaaq to find only a scattering of tents and a couple of incomplete huts.

'Some had to leave after one day of arriving here [in Qaanaaq], because we had no houses to keep us warm, and there were so many children! There were no houses in this area, only camping with the tent. Only tents with the snow coming in September and October! So it is very very hard for my family and our friends. Some go to Herbert Island, some to Kangerlassuasuq, or to Narssaq, and some asked permission to go down the fjord to

Qeqertat. So there are some four areas that we came to after moving out of Uummannaq in 1953. Without house, no house!' He shook his head, his brow furrowed with thought, his arms embracing the emptiness that they found when they first arrived here. 'And the Danish government will not talk with us about what happened before and after 1953.' He clenched his hands into fists and gently bounced them off his knees in frustration.

For years Uusaqqak has been trying to raise the issue of the effect this forced eviction has had on the people that were moved from Uummannaq, but up until now has been talking to deaf ears. Greenlandic politicians from the Home Rule were too scared of upsetting the Danish government, he believes, and none of them would champion his cause.

'So we have to go to court. We have very big understanding from the Greenland people, and the Danish people are beginning to listen to us now. [It is] very different now from ten to fifteen years ago; then they were not listening to us.'

In 1984 Uusaqqak was elected to the Home Rule Government, and stayed in office for eleven years, eventually representing Greenland at the United Nations. With permission from the Home Rule Uusaqqak went to New York in 1994 to talk to Danish government members; it was the first time he had had the chance to talk to them directly, and he wanted to use the opportunity of the United Nations stage to voice his concerns about the land rights issue as well as the future of the American Airbase at Thule, but, Uusaqqak said, he was prevented from doing so. 'The ministers from Denmark didn't want the whole world to listen to us. They said to me, "We will not have a discussion about this at this table. We will talk about this some other time, but not at this table!"' He scratched his head in disbelief.

'It was very hard for me. I didn't understand what was happening. But after we gave the Danish ministers our paper on what happened in 1953, one minister called me to his office and asked me, "Uusaqqak, what would you say if I gave you thirty-five million kroner in your pocket for you to take home and not talk of this, what would you say? I will give you cash. Thirty-five million Danish kroner!"' Uusaqqak looked wild-eyed and continued heatedly, 'But I said to him, "I am not talking about money, I want to have a paper that says what happened in 1953." So he said no more and asked me to get out of his office. We have not talked about it since that time.' He laughed derisively and shook his head.

'So what do you want?' I asked. 'Do you want the Danish government to give you the land back and the Americans to go?'

'Yes! Because our hunting area from the old times into now is getting smaller and smaller: Before 1953, before the white people came to the Arctic area, my family could hunt in their territory all the way over to Canada. We needed to hunt there because we needed skins to wear: polar bear skin. They have hunting areas that are special for polar bear over in Canada, and we went there every year. After 1953 a telegram came from the Canadian government saying that the Greenland people must never ever come back again to Canada area. But they didn't ask the Canadian people what they thought about this. No Canadian Eskimo go to this area; only Thule Eskimo hunt in this area! It is only the Thule people that have given these Northwest Territories their special names. So after 1953 they told us we must not come within three miles of the coast of Canada, then we were told it was six miles, and then twelve miles off the coast of Canada. So our hunting area was getting smaller. Then the American people came and built a rocket base in our village, and they told us that we could not come into the military area. They said it was closed to us. So I think that after fifty years I must fight about that, because this is *our* land.'

We sat in silence for a while, looking out at the molten gold of the fjord.

'Things are changing for the Thule hunters,' Uusaqqak mused eventually, tapping his pipe on the side of the log. 'Last winter was a real problem for walrus hunting; every year for the last few years the ice conditions and weather patterns have changed and last year parts of the fjord didn't freeze at all, there was open water all over the area –' he traced a vague map in the sand at our feet. 'Every year the sea ice is getting thinner. Even six or seven years ago the ice was very different, several metres thick, now we have dangerous ice.' He talked about how things had changed drastically for the community since we were last here, but he said emphatically that he was part of a group of hunters that were trying to ensure that the traditions of hunting were preserved, such as the use of dog-sledges instead of skidoos. 'We still hunt narwhal with harpoon –' he motioned the thrust of the old weapon – 'further south and in Canada they use rifles. That is bad. If we shoot the narwhal, sometimes they sink and we cannot keep them, so we cannot like that method with the rifle. It is very important for our future that we can balance hunting, so that the narwhal come back every summer, and in the future too. This is the best method that we have learnt from our fathers and grandfathers. Maybe we are the only ones left in the Arctic who use the old equipment. In Alaska they sometimes use the beautiful old equipment of the kayak – but I don't know what has happened for the hunters in Canada, they do not have these methods.'

Currently there are sixty-one registered full-time hunters in Qaanaaq (hunters of Thule have to register with the Hunters' Council to be permitted to hunt), and countless part-time hunters who have a supplementary job. The difference between the full-time hunters and their weekend-hunter counterparts is that the so-called '100 per cent hunters' are allowed to hunt walrus, narwhal, polar bear, seal, birds and fish, and on request are given additional time-restricted permits to hunt musk ox and caribou; whereas part-time hunters can only hunt seal, birds and fish.

The regulation of game hunting is one of the primary concerns of the Hunters' Council, to ensure that the area is not over-hunted so that future generations will not suffer; the hunters of the Thule district have always – for the most part, for it would be wrong to say that every hunter is flawless – wholly respected the animals with which they share the Arctic. They have learned to identify the nuances of animal behaviour and migration patterns so that they are aware if numbers have fallen in the summer visits of the narwhal, or the autumnal appearances of the walrus. The hunters are well aware that their own lives depend on keeping the stocks of animals, birds and fish in the area at a certain level, and still they do not kill more animals than they need to feed and clothe themselves. Restrictions are imposed on part-time hunters who are not permitted to hunt certain endangered animals as an additional safety net. But the hunters also need a buffer between them and the outside world who do not understand what it is like to live life at subsistence level. The Hunters' Council therefore is the mediator between the Thule hunters and some environmental agencies who are determined to curb the hunting rights of the people of Thule. Without representation, these hunters – who have an infinitely greater understanding of their own environment than most of the staff of these environmental agencies – may well have lost their already endangered traditions. Protecting the rights of the Thule hunters is even more vital in this age where 'progress' is homogenizing the world's most fascinating and valuable cultures.

'Ah, life is very hard for the hunter now.' Uusaqqak sighed, shaking his head, remembering what it once was like. 'What we need,' he explained, 'is permission to sell a quota of furs and ivory from hunting to people outside of the community. That is the only way that they will be able to survive.'

I asked: 'You cannot sell the ivory or the pelts at all?'

'No, it is not possible for us to trade the products of our hunting any more to the whole world. If you like some sealskin –' he jabbed a finger at me – 'and you want to bring it to your home in England, you must have permission to take the skin. We can only give [the skins and carvings] to people from South Greenland. People come from other parts of Greenland to buy our furs but we cannot give them to anyone else.'

A few years ago in a desperate bid to help the hunting community Uusaqqak travelled around Europe trying to promote the use of seal-skin in fashion. Now that they could not trade in furs they had more than they needed – the pelts were the by-product of their main staple food and it bothered them that they had a surplus of good fur which they could do nothing with. But like America and Canada, Europe was not interested. They needed help and understanding from the European Union, Uusaqqak said quietly, because otherwise the old ways will disappear and all the young people will have to turn to other jobs just to survive.

The subject finally wore him out and he started talking of my father, and that he was a great traveller and a good man. He had seen one of Dad's books on the Polar Eskimos – 'and the pictures were *beautiful!*' he cooed. He loved photography and he himself owned a couple of cameras, and even a Super-8 film camera, 'but,' he said seriously, 'it is too heavy to take hunting and makes it no fun.' I laughed and told him that my Dad had felt exactly the same way.

Uusaqqak's wife Inger came up behind us and he turned to include her. 'My wife,' he said proudly, 'she is a very good cook; she cooks for the hospital.' His eyes sparkled. 'Lucky patients!' he said with rolling laughter. She nudged him and handed him a bowl of steaming chicken broth which he sucked at noisily before pausing and whispering conspiratorially, 'Maybe I will get salmonella!'

Four people remained at the summer camp, and they waved vigorously to us as we rolled away from them into the fjord. It was a wrench to leave the little beach with its ancient memories and its protective bosom of a mountain behind. The sky was mottled, brooding darkly over the mountains but the ride back to Qaanaaq, although rough, wasn't as bad as it had been before. The girls and I perched on a thick reindeer hide, which slightly cushioned the bumps as we slammed into rogue waves. We rode tandem with Uuli whose boat looked like a crippled catamaran, with two kayaks secured either side of the deck.

Ilannguak and Arnarulunaguaq were waiting on the beach for us as we grounded a couple of hours later at Qaanaaq, relieved at our return. Arnarulunaguaq automatically grabbed some of my gear and helped me carry it back to Louisa's, commiserating with me as I grumbled that I didn't like being back in town. She deposited my gear and, declining a cup of tea, shot off back down to the beach with a brief hug and a smile.

I was ravenous, and desperate to peel off my clothes and scrub myself clean; my daily ablutions in the stream hadn't been enough. But my visions of cleanliness were short lived. The 'dump-truck' which emptied the town's filled toilet buckets hadn't been around for a few days and the bathroom stank of shit – a putrid gagging smell in the airless heat of the modern house. I opened the window wide and sighed thinking of the last few days where the whole Arctic had been my vista as I had gone to the toilet. Holding my breath I tore off my clothes and threw myself under the shower, dousing myself quickly with water and scrubbing myself until I was almost raw. I turned off the shower to save the rationed water, excessively lathered myself, turned the tap on again, and not a drip of water came out. No amount of turning on or off would produce anything. Shampoo in my eyes I staggered to the small basin and groped for the tap: nothing. The only water in the whole house was a single glassful that was in a small plastic bottle in the fridge. It was pure farce. I poured the precious glass of ice-cold water over my head and shrieked with the cold and the irony of the situation.

It suddenly struck me that I hadn't looked in the mirror since I had left and was taken aback by my freckles and dark-flushed cheeks, my wind-burnt lips and the white lines where I had been smiling and squinting in the never-ending daylight.

It was strange to be back. I felt so alive from being out in the elements and everything in Qaanaaq felt lifeless. Hans came in and pointed to my ruddy cheeks. '*Illit Eskimo*, you are an Eskimo!'

he exclaimed grinning. 'I am leaving too,' he added, brandishing a large fishhook. 'I am going fishing tomorrow!' I sat with him as he prepared his fishing rod and showed me his hooks. He was so eager to go that his sleeping bag and small backpack were already by the door. Louisa arrived a few minutes later, and she hugged me tightly. '*Ivariaqiikkit*, I missed you,' she said softly.

The next day I returned to the house from a walk to discover Ilannguak and Arnarulunaguaq waiting for me. Ilannguak was obviously excited and had some news. I asked if he had had good hunting and he nodded grinning, but it was Louisa who told me that he had caught a large narwhal. Arnarulunaguaq squeezed my knee and pointed at her husband telling me what a good hunter he was. I got out my map and asked him where he had been hunting and he was delighted by the question. With a gravity of tone reserved solely for hunting talk, he breathed deeply and smoothed the paper with great delicacy over the coffee table. He pointed to an area of the fjord further down from where I had been staying, and then urged on by my questioning expression started showing me all the places where the good hunting was. His hands were small and dark, tough and weatherworn, and yet his fingers were graceful and controlled as he made the most delicate of gestures, sweeping a blunt thumb-nail across the ice cap, over tough rock promontories and down treacherous glaciers. There was almost nowhere he hadn't been.

This deliberate yet exquisitely subtle use of their hands when describing a hunt is common among good hunters. The tales are in their fingers, and from their gestures they relive the intricacies of their communion with the animals and the environment. The hands of the hunter can describe in silent mime the subtle movement of a narwhal as it dives, the direction of the wind and the quality of the ice. This unique sign language, encompassing flutters of the fingers, wide sweeps of the palm with a flashing turn of the wrist or a curve of a finger, is crucial to any story. Ilannguak ran imaginary grooves through the map, delineating space and his voyages through the icy wasteland marked heavily on the map, *UNEXPLORED*; Ilannguak's thumb cut through it all. We all glowed with pride and fascination as we watched him etch out his life.

As always, Ilannguak's visit was brief, long enough only for a cup of tea or coffee and a chat. But this time they asked me to join them as they left. We walked in comfortable silence to the beach and pulled up a couple of boxes and an old oil drum to sit on, and simply watched the quiet activity around the scruffy pale blue hut that the brothers shared as their hunting cabin. Once, not that long ago, this bloodied and grotty hut would have been home to a hunter and his family, but now almost all of the older huts of the town are either just used as store houses or as a refuge away from home for teenagers.

The word had spread quickly that the couple had fresh mattak, and a slow stream of customers came to visit. A customer would walk up to the hut, nod at Ilannguak and either he or Arnaruluna-guaq would lead them up the rickety wooden steps and be gone for a few moments before re-emerging with a nondescript plastic bag as Arnarulunaguaq surreptitiously slid kroner bills inside a pouch she wore around her waist. She giggled when she saw me watching, and beckoned me inside to take a look. The rich smell of blood hit me as we walked through the door. Plastic basins filled with large slabs of blubber or dripping meat lay among an assortment of wellies and hunting paraphernalia. A large bloody knife skewered the pile of mattak closest to the door.

Qaanaaq was quiet save for the occasional howls from bored dog teams and the excited shrieks of young children at play. Louisa came home from work. Being five months pregnant, a day's work was draining for her and often she would come home and curl up on the sofa, falling almost immediately into a deep snoring slumber. Today though she wanted to talk.

'I miss you,' she said, and then held up her hand indicating there was more. With a combination of halting English and

Inuktun she explained that she had missed me when we returned to England when I was a little girl, that everyone had – in particular Aata, who sat silently with a heavy heart when we left, often looking out the window just in case we came back. She held my hand tightly, tears rolling down her full cheeks. Avatak and Maria too were very unhappy, she said: they would sit together and look out at our hut saying 'Ajor!' to each other. Maria missed my mother, she whispered hoarsely. And then finally I heard what had happened when Avatak died. Louisa patiently talked me carefully through it so that I could understand. She told me that as the shot rang out and her husband fell to the floor Maria had suddenly sobered, and when she realized what she had done she was consumed with grief. She was inconsolable. Maria was taken to a hospital in Nuuk and put on medication, 'for her mind,' Louisa said, tapping lightly on her forehead with saddened eyes. The children moved to Qaanaaq from Herbert Island and lived with relatives for the first year, then when Maria was moved to Ilulissat (then called Jakobshaven) the girls followed and stayed with other family there; Arquenguak and Ilannguak stayed in Qaanaaq to become hunters. The girls all gradually moved back to Qaanaaq, with Louisa being the last to return along with her husband Hans and her daughter Karen. She had lived in Ilulissat near to her mother for seventeen years.

We sat together for some time, holding hands, quietly steeped in reminiscences and letting the tears fall unhindered.

13. In Search of Happiness

The school was bustling as staff prepared for the new teaching year and I was easily drawn into the busy atmosphere that was such a contrast to the soporific stupor of summer camp. Watching the teenagers learn how to kayak and how to relax into their natural surroundings had made me wonder more about what the future was likely to hold for them, and the school seemed the obvious place to start.

Axel Lund Olsen greeted me effusively at the door to his office and led me cheerily through the school, our footsteps ricocheting down the empty corridors past countless classrooms in various states of preparation for the new school year, towards the back of the U-shaped building. Maps of the world hung on the walls next to class projects of the animals of the Polar Regions. In one classroom kayaks and dog-sledges made out of cardboard hung from the ceiling, moving gently in the summer breeze. Axel explained as we walked that the school was about to be rebuilt, and the new educational complex would include a state-of-the-art computer room and games hall where the children could watch films on a big screen, put on plays and hold discos. It was a world away from the schools that I attended on our various visits to Greenland. At one school I went to when I was nine years old, I remembered, all the students seemed to do was learn Danish and needlepoint. I myself became quite adept at beadwork.

'It is more comfortable here,' the headmaster said, waving me into the deserted staff room. Stale cigarette smoke hung in smoky veils over the mismatched furniture. Axel moved a guitar off a dark green armchair, took a swig of coffee and lit a Lucky Strike. He looked me over with keen eyes and leant back in his chair. 'So how can I help you?'

I thought I should introduce myself properly and gave him an extremely brief potted history of my association with the area before asking him about the children and their future. I had barely mentioned Qeqertassuaq when he interrupted me: 'Herbert Island is my home!' he declared, sighing '*Qeqertahhhaaaa . . .*' in a growl of phlegm. I looked at him surprised; I had never heard Herbert Island's only village pronounced so grittily. 'The very first moment I saw that hunting village I loved it, and as soon as I heard that there was a house for sale there I bought one. So now I say that I come from *Qeqertahhhaaa!*' He almost leapt out of his seat in enthusiasm. I noticed for the first time that he didn't look a Thule man; his skin was pale buff and his demeanour and confidence set him apart.

'I have dreams for Qeqertassuaq, I want to reopen the school – what a wonderful place to educate children!' I loved the idea. In fact, I was behind any idea to re-establish Qeqertassuaq as a thriving community. Encouraged by my enthusiasm Axel flung himself back in the chair and studied his clean fingernails. For a moment he took on the poise of a politician. 'And I want to use the old store as a – what do you call it? A drying out place? Yes, that's it, for alcoholics, for entire families of alcoholics.' His arms swept wide as if he were talking about the whole of the Thule district.

My eyes widened. I knew from our time living on the island that for decades there had been problems with alcohol in Greenland, but I did wonder if the problems were being exaggerated.

Axel sighed with the weight of being surrounded by non-believers and continued: 'The first hurdle is not to treat this as a taboo subject,' he said patiently; 'we need to fully and openly acknowledge that the community has a problem.' He shook his head slowly. 'At the moment the system isn't working,' he said stabbing a finger at the stained coffee table. 'But using Herbert Island as a rehabilitation facility would be perfect,' he enthused. 'They would be able to see Qaanaaq across the fjord, so they wouldn't feel so isolated, but they wouldn't be able to get hold of alcohol. It would be *perfect.*'

Some children outside kicked a football against the window of the staff room. Axel didn't flinch.

I asked Axel about how the young people felt about their future in Qaanaaq, and how many went on to higher education. Then the light fell from his face. From his expression I gathered the future for them looked bleak.

'Schooling in Greenland is a complex matter,' he explained, 'with too many directives coming from those that know very little about what was needed in the more remote settlements. It is time that it is acknowledged that the Thule people have a much closer connection with the Inuit of Canada and Alaska. Many people in Qaanaaq have relatives in Canada, and many people, not just the students, talk about their wish to go to Canada to meet their friends who they talk to over the radio.' He took a slug from his coffee cup. 'We have to teach Danish and West Greenlandic here, but most of my students want to learn English because so many of the movies we get here are in English – they like to watch many movies – and so they can talk to their Inuit friends in Canada. And if we want to integrate into the global community, which the people here will eventually need to do in order to be able to survive, then Qaanaaq people will have to learn English. You have to understand that Denmark and even West Greenland is a totally alien environment for the people here; Canada is closer to their roots.'

As for their future as a whole, Axel could not give me any answers. Things were changing so fast in the district, he said, that few seemed to know who they were any more. I agreed with him. There was an unsettled feeling to Qaanaaq, and fundamental changes in the community were happening so fast that the whole district seemed in turmoil. Their evolution from subsistence 'primitive' living to a modern way of life has taken just a hundred years, whereas it took the rest of Europe several centuries to evolve into what it is now. The Inughuit are reeling from culture shock.

He continued morosely: 'None of the kids who go for higher education come back to become school teachers. They stay in South Greenland. Things are easier for them there: life is easier! Trying to get any teachers from the south is difficult and expensive, and many cannot deal with the dark winters and the lifestyle here. We need more local teachers who know the area and who have sympathy with the community and the kids, but local teachers who stay here have only been educated to teach kindergarten or first school [primary school]. But we use what we are given.' He sat quietly for a moment before adding, 'And we have a problem with alcohol and local teachers.'

We left the staff room and Axel gave me a tour of the school. Inudliah called out to us as we walked into the dormitory area and grinned in her rubber gloves and overalls as she carefully washed down the walls. Children still come to board at the school from the surrounding villages of Siorapaluk, Moriussaq, Qeqertat and even Savissivik, and remain here until the school holidays. The bedrooms were compact and simply furnished with desks and narrow bunks, but they had a homeliness about them nonetheless. One of the bedrooms was waiting for its occupant to return from the summer holiday with his family; the walls were covered with pull-out posters from teen magazines, a small stereo sat on a small desk, and a colourful single duvet cover was neatly ironed and folded at the foot of his bunk.

It was a welcoming atmosphere, but understandably the first time children come here, like anywhere in the world, they feel disoriented and distressed about being away from their families, particularly as life in Thule has always been so family-centred, with the whole family sleeping together. It was some comfort at least to be sharing a room with other children – to join in the ebb and flow of group sleep. Privacy is still a modern phenomenon for this community. It was lucky for the children of Qeqertassuaq that they had had a school on the island in the 1970s so that they hadn't had to leave home so young. Lucky for me too; if the children had all gone to Qaanaaq for their schooling I would never have developed such a strong relationship with them. I asked Axel if the new arrivals found it hard to be on their own in the rooms and he laughed. 'Sometimes when the care staff go round in the mornings they find the kids have slept together in the same rooms anyway.'

The headmaster gently guided me back through the school then apologized, saying he had to attend to pressing school business. 'Help yourself to our facilities!' Axel urged generously as he walked away down the gleaming corridor. 'Our computers are in there; you can tell your family that you are back safely from your adventure at summer camp!'

A casually dressed man in his early thirties was already sitting in the computer room. I hadn't seen him before and assumed he was one of the Danish teachers. I asked him if I could use one of the machines. He looked startled and muttered something along the lines of 'Oh sure, um . . .' in an American accent and waved vaguely at the other monitors in the room, never taking his eyes off me. He falteringly introduced himself as Robert Biswas-Diener. He had a distinctive look, with bleached hair, a rough goatee and gentle eyes. I was surprised at both his accent and the fact that I hadn't noticed him around the town.

'How come I haven't seen you around?' he asked, reading my thoughts.

We looked at each other for a moment with a tinge of shock and gratitude at finding another native English speaker. Amazingly, he and two other researchers had been in Qaanaaq for almost the same amount of time as myself, and yet we had never bumped into each other.

He told me he was researching happiness, and urged on by my surprised expression he continued: 'Basically, myself and my colleagues travel the world studying groups of people who have very little materially, and try to discover what it is that gives them a sense of well-being.' The studies have so far taken them throughout Middle America to the Amish communities, to the prostitutes and street people of Calcutta and the Maasai of Kenya, and now the Inughuit of Greenland.

'Is there much happiness in Qaanaaq?' I asked. He gave me a wry smile and said they were yet to find out, but the prognosis so far was pretty good. He invited me to come and share a beer with him and his colleagues that evening so that he could enlighten me further.

I left the school as two young teenage girls walked past, one in platform boots and the other with streaked bleached hair. They looked at me blankly, the girl in platform boots struggling to keep her balance as she tottered on the arm of her friend. Their skin was pale and perfect, in complete contrast to my freckled and wind-burnt face. Unlike Little Tekummeq and Naduk, they had obviously not spent any time outside during their summer holiday. I turned and watched them walk into the school and wondered what they would be doing in ten years' time, and how different Qaanaaq would be.

There was little sense of adventure being back among so many modern amenities, but I made the most of them nonetheless and spent the evening cooking a large roast chicken that looked as if it had been frozen for a decade or two. It was ambrosial after the endless boiled meat concoctions of camp life. We had just finished our meal when Robert poked his head around the door and walked in. Louisa and Hans were almost beside themselves with surprise and curiosity and looked at each other grinning before standing up in greeting, but Robert had already made himself at home at the table. Louisa offered him tea and Hans produced the traditional Eskimo puzzle to work out, and stood delighting in Robert's bewilderment at the game that had baffled me when I first came to stay. We left Louisa and Hans and walked down to the meteorological station where the other researchers were staying, aware of the scrutiny and gossip that was already hatching at the window of my temporary home.

Joar Vitterso was an attractive and friendly Norwegian, who

had worked with Robert's father several years before on similar ethnological projects. It was not his first time to Qaanaaq and he knew a smattering of the language, so was a crucial member of the team. Joar was stunned when he heard of my family history, and stood quietly for a moment before he told me that he had followed my father's expeditions for years: 'I even bought the son of one of his North Pole dogs!' he exclaimed in his quiet Norwegian way. The three of us sat and talked like old friends. I had had eight weeks of using pidgin Inuktun, and I relished their intelligent conversation.

Louisa and Hans were waiting up for me when I got home as if I were a teenager out on a first date. Louisa got up and stood in the doorway, unable to contain her curiosity, looking closely at my face trying to find any trace of passion, but she was looking in vain. She followed me to the sofa and stared at me expectantly. I ignored her and felt her bubble with frustration until she finally asked me who Robert was. I laughed at her insatiable curiosity. 'A scientist,' I said finally after searching for the term in my language book, but I had no idea how to explain how he was studying happiness. That was not enough information for her, and she kept prodding me for more. Obviously not getting quite the information she wanted she started doing a peculiar imitation of people having sex. 'No!' I exclaimed, trying to explain that I had spent the evening talking to the two scientists, but that only encouraged her all the more, and she insistently carried on with her charade, miming an ejaculating penis and sperm swimming through the air so that my eyes were as big as saucers from the whole display, causing her to explode with giggles, and in turn had me helpless with laughter.

'No no!' she wheezed, finally pointing at the television. I turned to see a programme on the TV about artificial insemination which I hadn't noticed at all. It amused us both periodically for an hour, and finally I left to go to sleep, still hearing little bursts of giggles and sighs from downstairs.

★

I felt drugged with light as I pulled myself out of bed and sat quietly nursing a cup of tea until Robert came to pick me up to take me to meet a girl called Nuka Harper whom I had been hoping to meet since I had arrived, but so far had kept missing. Navarana was Nuka's mother, and her father was Kenn Harper, a Canadian writer and historian who had spent around twenty years in the Northwest Territories of Canada and in Greenland. His book *Give Me My Father's Body* about Minik, a Polar Eskimo from Smith Sound, who was taken with five other Eskimos to New York in 1897 by Robert E. Peary, had been on our bookshelves for years. In a bizarre chain of coincidences, I had happened to meet Nuka's half-sister in a smart bar in London just after Nuka had left after spending a month in the capital; heavily pregnant she had returned to Qaanaaq to be with her mother. Nuka sounded like a fiery and well-travelled character and I was intrigued to meet her, particularly as I thought she could give me a clue as to what the other young women in Qaanaaq wanted for their future, but I hadn't yet been able to track her down. It turned out that Robert had hired Nuka as an interpreter. He described her as 'fantastic – a punk-rock-chick Inughuit girl,' and arranged for us finally to meet.

'She may still be asleep,' Robert warned me as we ambled our way slowly through town; 'my colleague Andy, Nuka and her mother had a bit of a session last night.' It seemed that he was right; the house was silent as we arrived and no one came to the door.

We returned to Navarana's place after a couple of hours of walking around the town and this time Nuka and her baby were awake. Extremely attractive and slender, with large almond-shaped eyes, she greeted us with a casual 'Hi,' and carried on with what she was doing. The studs in her nose and chin glinted in the sunlight.

'My sister told me about you,' she said breezily as we made ourselves comfortable among a chaotic jumble of knick-knacks and souvenirs from around the world, but Nuka seemed preoccupied and didn't venture any more information. Heavy rock music played from a ghetto blaster to which her wide-eyed fourteen-month-old daughter was shaking her shoulders beside two large ornate elephants stuffed under a side table. Japanese lanterns sat next to the stereo under an old angákoq's drum mounted on the wall, and nearby an ornament rack was filled with tiny objects: miniature kamiks, a pair of wind-up boxing kangaroos, a thimble. Every space was filled with something. Photographs, beauty products and books were piled on the table. In the corner a narrow bed and crib were covered with a tangle of clothes.

'Hey Nuka, you been tidying up?' Robert exclaimed.

'Yeah, that place in Siorapaluk was so fuckin' dirty, that when I got back I just had to clean this place up.' Nuka's voice had a distinctive Canadian twang.

'We've just spent a few days in Siorapaluk doing some interviews,' Robert explained, 'but the place we stayed in was just so gross. It hadn't been cleaned in years, probably never in fact!' Nuka grimaced and changed her daughter Maija into a clean outfit: stretchy black trousers and a black T-shirt. She was dressed just like her mother.

A childhood friend of Nuka's peered around the door and silently joined us. She had the same streaked hairstyle as Nuka and was obviously trying to model herself on her more cosmopolitan friend. 'She is my oldest friend,' Nuka said, nodding towards the shy Inughuit girl; 'we even had babies at the same time.' The girl watched Nuka's every move with fascination.

Nuka was young and rebellious, a free spirit who craved experimentation in her life. 'The pregnancy was a mistake,' she said bluntly, 'but,' she added quickly, swinging a gurgling baby Maija over her shoulder, 'there was no way I could not have had her. I can't imagine not having Maija in my life now, just look at her, how she loves life. Yeah, being a mother rocks, but sometimes I feel like I am missing out on other shit.' Maija squealed in delight as Nuka dangled her upside down. 'Being a single mom I have to be the dad too!' Nuka laughed and lit up the room with a perfect smile.

Like her father and mother, Nuka loved to travel and had spent much of her childhood following her father around the Arctic, and then as she became independent, she started to see the world with her own eyes, and was not afraid of making a new life for herself in different cities, although it didn't always work out.

'I stayed with my sister in London for six months when I was pregnant and it was terrible,' she said. 'It was difficult and so different to the other times I visited. I couldn't go clubbing and do all the things I wanted to do as I had to keep myself and my baby healthy and all that shit.'

'What about Qaanaaq, do you like it here?'

'Qaanaaq sucks!' she retorted. 'I can't wait to get out of here. I am supposed to be going to Denmark for a job, but it keeps getting postponed – it's driving me crazy. It's like a prison sentence being stuck in Qaanaaq.' She got up suddenly: 'Can you watch Maija? I have to go do my laundry.' She picked up a binliner of clothes and disappeared.

There was something that had been gnawing away at me since I arrived in Qaanaaq, and with just a few days left before my departure, I had little time in which to ease my disquiet. I needed to find out what had happened to Maria after she shot Avatak. And if I couldn't uncover the specifics, I felt at the very least I needed to discover how the problems in the community as a whole were being dealt with.

The police station looked deceptively large from the outside, and on entering I was surprised at how cramped the place was. I was greeted politely by the Danish policeman who immediately asked me to take a seat and offered me coffee from his flask, apologizing that it wasn't very fresh. He cut quite an imposing figure; tall and trim with blond hair and intelligent eyes, with a revolver slung in a holster around his hips. He introduced himself as Mads Iversen and was more than willing to answer my questions although, he cautioned, he had only arrived in Qaanaaq two weeks before.

Mads Iversen was an affable man and, quite unprompted, started pulling out files of statistics and flicked through them for any relevant information, giving me a broad view of crime in Greenland as he went.

'The justice system in Greenland is unique,' he said, swinging in his office chair, 'and so far it seems to be working, although of course every system has its faults.'

There are 140 policemen in the whole of Greenland, and although for years the police force was entirely made up of Danes, most of the posts are now held by Greenlanders, with only twenty Danish officers stationed on the island, mostly in positions of seniority. All reports are still filed in Danish, as Greenlandic – which has always been an oral language – is almost impossible to write, so all Greenlandic police officers have to be fluent in Danish. Originally recruits had to travel to Denmark for training, but now there is a training facility in Nuuk, with many of the training officers originating from Greenland. The powers that be have realized that people who are indigenous to smaller communities have more sensitivity and natural understanding of the psyche and needs of the local people.

'Our system of dealing with crime and offenders in Greenland is based more on rehabilitation than incarceration,' Mads started to explain. Serious convictions for murder or extreme violence where the offender is not deemed to be a threat to the rest of the community – for instance if the crime was within a family or was a singular incident – will incur a sentence of six or seven years in Greenland but away from the community in which they committed the crime; the tribal justice system originally banished murderers from their community. But even now convicted criminals are not incarcerated twenty-four hours a day. For a hunter who has spent his whole life outdoors such a punishment would be likely to have an adverse mental effect, therefore the offenders work during the day, and at a curfew return to jail to sleep at night. Obedience to these rules is strictly observed. This form of punishment is the most sensible for various reasons: the Inughuit essentially believe that the human being is not infallible, and agree that crimes must be punishable and the perpetrator be repentant, but also that the state or the community should not be responsible for supporting someone who has committed a crime; therefore if the convict can work then he or she has to pay for their own survival. In the old days people who had committed a crime would still have to hunt for their food and clothing. For lesser crimes incurring a jail sentence of less than four months the criminal will stay in a local prison, but Mads admitted that sometimes this can be quite a problem, and invited me to look at the one prison cell in the Qaanaaq police station.

The cell was, as one would expect, a pretty miserable place. It was small and gloomy with grey concrete walls, a hard single bunk and a small slatted window set high up the wall. 'It is usually used for drunks who are being a nuisance, or people that are having a bad argument,' Mads said, his voice echoing dully in the small room. 'You can imagine, though, if we have a particularly bad night, we have to put them all in the same cell – it is an interesting way of settling fights sometimes.' He smiled wryly, shutting the door behind him and looked amazed as the handle came off in his hands.

I didn't imagine that there was much crime in a town like Qaanaaq and mused out loud that it must be a quiet place in which to be stationed.

'Quiet! No!' he said emphatically. 'In 1999 there was something like six rapes and two murders in Qaanaaq, which I believe, proportionate to the size of the town, was one of the highest crime figures in the world per capita at the time.'

Modern life in the Thule district had taken its toll on the community and there is an increasing number of rapes and domestic abuse, most of which is blamed on alcoholism, but there are deeper social issues that all contribute to the problems.

Mads believed that the Inughuit are struggling with their identity, and are desperate to be linked more with the Canadian Inuit instead of Denmark.

'I think many people here believe us [Danes] to be imperialists,' he said matter-of-factly. He was well aware of the problems of enforcing a law that does not have its roots in the traditional culture, but that finding an appropriate way to deal with crime in such isolated territories was always going to be an uphill struggle. 'Greenland Home Rule are trying to put together methods of law enforcement, but as they have no point of reference in their own history they are still looking to Danish, American and British examples, which simply do not work in the remote settlements. Ethnically, Nuuk is a million miles away from a place like Qaanaaq, and it may be that although the Home Rule is supposed to represent everyone in Greenland, it may not be in touch with the needs of the Thule people.' Mads stood by the window and swept his eyes over the town. 'The people here feel as though their lives are being governed by people who do not know what it is like living in such a remote hunting community, and this is difficult for them to accept, even though they acknowledge that rape and murder have to be punished somehow.'

Before Knud Rasmussen came to Thule, the Polar Eskimos had over the centuries developed various unique ways of dealing with crime. The Polar Eskimo language did not include any words to describe 'law' or 'justice' or 'crime', but they did have taboos, which became necessary social constructs that each individual and community had to observe. Without these taboos their way of life, and most importantly their relationship with the animals, would unravel, and starvation or famine could descend on the entire community. Maintaining the peace within the community was paramount, but as a whole they did not believe that justice could be achieved through punishment.

Disputes that were not as severe as murder were often traditionally resolved by matching adversaries against one another armed only with drums; each man would take it in turns to lampoon the other through cleverly worded but highly abusive songs. The listener was required to stand and take the abuse silently, without betraying any expression, even when his opponent repeatedly, for added effect, hammered his skull into his face; he could only retaliate when it was his turn, and then he had to be more brilliant, more abusive and filthy in his satire than his opponent. Ridicule and mockery is one of the most powerful weapons against the Eskimo psyche – the Polar Eskimos are a proud people, and mockery and laughter induce self-doubt and insecurity – the drummer who was not up to the verbal challenge would be regarded as mortally wounded and would lose the fight. The loser, thus shamed, would have to bear the brunt of public humiliation, but for most the teasing would be so merciless that his honour would not permit him to stay in the community where the tide of public opinion was blatantly against him.

But the old traditions were archaic, and justice didn't necessarily err on the side of the wronged – with the drum-song competitions if the perpetrator of the crime was quick-witted enough he was the more likely opponent to win, and his victim might have his suffering compounded further by having to leave the community himself. The ancient justice system was the law of the pack, and was potentially devastating for the whole Inughuit culture, for they believed wholeheartedly in revenge.

The Inughuit believed that a murderer or abuser was accountable not only for his crime, but also his entire family, and driven by passion before logic, the Inughuit became so entangled in their web of accountability that the hunters were constantly in fear of their lives from some unknown hand; even if they or their next of kin had never been involved in a blood feud before, a marriage into their family might tie them into a complicated vendetta even if they abhorred the concept of revenge. The situation grew so desperate in the district that a hunter travelling to another settlement, who was unsure if he had enemies in the village, would wait out on the ice until one of the old women came out to greet him and assure him of his safety; only then would he drive his dogs inland.

Rasmussen was deeply bothered by the blatant use of revenge as a means of justice, and called together the local hunters and proposed that a set of tribal laws be drawn up so that blood feuds would no longer be a necessary way of dealing with crime. The idea, it seems, was accepted with enthusiasm, and in 1920 the first Thule Law came into being and stayed in effect until 1951 when the Danish government revised all Greenland laws.

Even today the justice system in Greenland is still regarded as being one of the most progressive, and conversely, the most outmoded, in the world. The principle of rehabilitating offenders is central to the Greenland law. The Inughuit in particular believe that every person is essentially good, and that there must be some reason why that person has become troubled enough to commit a crime. They believe that with understanding and help, all offenders should be able to redeem themselves. Therefore the sentence of a convict is reached not simply by assessing the crime itself, but also by taking into consideration the circumstances which led the offender to commit it. This concept of embracing offenders rather than ostracizing them goes as far as having lay judges in each community – ordinary people who are respected and trusted in their community – who are likely to know both offender and victim, and who can try them with a much more rounded knowledge of their characters than a judge from another district (or culture), who has less of an appreciation of the dynamics of the community. Lay judges have no formal education in law. Should the offender want to appeal the sentence, the case is retried at the Greenland High Court with a judge who has had a formal law education, and who is most likely to be Danish.

I tentatively asked: 'What would have happened if, say in the mid-1970s, a wife in one of the smaller communities in Thule killed her husband?'

Mads looked at me curiously. 'Well, of course it would have

depended on the situation. The suspect would have been picked up by helicopter or boat and locked in this cell, and then she would have her trial here. If the suspect was found guilty, most likely she would have been taken to Nuuk or Ilulissat to open prison. If it was a really serious case, where the criminal was considered to be a threat to the community as a whole, she would have been sent to Denmark to be locked up in a secure prison, or would have been treated as being mentally unstable and put on medication.'

In a moment of great sadness I remembered Maria, the last time I saw her, showing my mother a phial of tablets as she tapped her forehead. 'They are for my mind,' she had said conspiratorially.

Louisa was cooking lunch when I arrived back at the house, and sensing my disturbed mood tried to cheer me up by pointing to the frankfurters she was boiling up. '*Uhuk*,' she said nudging them with a fork, '*uhuk, uhuk . . .*' getting me to repeat their Greenlandic name over and over again until I pronounced it correctly, after which she could contain herself no longer and shrieked that I was saying 'penis, penis, penis'.

'Hmm, *mammaktoq* – delicious!' I teased and she hooted up-roariously. I felt a wave of affection for this funny, lovable woman.

I was worried about my room-mate. Since her friend had left, Karen was getting increasingly bolshy, and I had spotted her several times hanging round a group of older boys who seemed quite aggressive. She would scowl or ignore me completely when she was with them on one of their aimless jaunts around town. As I left her room now I noticed a poster of a clean-cut boy band that had been there since I arrived. Now it was completely defaced with scrawls of 'Fuck you muther fucker get out of my hous [*sic*]', and Nazi swastikas scrawled on scraps of paper torn from schoolbooks littered her Coca-Cola duvet.

I wondered how I could broach the subject with Louisa, and

quietly went to join her downstairs, but she obviously had other worries and was sitting frowning over my language book. '*Agiri*, come,' she said softly and motioned me to the sofa. She looked at me, deadly serious. 'You no eat apple,' she said in English, wagging her finger. I was confused. A boy in another village, she told me, had died the previous day from eating an apple. 'They are dangerous!' she cried. 'Apple *ajorpok!*' It seemed like an extraordinary accusation towards an innocent piece of fruit, but then I wondered whether the boy had had an allergic reaction. There seemed to be no word in Inuktun for allergy, and so I tried to explain the symptoms of an anaphylactic shock in a jumble of English, Inuktun and sign language. Louisa jumped off the sofa in excitement. '*Eie*, that is how he died!' She pointed an accusing finger at the supply ship and the *kadluna* food. She quickly sobered and returned to my side and again told me that I must never eat apples again: 'Eat only mattak!' Later I found Louisa lying prostrate on the sofa, keening and wailing softly on the phone to the mother of the boy that had just died. Neither of them spoke, and I could hear the woman echoing down the receiver in grief.

I was walking towards the beach when I heard Hans Jensen calling my name. He was standing next to an army truck with a Dane at the steering wheel, amiably chatting about the events of the day and sharing stories. Hans had to leave but the Dane was happy to talk.

'I am Finn,' he introduced himself in a gruff voice, 'and yes, yes, I know who you are,' he added quickly before I had a chance to offer him my name. He had lived in Qaanaaq for twenty years, and had seen many changes during his stay. 'Oh the stories I could tell you!' he laughed. 'I would write them myself, but nobody here would ever speak to me again.'

It was an Inughuit hunter who had first encouraged Finn to come to Thule. 'I met this Eskimo in Denmark, and he told me to come up here; I had already been to South Greenland, but the man told me I had never been to the *real* Greenland, and that I must come up here and visit him in Thule.' Intrigued, Finn took him up on his offer and flew to Thule. 'In those days Qaanaaq was much, much smaller,' he said looking around him. 'We camped in Qaanaaq for one night and then took off down the fjord to a narwhal camp on a small island. And that was it,' he said wistfully, 'I fell in love and was lost.' He returned to Denmark, but he was smitten with Thule and couldn't think of anything else but returning. One day he woke up and made his decision, moved everything lock, stock and barrel to Greenland and has never looked back.

'You lived on Herbert Island, right?' he asked. 'Well, a few years ago I discovered that the store was for sale, so I bought it along with the house next door for DKK7,000.'

'You are joking,' I said incredulously, 'that is only about £650!'

'Haha, yes I know! So I am the landlord!' he whooped with glee. I asked him if he knew about the headmaster's wish to turn it into a local alcohol rehab centre and he said yes, they were already in discussions about it, but there was a long way to go before it could be properly put together. 'I don't want money for the house, but I need a new snow-scooter and I think that is a fair trade. I need it for the winter for delivering supplies to some of the small villages.'

He seemed genuinely passionate about community life, and was keen to promote more tourism in Thule, his premise being that it would bring more money to the people themselves so that they weren't so reliant on governmental handouts. Finn was trying to set up a tourism council, but time and time again the plan had fallen through as people seemed loath to commit to it. 'There are some people here who are already doing really well out of the few tourists that come; don't get me wrong, they work really hard for it, but they don't want to share the booty.' Finn, though, had bigger ideas. He had been researching the tribal co-ops in Africa and Australia and believed that the system would work well in Thule. Instead of the profits going into individuals' pockets it would go straight back into the community – 'and in turn may give some of the hunting community some of their dignity and pride back'. But it was a frustrating process: 'There is opposition in the form of enforced lethargy among those that could make it happen, because it would no longer benefit them.'

He mulled over the situation for a minute or two, and then he went on: 'Things have changed so much here, the people are not as nice as they once were. The land though is still very beautiful. I stay for the land,' he declared, looking out over the glistening water and mountains. I couldn't help but agree. 'Sometimes though,' he added, 'I do love the place but every once in a while you have to get drunk just to be able to bear it.'

'One-third of the entire sales of the local store are from alcohol,' Otto Christensen told me darkly over his melamine desk. Mads Iversen the police officer had suggested I visit the Kommunea offices to meet the social services officer for Qaanaaq and get more in-depth information on the community, but I hadn't quite expected such a cool reception, and as I sat under his steely scrutiny I almost wished that I hadn't bothered. Otto Christensen looked deeply mistrustful of my intentions.

'Myself and others high up in the community have tried to persuade the manager of the store not to sell alcohol, or at least to just stock "lighter" alcoholic drinks such as beer rather than whisky and stronger liquors, but the management don't see it as a profitable option and so will not agree,' he said flatly. His pale blue eyes didn't blink.

The six-week alcoholism treatment in Nuuk or Ilulissat is so expensive at DKK60,000 (around £5,450) per person that only a few can be treated at one time, but at present the current system has a low success rate. Currently only one member of the family can be treated at a time – often there are children involved and someone has to look after them – so the wife may be sent off first for six weeks, and then the husband may be sent off afterwards, but quite often by the time the partner returns the first partner has started drinking again. Only fifteen people a year can be sent to the alcohol programme, and out of those according to Otto Christensen only four or five seem to stay sober. 'It takes a strong person to be able to say no to their friends who urge them to drink again, particularly in the winter months when there is little to do and you want to drown out the darkness.' Otto Christensen chose his words carefully, and spoke without emotion. I wondered vaguely if he had always been so self-protective or whether his armour came with having worked with the darker side of life for so long.

Interestingly enough, more women than men have attended the programme. I asked Otto Christensen why he thought that was. He answered slowly: 'I think they have more interest in helping themselves but then again,' he added sombrely, 'when they are drunk it hurts less when they are beaten. Friday is payday here, and is the busiest day for women to arrive late at night with their children and the "Thule Scar".'

'The Thule Scar?'

'Black eyes,' he answered flatly.

For years Otto Christensen has been trying to sort out some kind of treatment centre in Qaanaaq but there are numerous hurdles. If they set up a centre in Qaanaaq the local community would have to pay for it, and without help from central government there is no way they would ever be able to afford it. I asked him what he thought of Axel's plans for a rehabilitation centre on Herbert Island. He gazed at me coolly. Perhaps the headmaster's ideal was too unrealistic, for Otto Christensen obviously didn't feel it justified a comment.

The first hurdle, he continued, was to find people who were willing to train to be care workers. Only 8 per cent of Greenlanders have had a secondary school education – which is not even to the equivalent of A-level standard. This is a big problem, Otto Christensen explained, when you begin to realize that most of the teachers and social workers have been poorly educated. Suddenly they have so much responsibility, and many simply don't have the fundamental training and support system of mentors or even a solid platform of basic knowledge to help them in this difficult work, and the pay too is unattractive. 'The result is that people leave their positions remarkably quickly, and find jobs in other fields instead of persisting at this occupation that makes such a difference in these communities.' His fingers drummed on the desk, and his eyes finally released me and played over the street outside. Thule is one of the main places that has suffered from 'brain-drain'. All those that have a good brain had been sent away for an education, and few have returned to help others in the community into which they themselves were born.

And then he told me about child abuse. Child sex abuse is the most frightening of all modern developments in the community. I had been expecting stories of alcoholism and domestic violence, but this was something new. When we lived in the area the children were cherished, and were never, ever, even disciplined let alone abused. And abusing a child sexually was simply unthinkable. My stomach started caving in on itself.

Otto Christensen said: 'The abuse is sexual, not physical in the way of beatings; I think that is significant.' I struggled to sit in my seat and hear the statistics that were now being spewed out over the table. It seemed as though it was a release for him to talk it out of his system and he wanted to make sure that I had a clear view of Qaanaaq as it was now, laid bare, prone and naked for inspection. His fingers rubbed against each other, clasped and unclasped. It was a blinding moment for me. Hearing this man talk rocked my world: this place that I had thought of my whole lifetime as being a place of beauty, safety, of familial warmth – most of all as a place that preserved above all else the utter sanctity of the child – was actually abusive, dark and lost.

Otto Christensen talked at length about the cycles of abuse, then promptly stopped and fixed me with a stare. He asked: 'How are you going to approach some of these delicate subjects?'

He smiled wryly. 'You know that some of the stories you may tell are public secrets.' I couldn't offer him a reply. He said: 'I don't envy you your task.' I was overwhelmed by the prospect myself.

14. A Midsummer Nightmare

The following day I was still unsettled from my conversations with Otto Christensen, and couldn't shake off the feeling that I was starting to uncover a more disturbing edge to this community. The scientists Robert, Andy and Joar too were encountering more than they had bargained for. I talked to them about my dilemma: what gave me the right to judge and make explicit in a book certain aspects of the community that the people themselves wouldn't even openly acknowledge. 'Where do you draw the line between telling the story as it is and protecting the people you respect or love?' I said, thinking out loud. Joar sat beside me on the worn green sofa with his eyebrows knotted, deep in thought. Robert untangled his hands that had been working together slowly: 'I understand what you mean; it's all very well writing that someone in the community is a habitual child abuser, but then naming your best friend as the culprit . . . that's another story.'

The door suddenly burst open and an Inughuit woman whom I had met a few days before unsteadily beamed her way into the room and crossed the floor in a couple of strides before hugging me enthusiastically and spectacularly knocking my drink out of my hands. It was Friday night. The woman made a beeline for Joar, and in response to his terrified expression we quickly decamped and made our way to Nuka and Navarana's house.

Our first port of call was the 'Gay Guy's House', as Nuka bluntly put it. Although there is a growing gay community in Nuuk and in a couple of the larger towns in southern and western Greenland, homosexuality is still quite a new concept in Thule, although according to some there are lots of bisexual goings on in Qaanaaq 'under the sheets'. But I thought that I had seen enough evidence of homosexual tendencies in and around Qaanaaq. Even on summer camp one of the late arrivals had been an effete, tall and uncomfortable-looking hunter with over-lapping teeth and a smudge of a moustache, who had a particular predilection for teenage boys – one in particular. The hunter kept lunging at the sixteen-year-old boy, wrestling him and grabbing him by the balls, or holding him in a fierce hug until he almost suffocated the unfortunate creature. At one point he rugby-tackled the boy, threw him face down on the sand and pretended to have sex with him. Later, at a card game in the hut, he kept leaning over and touching the boy's face, smoothing his thumb over the boy's mouth and sensuously rubbing a fatty piece of seal meat over his lips. The boy took the advances in good humour, shrugging the older man off him, sometimes embar-rassed by the attention, sometimes courting it. In Qaanaaq there was only one Inughuit who was 'out', and most of the com-munity refused to acknowledge that homosexuality even exists.

The 'Gay Guy's House' turned out to be a tiny single bedroom in a workingmen's bunkhouse with a communal kitchen and revolting excrement-encrusted toilet. Already the diminutive host had five guests enjoying his small bedroom-party, all of whom welcomed us with the fumy fervour of the deeply inebri-ated. Our host fluttered his eyelashes at us in welcome and continued to flaunt his effeminate manner at his friends from a rickety stool. In no time I was pressed into a corner by two young hunters who scrabbled at each other comedically trying to push the other out of the way. Both brothers were desperate to communicate that they remembered me when I was a little girl, touching my face and sobbing brokenly that I had aged so much, and holding their hearts tragically, telling me that many people had died since then. They planted great wet kisses on my cheeks and in between their tears they grinned with boundless happiness that we were all reunited at last.

I was looking for some kind of relief from Tweedle-dum and Tweedle-dee but there was little hope of rescue as the others had similarly been accosted and were now pinned in between new friends on the side of the single bunk, behind whom a couple clumsily groped one another. I had a moment's respite as the brothers disappeared to find more beer before a pretty young man came and blearily introduced himself. 'It is fate!' he proclaimed, that we were at the same party and were both wearing carved polar bear heads around our necks. 'We must dance!' The thumping techno wasn't my cup of tea and I politely declined, but my new friend could not be discouraged. Andy came to my rescue and gathered the young man into an elaborate tango and, taking his cue from some of the other young guys sang 'muther fucker . . .' over and over to the music. His partner looked faintly distressed and in a moment of soft clarity his shoulders drooped as if he had been deeply offended. 'I really love my mother,' he said, his lower lip trembling. Andy shot a look at Robert and me and turned back to the young man. 'I didn't mean anything by it, I am sure you do love your mother . . . oh shit.'

Our new friend took the opportunity to squeeze next to me and tugged on my pendant trying to look wise – or perhaps just focus – as he spoke in slow English. 'My polar bear is different to yours,' he said. 'Mine is dangerous!' he added with aplomb, nearly falling off his perch. At that moment a tremendously large woman threw open the door and swivelled her eyes greedily around the room. The tape reversed on the stereo and was suddenly blaring some thumping trash with a gravelly vocal screaming, 'Eat my pussy!' In the split second it took the three of us to exchange surprised looks the large woman was gyrating her rolls of flesh towards Andy who was sitting cross-legged on the floor, lasciviously thrusting her groin into his face with her hands gripping her thinning hair in an expression of ecstasy. At the same moment our host leapt up, and not to be outdone started grinding his hips in time to the music, turning round and suggestively pulling his jeans down, just a little bit at a time, revealing the perfect moons of his tight pale buttocks, looking back over his shoulder coquettishly to see if Robert was watching him. By now the couple behind us on the bed were groaning with passion and those that weren't able to perch on the side of the bed looked around desperately for a mate. The pretty young man whined beside me, 'You don't like me, you *hate* me.'

As quickly as it all kicked off it all stopped. Andy's corpulent admirer disappeared with a trail of drunken cohorts and the host, getting no response from either of the boys, suddenly picked up his keys and promptly dissolved the party saying that it was time to go to the disco. He wanted to dance.

Next door the scene was very different. The salmon-pink-painted house stood a few yards away from the door of the workers' accommodation, and a warm, flickering glow from the candlelight within gave a sense that it was night-time although the sun was still high and bright. We were passing the house without pause but were quickly stopped in our tracks by a high shriek of welcome behind us. We turned to see a large happy-faced woman filling the doorway, beckoning to us wildly. Our new hostess introduced herself as Jacobena and she quickly pushed us inside with entreaties that we must help her drink Martini. We plunged headlong into a homely room; heavy curtains blocked out the sunlight, a couple of bottles of wine and a large bottle of Martini glittered on the sideboard. Jacobena urged us to sit down and locked the door on a couple of inebriates who were pressing their way inside.

At the heavy wooden table sat another woman with unusually curly hair and a soft unchallenging face who grasped me tightly and told me her name was Magdalene. She cooed softly and stroked my cheek, saying something rapidly to Jacobena, and then turned to me saying she had met me several times when we were living on Herbert Island.

As the others started talking about the beauty of wrestling, Magdalene started opening up to me about her family. Her teenage son, she said quietly, had died three years ago: he had committed suicide. I held her hand tightly as a couple of stray tears dripped off her cheek, but she remained completely contained. 'I

am OK,' she said, 'I am just starting to live again.' My stomach
clenched as I listened to her and I wondered whether her son had
been a friend of Magda's boy, and whether they had somehow
influenced each other. She pushed her small glass of wine away.
'I don't usually drink. Maybe just a little with my friends.' She
looked merry but certainly not drunk, and I told her not to
worry on my account. Jacobena sighed loudly that we must
finish our drinks quickly and demanded that we all go dancing
immediately.

My eyes smarted as we left the darkness of Jacobena's house
and walked down the street, Nuka on one arm and Magdalene
on the other. The dogs in the town were restless and howls and
calls followed us as we slowly bent our way towards the small
town hall. As we crunched our way over the brittle dirt tracks
I heard someone call my name and turned to see one of my
childhood friends reeling towards us. 'Hello,' she said smiling
happily, 'wait for me!' I left the others and walked to meet her.
She was very drunk, she told me, and asked me slowly if I was
going dancing. Yes, I said, we would go together. She clung
onto my arm and smiled with intoxicated eyes, squeezing my
fingers until they started to go numb. Stopping and swaying for
a moment, she carefully prised a can of beer out of her pocket
and offered it to me, watching almost soberly for my reaction.
I took a small swig of beer, thanked her, and handed it back
smiling. 'We are sisters,' she said with a look of contentment on
her face that I had not refused the drink, 'we will share.' She
swung the beer so that it frothed into the ground at our feet.
'You know,' she said with a pause to drink again, 'they all know
you –' she pointed at imaginary people walking the street – 'they
remember you. They keep asking, "Is that *Kaari-gnaa*?" but they
are too shy to come and say hello.'

A group was standing in the fine drizzle outside the community hall, every single one of the party swaying in individual
rhythms. My friend would not let me go, partly for her own
support but mostly to protect me from the numerous advances

that descended on me as soon as we neared the hall. Within just a few minutes I had been offered either sex or marriage, or both, from both Inughuits and Danes.

'If you marry me,' one young Danish worker breathed, catching my hand and raising it to his thin lips, 'I will give you three houses.' He swayed, towering over me, his eyes blinking quickly under blond eyelashes. I had passed the man on numerous occasions since my arrival in Qaanaaq and said hello, but this was the first time he had ever acknowledged my presence.

My friend was delighted with the whole situation and was introducing me to everyone as her little sister, and whispered hoarsely in my ear, 'I love you *so* much.' I hugged her tightly and wished that we could spend more time together so that I could find out who she really was; it was difficult to recognize her in her inebriation.

The two of us, now also joined by Robert, were starting to attract a large group of locals who until now had been too shy to say hello, and now, liberated with alcohol, were all desperate to share a few words in jumbled Greenlandic with a couple of obscure English words thrown in for good measure. 'Fuck you,' someone said cordially to me in greeting, shaking my hand and beaming wildly. Slowly, ploughing his way through the well-intentioned fray, my friend's husband headed towards us, grinning with good humour and open arms. Prising himself between his wife and me, he flung his arms around me in a tight embrace with his back to his wife. 'Kiss me!' he cried; I offered him my cheek. 'No, *kiss me*,' he demanded, puckering up and tightening his grip. '*Na-aa*,' I said frowning and pushing him away. His face suddenly darkened and he became more and more insistent, pressing himself against me and pushing his face into mine. I pushed him away violently, until three of the group finally managed to drag him off me. Robert didn't know what to do and stood behind me for moral support, rooted to the spot.

My girlfriend's face was concerned but she tried to make light of the situation, placating her husband and pulling at his arm to turn him away from the rest of us, but he caught sight of Robert and became enraged. Launching into a verbal attack, he turned and spat at Robert, stabbing the air with his dark hands: 'Fuck you, white man, FUCK YOU!' One of the small brothers who had been weeping over me earlier made a brave effort to hold him back, but he slipped on the gravel and lost his grip, and the husband lunged at Robert who was standing rigid with astonishment and confusion. Both my girlfriend and I jumped in front of him and braced ourselves against her husband's chest, pushing him back and trying to calm him down. He momentarily submitted to the hands of the concerned locals before wheeling round on his heels, pointing at Robert's bleached hair and then flying into a weird jumping drumming dance, as if he were possessed: 'Fucking white man, muther fucker.'

It was all pretty short-lived and the hunter had soon burnt himself out and allowed himself to be dragged away by his wife who looked back over her shoulder at me as she walked with him, a haunting look of embarrassment and something akin to fear shadowing her eyes. She grabbed Robert's hand as they left, saying, 'I am so sorry, he is really *drunk*,' then turned to me, kissed me and ran back to her husband.

Seeing the look of shock and discomfort on Robert's face I suggested we leave but Magdalene overheard me and insisted that we still go into the disco. 'My other son works there,' she said, dragging us both unwillingly towards the door; 'he has got us free tickets.' Her son nodded to us in welcome: 'Hi, I am Piuartoq.' He was a good-looking, self-contained boy who spoke reasonable English, and was mortified at his mother's vivaciousness: 'My mother is drunk,' he said flatly, shuffling his feet. 'I don't drink . . .' His words trailed off as Magdalene danced with abandonment. 'You are so embarrassing!' he said to her sternly, gesturing that he was going to take her beer and throw it far out into the tundra.

The disco was completely dark apart from a few cheap disco lights that cast shadows over the figures that were slumped on chairs around its perimeter and lit the few that twitched and gyrated on the dance floor. 'Dance!' Magdalene demanded, pulling us by the hands and swinging us into the centre of the room. 'Don't worry, my son will look after you!' she laughed as she lost herself in the discordant pop music. Robert was immediately pounced upon by a tall young Danish woman and quick as a flash an Inughuit man I had never seen before slipped his arm around my back and grabbed my bottom; I moved away sharply and Piuartoq immediately pushed the man out of the hall in disgust.

Through the darkness I could see that the young woman was still crawling over Robert as he tried his utmost to fend her off. 'I'm married!' he protested, his mouth over-exaggerating the words over the music.

'I don't care!' the woman cried out. 'I know somewhere we can go!' He peeled her off him with some difficulty and was hot on my heels as I made my way outside.

Someone tugged at my arm as I walked out of the hall and I turned to see that it was Suakunguak, Karen's younger cousin. I was taken aback that she should be in such a place. She looked up at me, her face filled with apprehension, gauging if I was drunk or not. I put my hand gently on her shoulder and guided her out of the hall but she pulled on my sleeve again. 'Where's Karen?' she asked with a desperate look. I hadn't seen her, and Suakunguak's face dropped.

'Are you OK?' I called to her in Greenlandic as she ran off; she turned and nodded briefly before disappearing.

Andy and Nuka were sitting together outside the entrance, laughing and listening wide-eyed as Robert told them of his encounters with the enraged hunter and then the impassioned woman. Around them a crowd of people, both Inughuit and Danish, hung in a sort of suspended animation, cloaked in a haze of booze. To one side a small group of young teenagers drank surreptitiously, and watching it all were children between the age of six and ten, probably waiting for their parents who were on the verge of passing out. I struggled with a knot in my throat as I watched them, wondering what deep psychological effect these weekly scenes were having on this fragile generation.

When we were living at Herbert Island there was a points-rationing system for alcohol (for the Danish Administration in Greenland as well as other visitors to the area): as a monthly allowance the inhabitants of the Thule district were allowed one bottle of spirits, two bottles of wine, or twenty bottles of beer per person. Invariably the favourite among the Eskimos was a bottle of whisky that they would polish off in a single alcohol-sodden weekend. Now there are no limits on the amount of booze the Inughuit of Qaanaaq can buy, although it is different in the smaller settlements. A few years ago the community of Siorapaluk voted to see who didn't want alcohol, and who needed it. There was only one vote more in favour of alcohol, so it was decided that there should be a no-alcohol period of one year. The trial was a resounding success. Because there was no drink in the village the hunters went out hunting more, the workers turned up at work every day, and most importantly, life at home for every family improved. The effect was so positive that social services had money to spare for the first time in their recorded history. Encouraged by this the no-alcohol policy has stayed put, although there is a worry that beer and wine will once again be sold in Siorapaluk.

Robert walked me back to Louisa's, and I joked that considering our last couple of experiences we probably both needed chaperoning home, but as I was still shaken and wide awake by the time we reached my door we turned and walked back down to the meteorological station to have a cup of camomile tea.

Joar had returned to their digs early and gratefully joined us; he too had had a bizarre evening and needed some company. 'I have never turned down so many women!' he said laughing nervously. Robert agreed heartily: 'I have turned down more sex in this one night than I have in my whole thirty years – from both sexes!'

Sounds of debauchery drifted through the open window. I have never heard so many fights or raised voices in such a contained area. There was a dark, unpredictable feeling in the atmosphere, and everyone was unsettled by it, including the dogs that were baying eerily in the distance. I had a theory that perhaps it was full moon.

A loud knock at the door made us all jump, and we all sat bolt upright at the kitchen table. 'The door isn't locked,' Robert whispered hoarsely. The rapping at the door continued, now quietly, but persistently. We sat in silence, ears straining as the front door slowly creaked open and hushed whispers mingled with the sound of footsteps hesitatingly shuffling down the corridor. Although it was probably nothing to be afraid of, the night had already given us some strange surprises and, as Robert pointed out, in a town where all the inhabitants, both men and women, had a full range of hunting weapons at hand, this was not to be taken too lightly. It was, on reflection, pure comedy. Both Robert and Joar froze, their eyes wide with fear and anticipation, barely breathing and not moving a muscle as the footsteps closed in on the kitchen door. They were clearly the footfall of women. The footsteps stopped just short of the door, with one of the women telling the other to leave. A rapid discussion in raised whispers ensued, with one obviously winning the argument, as one pair of footsteps left. All was quiet. The kitchen door was still shut and the pounding of the blood in my ears was almost unbearable. Slowly, the footsteps came towards us again and the door swung open enough for the woman to poke her head through. Seeing us all sitting there in silence was too much for her and she stood in the doorway looking utterly affronted with her hands on her hips before gesturing extravagantly to Joar that she needed to speak to him. Joar felt safety was in numbers and insisted that she could speak in front of us all. She needed to stay with Joar, she said bluntly, to protect him from the other woman – who, it turned out, was the same woman who had been coming on to Robert in the disco. The situation descended into utter farce. Joar finally managed to get rid of the woman telling her that he could look after himself, he was tired and was going to bed; but for over an hour we were imprisoned by the endless knocking, calling and pleading of the two women outside. The men were beside themselves, tiptoeing around and hiding as the sex-starved harpies tried to look through the windows. Neither of the men could walk me home until they left, and I had heard too many fights and experienced too much unwanted attention that night to walk home alone.

It took almost two hours for the coast to clear, and by the time Robert escorted me back to Louisa's the town was a picture of serenity and peacefulness. It was hard to believe that all that we had experienced had not been a very peculiar dream. We walked, talking in low whispers about our bizarre evening.

'Why are we whispering?' I asked.

'So we don't get lynched,' he replied, looking over his shoulder.

We walked, still whispering, through the centre of town at 4 a.m., in broad daylight, with no darkness for potential over-amorous attackers to hide in, yet both of us were still on edge. 'Run, and don't look back!' I jokingly cried out to Robert just as a fight broke out between three people in the house next door. Loud music simultaneously broke out at various houses across town.

I went to sleep listening to cries and screams and breaking crockery.

The following morning I came downstairs to penetrating looks from Louisa and Hans. They had assumed that I would have a terrible hangover and Louisa had a big sister's 'I'm disappointed in you' look on her face until I finally managed to convince them that I hadn't been drunk like the other disco patrons. Louisa finally said: 'The whole town is ill, in their soul.' Hans added solemnly, 'For the whole weekend.' Louisa took me to the kitchen window and pointed at a house nearby where there had been a big fight. She said they had had to call the police. I thought of Mads Iversen and his new posting to this place. I hoped that the events of the last night weren't repeated every weekend. Again I wondered if it was full moon, or maybe a strange kind of madness brought on by the unrelenting light.

I felt safe and protected being in the house with Louisa and Hans, and was thankful that they weren't drinkers. I was drained. The experience of the last couple of days had taken its toll and I found myself encountering a desperate need to hold onto the safe and perfect ideal of our first time here and my Thule family.

Robert and Andy called by to invite me for dinner which broke the mood briefly, but later when I joined them at the meteorological station it turned out that we were all still swimming in the aftermath of the night before. Andy's usual buoyant self was clouded and down: he had returned to Jacobena's after the disco, he explained, and had discovered that every single person there had had a family member commit suicide; the evening had ended in them all weeping uncontrollably. We sat in a subdued mood, finally submitting to the silence that nagged at our consciences, all with eyes troubled by our individual thoughts.

I needed some fresh air after our meal and Joar decided to come with me for a walk to the beach as he had been taking refuge inside all day for fear of seeing the women who had been stalking him the night before. The tide was out and the town was quiet with just a couple of people walking among the rocks and seaweed-filled puddles.

Far from the town, almost at the rubbish dump we saw a small family cutting up the carcass of a small narwhal on the beach. We waved a cheery hello but we were greeted with suspicion, the adults muttering to each other in low voices before carrying on with their task. Two of the children ran up to within a few feet of us and stood rooted to the spot, not knowing whether to approach or not. It was a strange and unusual scene. The family were acting as if they had been caught doing something illegal and their dark looks were something I hadn't experienced in the community before. Their clothes were ragged and dirty, the children had strange temperaments and lopsided faces that gave a hint of deformity, and they huddled together in defiant protection of one another.

'Things have changed,' Joar said sadly. 'Not so long ago it was customary to invite passers-by to share in some food.' And he was right. It was engrained in the Inughuit psyche always to share one's catch, even if it is just the offer of a sliver of mattak to a stranger.

We passed the family again as we turned on our heels back to town. This time the adults didn't even bother to raise their eyes, and instead continued to gorge on the animal they had just slaughtered. The children again came running towards us, but still keeping a distance, with their faces and hands smeared in fresh blood.

Still needing to walk off my emotional discomfort, and with both of us enjoying our conversation, our feet took us far out in the opposite direction towards the cemetery. Joar talked a little about his project, and aired some concerns that had obviously been on his mind for a while. He was bothered that asking the Inughuit a wave of questions about their feelings might cause some people to look too deeply into themselves, and really question their state of happiness. He was worried that for a tribe of people who find it easier to suppress their feelings this soul-searching could tip the balance.

'What if,' he asked himself aloud, 'these questions cause people to find that they actually have no happiness?' He stopped in his tracks. 'What if this research causes more people to commit suicide?'

I had no answer, and we walked for some time in silence, frightened at the question. Silently I wondered both how he could get these people to define the level of their feelings (with which they were probably unfamiliar) with a few tick boxes, and how he and his other researchers could expect to gather the true nature of the Inughuit from questionnaires that asked things beyond the experience of the people they targeted. Long before we arrived in Thule, anthropologists had already been in the area studying all aspects of the local culture, and since then there have been a bewildering number of studies, many of which judged the people with the same questionnaires. My mother talked to a female anthropologist while we were here, and in the course of conversation Mum mentioned that she thought her friend Maria extremely intelligent; the woman retorted, 'What tests have you done on her?' Mum was appalled.

I also remember Dad being outraged by a similar study that was being conducted when we were in Thule in the early 1970s where one such question was: 'Who is your role model?' If the researchers had spent just a little time with the Eskimos before bombarding them with questions they would have immediately realized that their social structure was far removed from European leader–follower mentality. The Eskimos didn't understand the questions, and were bothered by them; they began to feel inferior because they felt that they *should* have a role model, whatever that was, and they were anxious not to offend the visitor by seeming churlish and not answering the question. It was a problem that was discussed behind closed doors. My parents were asked quietly, what did these *kadlunas* want from them, and what did the questions *mean*?

Joar fully understood the limitations of what he was doing but insisted that although they had used the same questionnaires for tribes in completely different areas of the world, they had learnt to adjust them to fit the temperament of the people they were interviewing. He went on to say that the data he had collected so far suggested that overall the Inughuit are extremely content with their lives, but he was confused because that conclusion didn't match with the suicide/abuse/alcoholism statistics, and had to admit that it was easy to misinterpret an Inughuit's level of contentment and balance. As an example he told me of an interview he had had through an interpreter a few days previously.

'The man was a great hunter, and seemed the perfect picture of contentment. He seemed at one with life, and yet the interpreter told me afterwards that the man had been considering ending it all, and didn't think that he could go on.' Joar was completely baffled by the experience. 'What was so strange was that the man had been smiling at me all through the interview. He looked like a happy man. I think maybe he was just making sure that I felt welcome in his house.'

15. Looking South

Children were playing boules in the dirt track as I strolled through the town. The children had no idea how to play the game properly, but were just enjoying throwing the smooth shiny balls up the hill, and cooing with delight as they rolled gleaming back towards them. One boy had obviously just been watching the European athletics championships on TV and was imitating the shot putt, causing mortal danger to his friends. Another had built a pyramid out of the sandy soil and was crowning it with his ball.

A jeep came rumbling down the hill and smartly dodged the scattered balls, the ill-tempered *kadluna* swearing silently at the children behind closed windows. Someone called my name over the roar of the engine; it was a visiting Danish ornithologist I had met a few times around Qaanaaq: 'Someone has caught a large narwhal!' he cried with enthusiasm. 'Go, see, it is on the beach.'

Until now I had only seen the narwhal alive in the distance, or in pieces up close, but here the majestic creature lay whole and graceful, lapped affectionately by small waves. Children, drawn as always to a spectacle, were all over the narwhal, splashing in the crimson water in their wellies; patting and slapping the side of the animal, feeling the firm texture of the skin and sticking their fingers into its fresh wounds. It was a big event. The narwhal was large and a great prize. People crowded on the lip of the hill overlooking the beach and the entire family of the hunter was rounded up to help.

Piuartoq looked fresh-faced as he slithered down the hill, smiling broadly as he walked confidently down the beach towards the narwhal. He looked transformed from the night before, relieved of his duties to keep the disco in order. Magdalene surfaced with a smile and came towards me with excitement, looking just as fresh as her son. We stood together marvelling at the size of the animal. Three generations of the hunter's family soon followed, with faces set with concentration, sharpening large knives and walking in a haphazard semicircle towards the beached narwhal with an air of determination.

In a couple of minutes they had surrounded the narwhal, and stood momentarily in silence, taking in the scene as if they were sending a 'thank you' to the animal, before congratulating the hunter who had caught it – Piuartoq's uncle – and getting down to carving up the meat. According to custom, the hunter who first harpooned the narwhal makes the first incision, and has the right to the tastiest and largest portions of the meat.

Quite often it is not just one hunter who brings a narwhal to the beach – the carcass is heavy and cumbersome, so if there are several kayaks in the water when a narwhal has been harpooned, the other hunters will quickly skim their kayaks towards the kill to help bring the animal in. It serves them all to help one another as the meat is shared between any hunter who has harpooned the animal or helped bring it to shore.

Deftly, and with great precision, the hunter who had caught the narwhal slit it from throat to tail and then the other men of the family joined him, including Piuartoq's grandfather, who wheezed and rolled his way around the whale, bent double with the weight of his years, with his hair carefully parted in a greying sweep of a fringe. No time and no meat or blubber was wasted. Piuartoq laid out a large blue tarpaulin on the beach on which the meat was to be piled, his baseball cap bobbing up and down as he worked alongside his family. It was the first time that I had seen anyone of his age in Qaanaaq being involved so whole-heartedly in the hunting way of life. I wondered if he would become a hunter like all the other men of his family before him. Magdalene parked two wheelbarrows alongside the narwhal and quickly helped her ageing father pick up a large piece of mattak.

The hunters were so familiar with the way the meat and blubber should be cut that the whole process was done in silence, each man honed in the skill of division and butchery. It was believed not so long ago that if a hunter was slightly off the mark when he divided up the carcass of an animal, it was evidence that he had lied that same day. Those crowded around him would say that he was a man who by failing to speak the truth had wasted his thoughts, and had thereby forgotten that all animals are created with joints, which serve to divide them.

The women scurried around the hunters, taking the steaming geometric slabs of meat off the men and carefully piling them in sections on the tarpaulin. It was a remarkably quick process. The mattak was cut into even rectangular strips, turned over, and the excess fat cut off in a flourish before being loaded into the wheelbarrows, which were continuously wheeled back and forth from large wooden crates out of the tide's reach. The old couple were just as busy as everyone else, working in a steady, methodical rhythm, carving the meat, and then taking it in turns to scramble up the steep slope to their rickety meat rack, on which they carefully hung some choice cuts of the meat and the guts, which looked like long lumpy sausages, well out of reach of the dogs where they could dry out.

I felt quite redundant standing on the periphery of all the activity, and remembered Mum telling me the story of when a couple of walrus had been caught by the hunters from Herbert Island. Feeling somewhat like a spare limb she asked Avatak if she could help them. 'Yes,' he replied, and much to the merriment of the gathered crowd, handed her the bloodied penis of the walrus, 'you can clean that!'

Blood streaked across the beach as soon as the inner cavities of the whale were opened up. Intestines floated in lakes of dark scarlet, swirling as if in a current as the carcass rocked with the movement of the knives. The sad wise eye of the narwhal looked glazed now, and I walked a distance away, feeling slightly nauseous from the whole experience.

Before I got too far away I was startled by an old man who was waddling towards me, hollering. He smiled broadly as he called out, and I turned to make sure that it was me he was calling. He laughed thinking that I was fooling around and offered his hand bearing a few small morsels of the fresh mattak, perfectly prepared, for me to eat. It would have been unthinkable to refuse and I accepted gratefully; it was a generous gesture. He watched as I put the mattak in my mouth, and waited for my response: '*Mammaktoq!*' I mumbled with my mouth full. He chuckled, pounded me on the back and walked back slowly to the carnage.

Piuartoq joined me, holding his bloody hands away from the sides of his new hip-hop trousers: 'My grandfather used to teach me to hunt when I was a child,' he told me as we watched the scene. 'My grandfather even took me out several times last summer to teach me how to kayak, but I was scared out there!' Piuartoq laughed, and it was the same story with other hunting skills. 'I don't want to be a hunter, it is too hard!' He smiled broadly, his peroxide blond hair glinting in the sunlight.

I asked him what his plans were for the future if he didn't want to become a hunter. 'I am going to go school in Denmark,' he answered, adding quickly that he was going to come back to live in Qaanaaq when he had finished his studies. I was surprised. Piuartoq was an intelligent and vibrant young man and I questioned what prospects he might have in Qaanaaq, but he was unfazed. His family were in Qaanaaq and playing football, making rock music with his band and organizing the youth club were enough to keep him entertained. 'I have been making some clubs in Qaanaaq and Upernavik, and that is what I want to do. I will have to get a job, but the children are so important, they need somewhere to have fun. I love football, and I want to teach that to young children too.' He had to come back here, he continued, because, 'this place is beautiful – look! This is why so many people come back. And because it is so quiet. The big city vroom vroom is not so good for me.'

Piuartoq's grandparents took a rest from the hard work and joined us as we watched one of the hunters saw off the narwhal head. Piuartoq's great-grandmother had come over with the migration led by the visions of Kritlaq the angákoq, and the old couple were proud of their heritage; they were the descendants of the life-blood that evolved into the Thule people. Piuartoq's grandfather, Orle, was born near Etah, when people still lived that far north. My mind rewound to hazy fantasies of the ancient people who lived in a world we can only dream about, where they truly lived among the spirits of the animals, and of nature itself.

'There are fewer hunters now,' Orle said slowly as Piuartoq translated, 'and many of the hunters in Qaanaaq just get drunk, and then they cannot hunt.' Piuartoq added: 'It is mainly because it is a little town. There are so many people that are drunk here.' His grandfather continued: 'In places like Siorapaluk or Qeqertat there are still some good hunters though.'

I asked if hunters still travelled to Canada by dog-sledge to hunt, and he and Piuartoq said yes, but not so many as before. 'I cannot go to Canada now,' the old man said, and wheezed again. He was getting too old for big trips like that, Piuartoq said; now he was just happy to fish in the fjord. Orle looked at me for a moment as if he had only just seen me for the first time. 'I can see your father in your face,' he told me, patting his cheeks and laughing. His hands flashed over the horizons as he spoke. I asked Piuartoq what he was saying, and Piuartoq just smiled and said, 'He remembers your father very well.' Orle was one of the many hunters that Dad had met on his long hunting trips in the district, and the two of them had smoked their pipes and drunk tea together on the ice many times.

A group of Danish men had gradually congregated around the carcass, nodding and laughing with Mads Iversen who was now off duty. He noticed me and came over to talk. He looked grey with exhaustion.

'I only had two hours' sleep,' he said, adding drolly: 'It was a busy Friday night.' He introduced me to the other men who were from an environmental organization, commissioned by the government. They were studying in particular the migration patterns and numbers of narwhal pods around the coast of Greenland; the studies were conducted by taking aerial photographs of the waters, then running them through various computer programs to count how many narwhal were in each pod. It was the first time that they had seen the hunters preparing the meat of a narwhal, and it had opened their eyes considerably.

'It is amazing how economical they are with the way that they handle the narwhal,' one of the men said to me in amazement. 'There is nothing left!'

We looked around us; the inedible excess fat from the blubber was the only waste from the hunt. The attitude of the researchers towards the hunters of Greenland had until that moment been pretty negative, their judgement tainted by the 'big town' Greenlanders who seemed to have, in their eyes at least, little respect for the environment. But this was the first time that they had spent any time in a High Arctic settlement, and they were impressed by the skill of the 'real' hunters. Here they could see for themselves that the narwhal had been caught by harpoon and kayak, not by motorboat and rifle, and watching the skill and proficiency of the hunters in preparing their catch, they had to admit that they needed to take a different view of the local hunting of narwhal.

I asked one of the researchers if numbers of narwhal were in decline, but he found it difficult to answer as their research had not yet been compiled. But what he could tell me, he said quietly, not taking his eyes off the hunters, was that he had had a suspicion before coming to Qaanaaq that the hunters were killing more than they needed. He paused, transfixed as one of the hunters started removing the tusk from the narwhal head. 'But I have to admit that I think my view on that has just been changed.'

★

It was 5.20 a.m. and I was restless with thoughts of my imminent departure. The family's body clock was completely out of whack: Karen was just crawling into bed, Louisa was noisily making breakfast downstairs and Hans was snoring loudly next door. I was completely tangled up in my thin duvet because I had been dreaming of fighting for the rights of lost tribes all night. Over and over again the tribes were being betrayed, and I continually wrestled the faceless beings that were destroying them. I lay completely motionless, exhausted. The air was still and my muscles were knotted, as if I were in a vacuum.

It was my last day, and I spent hours visiting different houses to say my farewells, but no one was home. Baali, Kristian, Magda, Gideon and Ilannguak had all gone off hunting at a moment's notice, Arquenguak and Tukúmek had taken the priest to the funeral of the boy who had eaten the apple at another settlement; Uusaqqak was in Quebec, Najannuaq, Edo and Savfak were nowhere to be found and Louisa and Hans had gone to bed early. Dispirited, I packed my bags and crawled into my small bunk for the last time under Britney's shadow. A shaft of light flickered on the wall as the baby-doll pink curtains fluttered in the cool breeze. The sound reminded me of bird wings in flight and I thought of the retired Danish ornithologist I had met at the beginning of my trip. Sven and I had found in each other a common thread of experience: he had spent a couple of years in the area as a young man and his return trip was a dream that he had nurtured for decades. 'There is a saying in Denmark,' he had mused, 'that is difficult to translate into English but essentially translates as: "walking the grass you have walked before", meaning that it is necessary sometimes to go back to places that have been special for you. I think you know what I mean quite well.' Sven had wanted to bring his wife with him, but she didn't like the cold, and besides it was his memories that they would be chasing after, not hers. It had been unfortunate, yet inevitable, that the reality of modern Qaanaaq didn't match up to his dream.

There was only one old hunter left whom he had known from his time there and he was too old to travel now.

'I have known four generations of some of the families here,' he had said, looking over the coloured houses, 'but the sons have no interest in taking out an old man, and the children are just so spoilt. They are more interested in TV,' he had said mournfully. 'I feel very sad here now.' His voice trailed off, and his eyes had filled gently with emotion. 'There are no great characters in the district anymore. No Wally Herbert or Jean Malaurie, or the people I used to work with.' He vowed that he would never return to Qaanaaq again. But he had whispered to me with the insistence of the elderly who feel they have some great wisdom to impart: 'Even if the revisiting isn't what you hoped it would be, it makes those memories from before even more precious.'

I sat outside Kangerlussuaq airport in a daze, already thrown by culture shock. I had been in Thule for two months and even though I had mostly stayed in modern Qaanaaq, I was unprepared for the comparatively bustling civilization of southern Green-land. Opposite me a buxom Danish woman with cropped blonde hair looked at me suspiciously, nursing her electric blue sealskin handbag and clutching a thick cigar in puffy fingers, encasing me in a wreath of stale smoke. I was in the realms of the wealthy Danish residents and the outdoor-enthusiast tourists, who expected everything to be done for them. How different it was further south from Thule.

I had left Qaanaaq in no haze of emotional turmoil. Only Louisa shed a few tears, but we had agreed that we would not agonize over this goodbye. I had enjoyed the Arctic summer in Thule, and I would be returning within six months to experience the ice of early spring. But in Kangerlussuaq I once again found myself in limbo, equidistant between the two places I called home, and lost in some strange void of emotions – I had no idea of how I felt. I wandered out to the signpost where I had gained some inspiration when I was heading north, but it gave me nothing. I felt only the chill of the wind plucking my bare hands and head. I plunged my hands into my fleece – my gloves were packed and being loaded onto the plane bound for Copenhagen – and felt something in the bottom of my pocket. I pulled out a small envelope that had been fashioned out of a piece of paper torn out of an old schoolbook. On the top was written KARI in bold letters. Inside the paper was a small bone pendant crafted into the shape of Greenland, strung on a leather thong. I spread the paper out over a nearby bench, and in the rough handwriting I read: 'Dear Kari. Thank you. I love you. Karen.'

I laughed out loud. After all the sleepless nights and dark looks my young room-mate had finally thawed. The character of the Inughuit was truly complex, and I could not wait to return.

PART TWO

Return

'To the desert go prophets and hermits; through deserts go pilgrims and exiles. Here the leaders of the great religions have sought the therapeutic and spiritual values of retreat, not to escape but to find reality.'

Paul Shepard, *Man in the Landscape:*
A Historic View of the Esthetics of Nature

16. Iceward Bound

Light poured in from the windows of the 747 as I once again flew out of Copenhagen and headed back towards Thule. It had been six months since my summer in Greenland and I was on my way home again, this time in search of snow.

I studied my Inuktun dictionary and found myself looking at a section dedicated to different forms of ice and snow: *nilak* – freshwater ice, *hiku* – ice on the sea, *kaniq* – rime frost, *hikuaq* – thin ice, *ilu* – ice on the inside of a window or tent, *hikuuharhiit* – pack ice, *hikuliaq* – new ice, *manirak* – smooth expanse of ice, *maniillat* – hummocky ice, *kassut* – floating ice, *qainnguq* – solid ice attached to the shore, *qaniit* – falling snow, *matsak* – wet snow, *agiuppiniq* – snowdrift, *qimiarhuk* – snowdrift against an iceberg . . . the list seemed endless.

The turbulence of pre-expedition chaos had left me reeling – funds had fallen through ten days before departure, and the prospect of a film to accompany the book tripped me up and pushed my departure date further and further down the calendar. Small worries nagged at my dreams and dragged me mid-sleep from my bed to find a notebook and scrawl incoherent messages to myself. But seeing the light of the ice once again I found myself slipping away from the melodrama of the past few weeks and back into this remarkable world.

This journey was going to be very different in many ways. Seasonally it was early spring rather than late summer, which meant that I was heading towards temperatures that would be between −15°C and −35°C; and this time I had my partner Laurence with me to experience, just as my parents had, what filming was like in the extreme north.

As we headed north the air changed and crystallized. At

Kangerlussuaq flurries of invisible ice tickled our throats and made the passengers wince as they gripped the railings of the metal steps with their bare hands and felt their skin burn with cold as they descended to the frosty tarmac. A scrolling LED display inside the airport said the temperature was −6°C. Further north at Ilulissat − where I had arranged a two-day stay in order to acclimatize to the dramatic temperature change − the temperature was down to −12°C and we still had several hundred miles northwards to travel before we reached Qaanaaq.

An impenetrable bank of cloud hovered just above sea level as we arrived in Ilulissat, and almost immediately it took hold of the town. The blue-fissured cliffs of the icebergs choking the Ice Fjord which had been in sharp relief just half an hour previously were now almost translucent, bathed in the softest hues of pale grey and cream and shifting in the freezing fog like ghostly mammoths of the Ice Age. The constant crooning of huskies tethered near the mouth of the fjord drifted with the low cloud as they sang to each other over the rattling of their chains; Laurence shuddered at their disembodied voices, but I found their harmony strangely comforting and fell into an easy sleep.

I woke as the fingers of the Arctic breeze found their way through the bedroom window. A small pile of snow had silently crept in during the night and was softly piling up on the window-sill. The nearby rock face was almost invisible through the drifting snow of the light blizzard. It was a chilly welcome back to the Arctic. The huskies below the window were now silent, curled up in tight balls against the snow, sleeping with their noses tucked under their tails with small snow drifts curling around their backs. In tantalizing moments the rock face would reappear, its scarred face pockmarked and lined with the driving snow, looking as monochrome and perfectly cross-hatched as a copper-plate etching. Snow and ice had drained colour from the world.

The small Dash 7 was already almost filled with supplies and post bound for Qaanaaq, with only eight seats for passengers at the rear of the aircraft, and two double seats at the front. Olive-green army-issue tarpaulins covered the mysterious cargo strapped to the vacant seats. At the very back of the plane sat an elderly Inughuit couple wearing wary expressions at this unfamiliar form of transport. The skin of the old man's face was honey-coloured beneath an extravagant beard with no moustache or sideburns; he looked like an ancient Japanese master of the Tao. His wife perched beside him, her small bright eyes flickering nervously. In her lap she nursed a pair of sealskin mittens trimmed with tufts of polar bear fur.

Laurence and I kept our faces pressed up against the window as we flew the final leg back to Thule, and the further north we flew so the black pools of water shrank and became thin dark ribbons against a world dominated by whiteness. With each mile the crevasses grew fewer and the stranded icebergs looked fused to the vast icescape surrounding them. The hostess delicately placed an in-flight magazine on our laps as a makeshift table and handed each of us a plastic box containing some rare meat and a potato salad drowned in mayonnaise. 'Welcome to Greenland,' Laurence muttered grimly as he unwrapped a bloody wrapper from the meat, which dripped blood on the floor and oozed unappetizingly on the lid of his lunchbox.

Qaanaaq arrived quickly. Herbert Island lay waiting on my left, wreathed in soft folds of low cloud. Trails of dog-sledges swept across the ice connecting my childhood home with the new town of Qaanaaq. The fine pattern of tracks appeared like a frosted spider's web in negative. A flurry of excitement rose in my chest as I pictured us travelling by dog-sledge back to Qeqertassuaq.

I had none of the worries on returning to Qaanaaq that had troubled me when I visited it the previous summer, and there was no great emotional welcome this time, but Hans Jensen from the tiny hotel was waiting to pick us up with open arms and a ready smile. He was one of the few members of the community who had a vehicle, and who was not out on the ice hunting.

The frozen fjord stretched into the distance – blue and grey-white with elephantine icebergs frozen fast ever since the first ice formed four months before. Dappled light fell over the scene, gliding smoothly over the frozen world. My spirit soared at the staggering beauty of it all.

The town was strangely quiet as we drove on the frozen track past the smouldering rubbish tip and into the northern part of Qaanaaq. There were few teams of dogs tethered in the town, and the land seemed utterly devoid of people. It was perfect hunting weather.

Qaanaaq looked almost pristine in its fresh winter coat. Although there hadn't been any snowfall in the last couple of weeks, there had been a sufficient dump of snow a month before, which in places had been sculpted into snow dunes that had buried trucks and parts of houses. As we neared the hotel Hans pointed to a fleck of red paint under an enormous pile of snow. 'Look, there's my other truck!' he chortled to himself and shook his head in amusement. 'We had a big storm at the beginning of February, and we lost half the cars in Qaanaaq! It is a good job that I didn't park this one in the same place or we would have had to find some dogs to bring you back from the airport.'

The hunters of Qaanaaq and their wives had been busy. Meat racks dotted around town bore up dark carcasses on their rickety legs, and numerous sealskins were stretched as tight as drum-skins on simple wooden frames outside several brightly painted houses. In the distance two yellow trucks collected ice from icebergs to melt for the town's supply of water. Those houses that did not have running water had boulders of freshwater ice outside their front doors, well away from where the hunters tethered their dogs so that the ice would not be spoiled.

Immediately Laurence and I made our way down the icy slope in front of the hotel to Baali's house. Puppies tumbled towards us as we approached, thick with coarse fur and rolls of puppy fat. Knocking quietly, I opened the front door to the amazed faces of Kristian and Little Tekummeq, who promptly squealed and almost knocked me over with a bear hug before running back inside to telephone someone, excitedly babbling that I had returned. Kristian grinned broadly and gathered me up in a tight hug before pointing to his freshly shaved head. He laughed at himself and urged us inside. As he turned I could see patches of bare skin where he had shaved too closely.

Within minutes Baali, Magda and Edo had descended on the house, holding their hearts as they gasped for breath after running to greet us. We fell onto the sofa laughing, trying to catch up on news while they looked Laurence over, intrigued by the man I had brought with me, and trying to pronounce his name. 'Just call me Lozza,' Laurence volunteered. 'Rozza!' they all repeated with enthusiasm.

There were so many things we wanted to say, albeit in basic language. We pored over pictures from my trip in the summer and the twins argued over which one of them was which in the photographs, then Magda told me again about the photographs that Edo had taken of their mother when she died. Baali went to a cupboard and pulled out a set of three macabre close-up photographs of Maria's face immobilized in death. They gazed at the photographs with no emotion, and then quickly changed the subject and told me that Ilannguak was out hunting, and that he and his companions had caught a couple of polar bears and several caribou. The girls could not wait for him to return. Ilannguak had been away for nearly two months, Magda said, and they missed him very much. They were so worried about him that sometimes they cried at night.

Baali had been quiet for some time studying a handful of typewritten notes that I had printed out to help with my Greenlandic. She looked up and smiled and rooted around in drawers for a pencil and slowly put together a sentence in English beside the Greenlandic. We sat expectantly watching her until she produced the paper with a flourish. It said: 'We are going dog-sledging on Saturday.' 'Rozza' and I were invited to join them.

★

We crossed the rolling gateway of the tide crack – a chaotic ridge of blue-grey boulders that define where the sea ice struggles to grip onto the land – and walked out on the ice itself, knowing that with each few steps the water below us was plunging deeper. The track in front was strewn with the scattered lumps of freshwater ice that had fallen from the 'ice truck', and they gleamed as the sun caught them. It looked as though we were walking on a road of rough-hewn diamonds. The snow too was not to be outdone and glittered with minute spectra of colour, shimmering with light. I turned to see my excitement reflected in Laurence's eyes. Together we felt the ice creak underfoot. He murmured almost imperceptibly, as if he was afraid that his voice could crack the frozen carpet: 'This is . . . unbelievable . . .'

Children played far out on the ice, cycling or running on the pale-blue crystal road past endless teams of dogs tethered to ice darkly stained with frozen excrement towards a large area that had been cleared of snow and polished into two skating rinks. The sound of their chatter drifted towards us on the chilling breath of the ice. The children were in their element, sharing bicycles and ice-skates – no matter how big or small the boots might be for them – weaving in and out of one another dressed in a wide range of ski outfits. None of them wore furs in the −17°C temperature. The fallers quickly picked themselves up, casually nursing bruised knees and elbows and launching themselves out on the ice again. At the first sight of new visitors they sped towards us, pulling on our clothes and calling for our attention as they spun off happily again, the older children picking the little ones up and skidding with them across the ice and back. The water beneath the two-metre-thick ice on which they skated was a thousand metres deep.

Beyond the children gargantuan icebergs rose out of the ice, one of which was perhaps four or five times the size of Qaanaaq and probably weighed as much as a million tons; it had broken free of a nearby glacier in the late summer and had ground to a halt on the floor of the fjord before the ice had frozen around it and held it captive. The area around the foot of the iceberg was treacherous; the iceberg, being so heavy, did not move with the slight ebb and flow of the tides, but the ice around it did, causing it to weaken and crack – you have to be extremely careful and wise to the nature of ice to be able to walk right up to an iceberg even if it looks as though it is fused solid. The roar of diesel engines was amplified over the frozen waters as a large digger and the ice-collecting truck buzzed around an iceberg. Only the Inughuit would know which icebergs they could drive up to without disappearing through the ice.

After a couple of hours of being on the ice Laurence and I wandered back towards our new home – a shabby hut with no running water that reeked of kerosene and at one time was known to be the local knocking shop – past a large modern yellow building that nestled between the small rickety huts of the 1950s. Urgent cries called us towards the entrance of the warehouse and as Baali waved from the open door Naduk and Little Tekummeq came racing towards us and tugged on our sleeves to follow them inside.

Kristian and his childhood friend Avatannguak looked up with ruddy faces and beckoned us jovially towards the sledge that they were making in the large carpentry workshop. Scattered around were other half-completed sledges and basic woodworking tools. The men had been working hard and the sledge was almost in its final stages. Laurence watched fascinated as Avatannguak masterfully lashed the slats of the sledge platform to the deep runners with strong nylon cord, the man's face turning puce as he tensed his arms and pulled each individual loop taut – lashing the various joints together rather than using nails or pegs gives elasticity to the sledge over rough terrain.

Avatannguak's face gleamed with good humour as he noticed Laurence's eager interest. '*Agiri!* Come, come!' He moved to one side and handed the rope to Laurence before carefully showing him how to bind the sledge pieces together. Laurence was a quick learner and in no time had picked up the technique, but the speed in which he lashed the wood together had Avatannguak pounding him on the back. The men laughed: there was no sense of urgency, they said; take more time and the knots would be stronger. Laurence finally handed the job back to Avatannguak and as he turned to pick up his camera the hunter surreptitiously scrutinized his work – if the knot was not good enough he would have to redo it for safety's sake. He nodded in surprise. It wasn't at all bad for a beginner. He turned to Laurence with a flash of white teeth and shook his hand. '*Pidluarit!* Congratulations!' he said laughing and gave him a thumbs-up: 'Verry good!' he exclaimed in English and moved to the next slat of the platform.

Before wood was brought to the area from the whaling ships and various expeditionary parties, the Thule hunters had to be rather more ingenious with their use of available materials. Dog-sledges were constructed from pieces of bone lashed together with thongs made from the skin of a bearded seal, and the runners were often made from whale rib or narwhal tusk, then covered with strips of hide or sealskin (with the fur facing in the right direction), or even fish laid head to tail. The fish or the hide was frozen to the runners and more ice formed over the top; water was applied thinly with a piece of fur, and as it froze the ice was painstakingly built up layer upon layer, until there was a thick even coating of ice the full length of a runner. By the time we came to live in the area the runners were mostly made of steel, but the runners were narrow and needed constant maintenance. Narrow runners were useless in thick snow, so almost all the hunters carried a supply of thick pads torn from babies' nappies, which they would freeze to the existing runners to increase their width. Like their ancestors, the hunters applied layers of ice over the padded runners and then finally smoothed the ice down perfectly with a wood plane.

These days the sledges use more modern materials: imported wood for the frame and platform, durable plastic for their runners, and nylon cord to bind them together, but the design of the sledge in the Thule district is still the same as it has been for centuries.

The icy breeze burnt our faces and droplets of moisture quickly froze on the fur trimming around our hoods, weighing down the delicate strands of dog and wolf fur with frosted beads and freezing our nostril hairs until they were brittle and spiky. I cried out with excitement as we shot over the ice and immediately felt the lining of my lungs freeze. Kristian and Laurence chuckled like schoolboys. Baali and I clutched onto each other with our cheeks frozen into wide grins. Beneath the hard cobalt blue sky Kristian's team of twelve huskies fanned out on their twenty-foot-long traces, tails held proud and purple-pink tongues lolling to one side.

We were speeding across a well-used dog-sledging highway and the ice was hard and rutted beneath us from a season of sledge travel between Qaanaaq and the smaller settlements further down the fjord. In the distance other parties of hunters and their families were dotted over the ice, fishing, sledging or meeting for a brew of tea or coffee in the white wilderness.

Kristian pointed to a small hut sitting on the ice in the distance. 'My hut!' he exclaimed. The dogs knew where they were going and echoed our excitement as they tore across the ice towards the wooden box, before skidding to an obedient halt directly outside it with their eyes blazing and tails wagging. There was no need to secure their traces to the ice; the dogs quickly settled down, curling up into tight balls with their noses under their tails and watching our movements closely over their thick brushes of fur. They would only run off if they caught the scent of a polar bear.

Kristian's little blue hut sat isolated on its runners in the middle of the fjord surrounded only by vistas of ice; he had built the hut in Qaanaaq with Avatannguak, and had pulled the little house out to this perfect spot with the dog team the two friends shared. To one side of the hut stood an enormous fisherman's reel, with a handle either side of a large bobbin that must have had several hundred metres of rope wrapped around it; on the other the snow had been cleared to form an elegant arc of smooth ice where Naduk and Little Tekummeq could skate.

In no time Baali had lit the small Primus stove in the tiny hut and Kristian immediately started to chip away at the one-metre-thick ice nearby with a heavy iron lance. It was strenuous work and we all took it in turns to excavate the hole or to shovel the freed chunks of ice to one side. After forty minutes a half-metre-wide hole was clear of ice and we retired to the hut to warm up and to prepare the bait for fishing.

From under the sleeping platform Kristian pulled out a small cardboard box, which was filled with coils of green nylon string connected to carefully ordered rows of small fishing hooks that bristled around the top. Kristian hummed happily and produced a plastic bag of bait – tiny strips of fish – and showed me how to thread the bait so that it would not fall off the hook. Eighty baited hooks later we returned to the hole outside. Kristian fastened one end of the baited fishing line to the end of the rope from the fisherman's reel, secured the baited end to a large rectangular metal plate, and dropped the weighted line into the hole. Rapidly the twine spun out and Kristian quickly separated the hooks as the pieces of bait plopped into the gelatinous water.

By the time we had finished the hole and sunk the lines I was rigid with cold, and gratefully beat a retreat to the little hut with the others close behind. 'I should have built the hut with a hole in the floor so I could fish without getting cold!' Kristian muttered, rubbing his hands vigorously together. I laughed, teeth chattering and distributed steaming pot noodles to everyone.

'Maybe in two hours we will have some fish!' Kristian said grinning, picking up the small plastic clock off a ledge in the hut and willing the hands to go round faster. He smacked his lips, turned on the radio and danced in his seat, asking Baali and me if we wanted to join him in a polka. Baali smiled and changed the radio station to a local frequency that was broadcasting the meetings taking place in Qaanaaq with the delegates from Nuuk. Earlier, as we had been chipping away at the ice, a plane had flown overhead. We had stopped what we were doing to watch the shadow of the silver bird streak over the ice, and had squinted in silence as the plane had arced towards Qaanaaq. I was surprised as there were no planes scheduled to land that day. But now, over offerings of dried prawns and Danish pastries, Kristian and Baali were eager to talk about what was happening.

In 1968 a B-52 bomber carrying four thermonuclear bombs crashed in the waters just outside the American airbase, contaminating the local area with radioactive material. Local hunters were called in to help with the clean-up operation, including Kristian's father. Kristian's face clouded as he told the story: many hunters were called to the area, he said, because the Americans and the Danes did not want to get involved, and all those hunters became crippled with disease. Baali's eyes brimmed with sympathy, and she continued the story as Kristian stopped and stared frowning at the floor. 'Kristian's father,' Baali said softly, 'became covered in sores.' Kristian nodded blankly then suddenly, emphatically came to life again and ran his fingers over his arms, torso and legs showing where he had been affected. Eventually he was confined to a wheelchair and finally, I gathered, he died of cancer.

In 1957 Denmark, a NATO ally, pronounced its territory – including the autonomous region of Greenland – to be a nuclear-free zone. The Danish government declared to their electorate that not only would they resist developing their own nuclear programme, but also that they had banned the allied forces from bringing nuclear weapons into Danish (and therefore Greenlandic) territory, or even through its airspace.

However, the American airbase at Thule was to play a pivotal role in the Cold War stratagem. All aircraft flying between the US and the Soviet Union passed over Greenland. Handily, Denmark had already granted permission for the US to build stations in Greenland before the Second World War, and with the infrastructure of military stations already in place on such a pivotal route, it was inevitable that the US would want to make the most of their investment. As the severity of the Cold War increased, so the back-room negotiations between the US military and the Danish government intensified. Unbeknown to the Danish and Inughuit people, the US military gained secret permission to fly B-52 bombers over their land, twenty-four hours a day for ten years, carrying nuclear weapons, in case the Soviets made a pre-emptive first strike. These regular missions were code-named Butterknife V.

It is quite feasible that Butterknife V would have been kept secret until today, had not the B-52 caught fire and crashed into the ice of North Star Bay, seven miles southwest of Thule Airbase. The impact of the crash on 21 January 1968 exploded the standard weapons and ammunition on board, and blew apart – without fully detonating – three of the four thermonuclear weapons on board, blasting lethal plutonium, uranium, tritium and americium dust over the area, and sending a 2,200 ft smoke plume into the air. The US military claimed that all the weapons had been accounted for; however, they did not say that all four had been recovered. A leading Danish newspaper *Jyllands Posten* says: 'Detective work by a group of former Thule workers indicates that an unexploded nuclear bomb probably still lies on the seabed off Thule.'

An official clean-up operation – dubbed Project Crested Ice, or 'Dr Freezelove' by the Americans – was launched a month later, by which time the local Inughuit hunters had already visited the area, unaware of the dangers of radiation. American soldiers, who came directly from Vietnam, joined Danish and Inughuit workers as they struggled in the winter darkness in temperatures between −30 and −55°C to clean the area, and over the following eight months loaded 10,500 tons of contaminated snow, ice and debris into oil drums and shipped them back to the US. To the workers it must have seemed an insurmountable task; decontami-nation equipment failed in the extreme conditions and in their hurry to clear up the worst of the mess safety measures were not strictly observed. On top of that, two polar hurricanes, blowing at a force of 100 miles per hour, were said to have hit the immediate area of the crash on 24 and 27 January, making it impossible for the workers to limit the area of contamination.

According to Sally Schnell, co-founder of the Thule Association, 'Only four weeks after the crash and before the clean-up and the investigations had really started, the Danish-American Commission of Investigation released the following statement to the press: "It is agreed that under the present circumstances the radioactivity spread in the area does not constitute any danger for human beings or biological species, and nor is there any risk to be expected in the future."'

However, as time wore on, those who had been involved in the clean-up operation began to get sick. A Danish stevedoring team was responsible for transporting the contaminated snow-filled containers from the site to the ship; a representative of that team recently told the Thule Association that out of the crew of sixty-three, only three survived. Sally Schnell went on to say: 'From among the office personnel in the Transportation Department, Danish Construction Corporation, working in the buildings on the pier, none is alive today. It is also food for thought that after the stevedoring in the summer of 1968, the buildings and everything on the pier were purposely set on fire and destroyed.'

When interviewed, the Thule workers said that there were few precautions taken to protect the Danish and Thule workers, and that only the Americans and the health scientist from Riso National Laboratory wore irradiation detectors. Ninety-eight Danish-Inughuit workers were diagnosed with cancer. Two hundred workers subsequently sued the US government for negligence, but their claim was unsuccessful. Four American ex-servicemen sued their government for illness resulting from the Dr Freezelove operation. Their claim was disallowed: military personnel cannot sue their government for putting them at risk.

Kristian and other family members of those hunters who helped with the clean-up of the B-52 wreckage, powerless in the shadow of military secrets, are still fighting the denials of the Danish and US governments that Dr Freezelove was the kiss of death for their kin. Although the main reason for the big meeting in Qaanaaq was to discuss the issue of a radar upgrade to the American airbase, the families of those who were involved in the clean-up operation were hoping to find out some answers about what really happened at the time of the crash and finally to get someone to admit that the cause of their fathers' illnesses was radiation poisoning and, more importantly, to try to discover if a nuclear bomb still lies silent, deathly, off the coast of Thule.

Baali chewed a dried prawn contemplatively, watching her husband who once again was lost to his thoughts.

Hearing Kristian's story of his father and of the crashed B-52 bomber reminded me of the conversation I had had with Uusaqqak at the summer camp about his fight to regain his ancestors' land. I was keen to see him again and hear how his campaign was going and Laurence and I resolved to visit him on our return to Qaanaaq.

'Qaanaaq is like a campsite,' Laurence mused as we walked through town. 'It feels like a temporary place, as if this place is not really where the people call home.' His comments rang stark and true in this confused place. According to Uusaqqak, the founders of Qaanaaq built this new town out of desperation with a sense of betrayal, and deep down the town seems dogged by these unfortunate foundations. Qaanaaq had none of the soul of the ancient settlements.

Turning off the main ice road through town, we wandered along a waxy path strewn with ice rubble and stepped over sleeping husky pups as we headed instinctively for a small cluster of older-looking houses. The house directly in front of us had a good-sized motorboat on a trailer in the garden, and bundles of fur clothing and skins filled the small porch. The furs released a warm distinctive fragrance as I brushed past, as if they were hungry to be worn and used.

The door opened to Uusaqqak's rumpled and confused face. He peered at me inquisitively, his hair standing to attention in a wild unruly quiff and his threadbare lumberjack shirt hanging wonkily off his shoulders. 'Ah! Wally's daughter!' he exclaimed, pulling me into a rough embrace. 'I didn't recognize you with all this!' He tugged playfully on my down-filled parka and quickly urged us into the warmth of his house.

He nodded darkly as I quizzed him about the B-52 crash. 'The water is radioactive now, and it is spreading. So it is not so good a future for my family. Because we are not the only people who have a life in this area. We have many, many birds and animals from north to south; many billions of birds, but not only birds, we have animals: walruses and seals, who are eating the molluscs from under the water in this area of radioactive waste. I heard on the radio we must not eat so much meat from animals, because it may be dangerous for our health, because they don't know what the animals are eating.'

'So the animals have also become toxic?' I asked.

'Yes!' he said emphatically. 'We cannot be 100 per cent sure of our area or the animals now. They tell us that we cannot eat mattak and other meat. And I am afraid that there is more that we don't know about: maybe there is more radioactive material in Thule Airbase area.'

'But didn't the Americans try to clean up the radioactive pollution?'

'No! [They cleaned] only on the ice in this area, but never ever *under* the water. [The polluted area] is bigger now. We can see it on the maps of the people who have made some reports, but the Americans will have nothing to do with what happened. We have no control over what happened after 1968. I had a meeting with the people from the Pentagon in Washington in 1997. They said they were going to give us information with a picture, and they showed us pictures of the radioactive pollution coming all the way from Russia down East Greenland. But still to this day they have not given us information on *our* area. So when I came back from Washington I talked with my friends all over Greenland to try and make them aware of the radioactive problems in our country. But they will not listen to me. I have given the East Greenlanders a warning about [the pollution in their area] but they do not understand about radioactive things because they have never been given the information.'

I ventured: 'But even if you got the land back, and the Americans moved away, there would still be so much radioactive pollution there that surely it would be bad hunting for you there . . .'

'It's true, it is not so good a future for the young people. We think that there is a bomb under the ice poisoning us and our animals. There is a big question about that. I feel that I have a responsibility to our family in the future, we must do what we can do for them before it is too late. But they will not tell us how much poison there is!' He ineffectually drummed the air with his fists, and then stopped, looking seriously at his grandson playing quietly beside him and smiled sadly. 'I try and fight for their future.'

17. Nanuq – the Ice Bear

It was about 2 a.m. when we spotted the dog team rounding the tabular iceberg guarding the town and heading towards us. Ilannguak had been gone for several weeks and was finally home. His hunting companion, the son of Pauline Peary and her husband Qissunnguak, had arrived several hours earlier in a spectacular showcase of dog-driving skill, clothed in full long-range hunter's clothing – a tugto (reindeer) parka, polar bear pants and thick sealskin and tugto kamiks – and had driven his excited team right through Qaanaaq to a beaming reception of friends and family. But Ilannguak's arrival was much more subdued. The temperature had plummeted with the light – it must have been around −25°C – and the residents of Qaanaaq were asleep, unaware of the hunter and his prize quarry.

Ilannguak looked utterly shattered from his trip and there was little of the sparkle that normally glinted in his eyes. We gathered in a clutch of polite concern around him. The twins grinned with pride as they helped their older brother unload the precious furs from the sledge before pulling back an old tarpaulin to reveal expertly butchered portions of meat that covered the entire length of the twelve-foot-long sledge. At the front of the sledge like a macabre figurehead lay the solid skull of a male bear, rudely devoid of its fur. From the size of the skull it looked as though the bear must have weighed at least half a ton.

Polar bear hunting is notoriously difficult, and only the cream of the Thule hunters attempt to hunt the Great White Bear, particularly because of the distances the hunters have to travel in order to find the bears, for although they have been spotted occasionally around the region of Qaanaaq and Herbert Island, the bears are more often found north of Thule, and on the Canadian coast and Ellesmere Island (although Thule hunters are no longer permitted to hunt in Canadian territory). Now there are few hunters who would attempt the journey towards Canada – the ice conditions would most likely prevent them even if the Canadian Mounted Police didn't. But in my father's day the best hunters would frequently travel towards the Canadian coast.

The journey by dog-sledge towards Canada and Ellesmere Island was fraught with danger. The ice conditions were notoriously unreliable, and the 'ice bridge' – a knuckle of ice which could only be used during the frozen seasons of winter and early spring – north and south of which was mostly open water or dangerously thin ice – had been known to break up without warning, carrying passengers of hunters and dogs as far as Labrador (unless the marooned hunters managed to leap onto neighbouring floes and hopscotch to land when the current took them past Savissivik). Now that ice conditions in the Arctic are deteriorating, the ice bridge is even more unstable, and the hunters have to make do with the hope that they will find bears on the far north-western reaches of Greenland's coastline – an area that has been uninhabited for centuries.

Out in the Arctic wilderness, more than three weeks' sledge drive away from the settlements of Thule, the hunter takes on the mantle of his ancestors and, shedding the modern trappings of civilized life – films, music, pornographic magazines and alcohol – his senses become heightened and he moves with the predatory lightness of a cat. The hunter knows which are his best 'bear' dogs, and the leader or King Dog is likely to be one of those elite hunting animals. At the first scent of a polar bear the dogs go wild with excitement. As they race across the ice the hunter hauls in his best dogs one or two at a time, pulling the traces in hand over fist bracing himself with his feet against the curved bow of the runners. With his razor-sharp knife, the hunter cuts his best dog's traces as close as he can to the dog's harness – if the traces are left too long the bear could trap the dog by standing on the trace; my father has even seen a polar bear walk carefully and menacingly up the trace as if it were a tightrope before mauling the trapped and cowering husky.

Cut loose from the sledge the dogs tear across the ice to the polar bear, surrounding and baiting it until the hunter catches up. The polar bear raises itself up on its hind legs and lashes out with its huge paws at the dogs. The dogs have to be as quick-witted as the bear, for there is no dog that could survive the powerful strike of a bear's claw. As the dogs keep the polar bear trapped and distracted, the hunter quickly finds his rifle – or a lance in the days before firearms – aims and shoots. When we were living on Herbert Island there were stories of some of the elite hunters who still preferred to use the lance when hunting polar bears, but using the lance required phenomenal skill and daring. The hunter armed only with a four- or five-foot-long spear of driftwood, bone or narwhal tusk would always approach the bear from the left, as it was well known among the hunters that polar bears were left-handed, and dive in at the crucial moment as the bear rose to attack, plunging the lance into its heart or side before leaping away to avoid the blows of the enraged animal. A hunter will always try to kill the bear with a single shot to the heart, unless he is being attacked himself and cannot get a good enough aim. But a single misjudged strike or leap and the hunter would be dead.

The polar bear (called '*Nanuq*' by the Inughuit) has always played a vitally important role in the lives of the Polar Eskimos; not only for their meat and fur, which is one of the warmest and most durable of all furs from the Arctic, but also for the bear's role in their culture and mythology. The Polar Eskimos believed the polar bear could understand and sometimes even speak with human tongue, and there are many stories throughout the Arctic of polar bears that could change into human form. It is hardly surprising that the Polar Eskimos believed in the polar bear's power to shape-shift; the polar bear can comfortably stand upright on two legs, has a highly developed intellect, and when skinned the naked polar bear with its limbs, finger-like claws and huge torso looks freakishly like a giant human. There are even some ethnologists such as Jean Malaurie who believe that the early Eskimos learnt how to hunt and build igloos from watching the polar bear.

The hunters of Thule are the last to hunt the polar bear for its meat and fur, all of which they use. Unlike some other hunters in the Arctic with 'big game' permits who hunt with snowmobiles – chasing the bear until it is exhausted, whereupon it is impossible for the hunters to miss their target – the Thule hunters still use dogs when hunting polar bear. Using this method means that they have as much chance of losing the bear as catching it, but it is the only respectful way to hunt. To them polar bear hunting is a time-honoured skill, the rewards of which are furs for essential clothing and good meat as well as the respect from their community for being accomplished hunters. Only full-time registered hunters are permitted to hunt polar bear, and when there is more than one hunter on the hunt, they still observe the traditional rules of division of the fur and meat. Still, the hunter who had the first strike or shot at the bear can claim the entire skin if he declares at the point of skinning, 'I skin with claws.' This, however, is thought of as being greedy, which is a shameful offence. Mostly the hunter who killed the bear single-handedly or who had the first strike will take the head, the forelegs and the upper part of the body – the hunter will measure with his whip the length of his thighs, and take enough fur from the neck to his mark on the fur to make new polar bear pants – as well as the precious long mane fur which is highly prized and used by the women for the tops of their long kamiks. The hunter is also entitled to his favourite parts of the meat such as the testicles of the bear.

Ilannguak moved slowly, methodically, as if every muscle was screaming with fatigue. His face had been ravaged by the weather;

his skin was raw and blistered on his left cheek and his hands were knotted and blackened. His mouth worked at words, but his face was still frozen, and he looked bewildered at the attention of our small group after weeks of isolation in the wilderness. Someone's mobile phone rang, and it was immediately handed over to Ilannguak who murmured quietly into the receiver before quickly handing it back to its owner. He was not yet ready for the modern trappings of life in Qaanaaq. Magda pointed to his polar bear pants. 'They are new!' she exclaimed, and then with a small frown as if she were working out a puzzle she tugged on the back of her brother's anorak. 'What happened?' she asked him, her voice flickering with concern. For the first time I noticed that Ilannguak's thick anorak was blackened and burned through in places, and I wondered why he was not wearing the usual tugto parka when it was so very cold. With just a couple of words and gestures Ilannguak explained that his stove had gone up in his tent, setting his clothes alight. His polar bear pants and parka had been ruined and he had had to try and sew some new ones for himself. As Ilannguak bent over to pick up the last few pieces of meat off the sledge the women's eyes followed him, surreptitiously inspecting his handiwork on the seat of his fur pants.

Ilannguak at that moment personified the true hunter to me, and my admiration for him and Pauline Peary and Qissunnguak's son only increased my desire to get out into the wilds. Both Laurence and I were desperate to escape Qaanaaq. In every direction was the prospect of adventure, and all the while Herbert Island mocked us with its stark beauty and hidden stories. I was irresistibly drawn to it. It was North to my internal magnet. But our quest to journey to my old home was booby-trapped with challenges and hurdles. I tried all the contacts that I had in Qaanaaq, and not one of them could, or would, help us get to Herbert Island, and certainly not further north to Siorapaluk and Neqe. Ilannguak was recovering from exhaustion, Magda's husband Gideon was constantly booked up to take tourists up and down the fjord on day trips, Kristian was working for the Kommunea, and Arquenguak and Tukúmek had lost all their dogs to distemper. Arquenguak was a broken man; his dogs were his lifeline to his livelihood and his freedom, and the shock of their death had made him sick with despair.

With none of my friends available to take us over the fjord and fooled by its apparent proximity, Laurence contemplated borrowing a couple of children's bicycles, and failing that to walk, man-hauling the equipment and survival gear on a make-shift sledge. 'Perhaps we could borrow Navarana's ice-collecting sledge and modify it slightly,' Laurence suggested optimistically. I wasn't so sure if it would work; the journey by motorboat to Herbert Island had taken three or four hours in the summer, and the ice wasn't compact and smooth the whole way and neither of us was experienced enough to know where the thin ice was likely to be; it would be an arduous trek and we had no radio with which to call for help should we get into trouble.

The idea was quashed almost as soon as we thought it: 'Imposs-ible!' we were told vehemently as we mentioned the idea to a couple of people. 'There is open water outside the settlement; you will have to walk several more miles to get around it.' But just as I felt my little silver thread of hope break we found we were in luck. Inudliah's husband was suddenly willing to take us to the island for the going tourist rate of £100.

Inudliah called out shrilly as she saw us walking towards her house and scampered down the steps to help us with our gear. She rubbed my arms effusively and twittered with concern asking if we would be warm enough, before disappearing only to reappear a few moments later with two threadbare blankets and a flask of tea. The temperature was hovering around −14°C, but any windchill would make it considerably colder. A sharp wind along with the speed of the dog-sledge could plunge the tempera-ture to around −50°C. There was only a light breeze at that moment, but the weather in the High Arctic is unpredictable, and we could not be certain what conditions we would be facing by the time we were ready to do the five-hour sledge journey back to Qaanaaq.

Inudliah's husband smiled roundly at us as he waddled casually between his dogs and slowly untangled their traces with bare rough-hewn hands. His polar bear pants were patchy on both his knees and his behind from years of use; around the worn patches the polar bear fur stuck out comically like duck's tails.

'Be *carr*-ful Kaari,' Inudliah warned with the English expression she had learnt as a child from my parents. I smiled at the familiar call, but Inudliah was straight-faced. She pointed at a large black husky which was probably the lead dog. The dog was dangerous, she said grimly, stay away from it. The others, she added in a lighter tone, were all friendly. She kicked one fondly up the backside.

A young voice called my name in the distance. I turned to see Tukúmek and Erich holding hands and half-running towards us. Tukúmek waved enthusiastically and grasped my shoulder, panting, a few moments later.

'Erich wanted to say hello to his Aunty Kari!' she said between gulps of breath, laughing as she talked. Erich grinned and gripped my waist firmly with both arms, whispering, 'Aunty Kari, Aunty Kari,' in English into my parka. 'You see, my son is learning your language very well!' she exclaimed, and peered around me at the sledge on which we were about to depart. I told her that we were going to go to Herbert Island, and she cried out with excitement. 'Oh, I wish we still had some dogs, then we could come with you!' Her bottom lip stuck out with disappointment. She took my gloved hands in hers and shook her head. 'These will not be warm enough,' she said inspecting my modern hi-tech gloves. 'Take these, you can give them back to me when you get back.' She slipped her sealskin mitts off her hands and handed them to me with a smile.

A holler from Inudliah's husband sharply ended our conversation. The dogs were off. Inudliah bellowed behind us in a commanding tone far removed from her usual high soft voice and she urged us quickly after the sledge which was careering away from us through the town, bouncing wildly over boulders of ice and exposed rock. I vaguely heard Tukúmek join in her calls: 'Hold on . . . rope . . .' Laurence and I raced behind the sledge, trying in vain to guide the sledge over the uneven ground. The hunter ran beside the dogs with bowed legs, slipping and sliding down the hillside of Qaanaaq towards the tide crack, all the while roaring at his team trying to keep them under control. At his command we leapt onto the sledge, both of us clutching cameras in one hand and trying to grasp the straps of the sledge with the other. At the same moment it lurched sharply to our vulnerable side and catapulted both Laurence and myself off the sledge and into a pile of ice rubble. Mortified, we scrambled quickly over the tide crack and leapt back on. I laughed at the comedy of the moment, but groaned inwardly that at least a quarter of the town must have seen us fall off the sledge. I was bound to return to some open-faced teasing that I had forgotten the very basics of Inughuit daily life.

The hunter was still just ahead of us, and threw himself onto the sledge as we whipped past him, turning to grin at us, puffing from his exertions as he made himself comfortable. It was going to be a long ride. In front of us the dogs took it in turns to empty their bowels as they ran along – the beginning of any sledge journey involves a period of pungent aromas from the dogs. Some were dragged alongside the sledge, whimpering in their struggle to keep up and defecate at the same time, their eyes darting towards us in an almost human look of embarrassment.

The ice was deserted. Noticeably fewer hunters were going out every day as the ice started to weaken and crack, and so we cruised alone under the vast dome of a frozen sky, the only sound coming from the *shhhhhhh* of the runners, the quick breathing of the dogs and the occasional call from the hunter or a snap from his whip. In front of us the dogs settled into a steady trot and weaved in and out of one another, making and breaking alliances as they nuzzled up to a team-mate or growled at another, their excrement freezing to their traces which after an hour or two were knotted in complex patterns as if they had danced around a maypole.

In time we fell into a strange meditation; the motion of the sledge was hypnotic and for the first time since our arrival Laurence looked at peace, the cameras had been put away and he was marvelling silently at the icescape surrounding us.

As we slipped by the frozen cathedral icebergs I found myself transported back in time to my childhood: I was nine years old and my parents, my sister and I were returning by dog-sledge to Herbert Island for the first time since we had lived there. I was excited to be going back but the journey from Qaanaaq had taken an eternity and I was numb from the bitter cold. I hadn't liked Qaanaaq then; I had been almost attacked by huskies, a local drunk had tried to kick down the door to our accommodation, and I was confused when I met people I had once known from Herbert Island who had moved to the mainland. But as we neared Herbert Island I had felt something different: a strange excitement at the hard familiar lines of the island. The two hunters taking us there pointed beyond the running huskies: a dog-sledge was heading directly for us, and was travelling at an amazing pace. The sledge was being driven by two teenage boys, who shouted and waved wildly as they came careering towards us. The next hour was a blur. In a flash they pulled me off the sledge, spun their dogs around and shot off with me back towards the island, leaving my parents and Pascale far behind. My young kidnappers were elated. I was terrified. It had been years since I had been in Thule and we had all grown; I had no idea that these two wild young men were Arqenguak and Ilannguak. As we hurtled towards the settlement the boys grinned at my terrified face, in turn rubbing my frozen arms and legs with such vigour that I was shaken like a rag doll.

By the time we reached Qeqertassuaq my legs were like jelly. I was immediately scooped up by the waiting crowd and bundled in great excitement to Aata's hut whereupon my boots and mittens were quickly pulled off and several pairs of hands rubbed my hands and feet until they were raw. I smiled with a rush of warmth at the memory. I had been overwhelmed with confusion at the time, but now I wished that I could relive that moment.

Herbert Island rose magnificently out of the ice to our left, its naked rock face glowering darkly at us with the ill-tempered humour of a grumpy pensioner. My heart swelled as I saw it and I looked back at Laurence to share the moment. He looked back at me with shining eyes. The hunter's back had straightened, and for the first time since we left Qaanaaq he seemed alert and tense. The ice was thin around the settlement, he told me, and in places was just a couple of inches thick.

'*Auretiiit!*' he bellowed at the dogs and they stopped abruptly. The lead dog stood proud and alert; the others lay down in clouds of breath vapour or pawed at the snow, gulping up the fresh white crystals and waiting for the hunter to guide them between the thin patches and over the knuckles of ice that bridged the gap to the land.

We had timed it perfectly. The settlement, which for most of the day had been in shadow, was now bathed in soft afternoon light. But it was still deserted, and without the presence of Baali and Magda the place seemed lifeless. We clambered stiffly off the sledge and walked through the abandoned village.

Laurence was in awe. 'Where is your house?' he asked, casting his eyes over the scattering of small hunters' huts. I pointed to our little red hut and his eyes opened wide in surprise. 'You lived *there*, for two years?' I laughed and led him to it.

Nothing had changed in the hut since my visit the previous summer, but the atmosphere seemed somewhat different. Perhaps it was because I was sharing it with someone from my life in England who had no connection with the place, but as I walked around the tiny hut and told him stories of its history I found that finally I connected with it. The place reached out to Laurence too. The pictures of our time in Greenland were now pulled into sharper focus, and he had the strange experience of déjà vu. He grinned and inspected Dad's handiwork on the shelves, and sat with me on a small bunk in the corner, trying to picture the family living in this strange cold little space. It was a revelation for me to see this familiar world through his eyes. Through Laurence I saw the place as my mother must have first seen it, and I saw my old home for what it really was: a grotty, tiny hunters' hut in the middle of a frigid wilderness. We sat shoulder to shoulder amazed that my parents had ever undertaken to live in such a hostile and extreme environment with a ten-month-old child.

The hunter came in behind us, sat down sheepishly on one of the chairs, plucked a comic off a shelf, opened it up on the knees of his polar bear pants and started reading. We were aware that we had very little time. The ice was thinner than we had thought it would be, and if we left it too late we could be stranded. We both hoped that circumstances would keep us there, just for a day or two, but our concern for the hunter and our agreement with him prevented it.

For the next couple of hours Laurence and I immersed ourselves in the abandoned village sharing its memories. We visited Aata's house, and sat in its welcome silence, taking in the rope that hung beside the doorway, black with ancient grime and the blood of hundreds of seal or walrus carcasses that had hung from it over the years; the ancient oil stove and his faithful old green armchair. In one corner his 'drum' still sat next to a pair of misshapen trainers, and I smiled and could almost hear his '*ajajas*', see the swing of his hips, his bowed legs and his angled back from years of meditating beside breathing holes in the ice, and hear the sound of the side of the brush hitting the dustpan.

We weaved through ancient meat racks and scrambled in and out of huts ravaged by storms and then, finally, stood silently on the lip of a hill and just simply gazed over the vistas of wilderness surrounding us. Laurence was thoughtful. 'This place is so desolate,' he said, as if thinking aloud. 'Why choose to live *here*? Why does *anyone* choose to live here? It's beautiful, I give you that, but it's just so bleak and cold and isolated. I have never felt so isolated in my whole life.'

It seemed as though no time had passed at all when we had to leave the island. The hunter was bored and impatient to go – there was no hunting to be had immediately around the abandoned village, the ice was thinning by the minute and besides, it was Friday night.

Even just three hours on the island had made a huge difference to the ice surrounding the settlement and we found that the ice, which was thin on our way over to the island, was now covered in pools of water. The dogs sensed that they were not on a firm footing and whined and whimpered as the hunter called commands at them from the sledge; slowing them down over the bending ice so that the runners would not pierce the wave that buckled in front of us, or urging them to take off at speed over brittle ice so that we barely grazed the surface.

Then the hunter called softly to the dogs to stop: '*Auretit, auretiit,*' his voice rasped, blending with the sound of the runners as they ground to a halt on the herringbone pattern of wind-driven ice. The left runner slopped in a large puddle of indigo water as the hunter gingerly got off the sledge and pulled a metal lance out from where it had been strapped to the platform. The dogs danced on their front paws and snapped at the air, looking back at the hunter, obedient, watchful. The hunter minced forwards on the pads of his kamiks, patting the air behind him, ensuring that we didn't get off the sledge to follow him. I wondered how deep the water was under the left runner. Dark patches appeared around us, glinting steely blue and menacing; the ice groaned quietly beneath us, bending and darkening with our weight. The hunter prodded the ice with sharp inquisitive strikes of his lance, then moved forward a couple of yards and prodded again. In one place a strike of the lance would send a few tiny shards of ice into the air; in another the lance would plunge into mush ice. The dogs, now bunched together in a narrow line like schoolchildren on a day trip, followed lightly on the heels of the hunter, moving as one and sensing the gravity of the moment. Laurence and I waited powerless behind on the tilting sledge, edging closer towards the dark water, clinging to the equipment and preparing ourselves for a wild leap if the sledge finally broke through the thin membrane of ice that was the only thing between us and the deep freezing waters of the fjord. Quickly now, the hunter pressed forward on a narrow ice bridge, aware of the lurching sledge and our precarious situation, and with an urgent call the dogs ploughed forward. The back of the sledge careered to one side, skimming the water and crashing over a ridge of ice boulders and onto a firmer surface. For a few hundred yards we continued in this stop-start fashion through a labyrinth of thin ice, until finally both hunter and dogs found a more solid surface. The hunter leisurely ambled back to the sledge, replaced the lance and with a crack of the whip we set off once again at a steady trot.

We returned to Qaanaaq at 3 a.m. with the sun resting in the crook of two mountains, bathing the landscape in the soft pinks and delicate violets of a four-hour sunset.

Wafts from the rich meat stew hung in the air as we struggled out of our layers of clothing in Navarana's narrow hallway. Candles were already lit on the table and the top of a bottle of fizzy wine had already been unscrewed. Laurence was about to return to London and Navarana had insisted that we try polar bear meat before he left. Navarana sat us straight down at the table and continued stirring the meat in a large tin saucepan on the hob.

I cast my eyes over the multitude of photographs of her daughters stuck to her fridge. Several were of Nuka and baby Maija with Andy in their new American home, beside them fridge magnet words in Inuktun nestled in haphazard sentences. A mirror hung by the door on which Kevin Spacey had signed his autograph in red lipstick – Navarana had interpreted for him on his brief visit to Qaanaaq a year or so before on a leisure tour around the Arctic, and his autograph had pride of place.

Soon the table was laden with food; plates of steaming polar bear meat on the bone, bowls of white rice and bright yellow curry sauce. 'Eat!' Navarana insisted, pushing the fragrant meal brusquely towards us. 'The meat comes from your brother and Qissunnguak's son.'

Bear meat has long been regarded as a delicacy, and not just by the Inughuit; several explorers and merchant whalers to the district wrote that the meat was as good as young beef, and lightly roasted bear steaks were a particular favourite among the Roman elite – although many paid for their extravagant meals with their lives. Bears are often infested with trichinae, a deadly parasite, which is easily passed to humans by eating flesh that has not been cooked properly. Early explorers to the area were also to find out to their cost that the liver of the polar bear is extremely toxic; it contains such high quantities of vitamin A that those who eat it can die of hypervitaminosis. Dutch sailors marooned along the coast of Novaya Zemlya in 1596 told of a bear that 'desired to tast a peece of some of vs'. They killed it with their lances 'but her death did us more hurt than her life . . . [for] we drest her liuer and eate it, which in the taste like us well, but it made vs all sicke . . .' Three men were so sick 'we verily thought that we should haue lost them, for all their skins came off from foote to the head . . .'

The meat was tough but delicious, and as we feasted Navarana frowned and chastised herself for not cooking the meat for longer to make it more tender. 'I boiled it for hours and hours, the Thule way,' Navarana said chewing on a piece of hard fat, 'but maybe I needed to cook it longer.' She laughed when I said that I liked to eat seal meat with tomato ketchup, and told me to take more curry sauce: 'I love curry with polar bear meat. We Thule people like spicy things, tasty things. That is why we like to eat rotten meat and kiviak – it tastes so good!' I looked over to

Laurence who grimaced slightly as his teeth crunched on a piece of gristle. Navarana scolded him light-heartedly: 'We love the fat and those tough bits, they're the best! They are good for you, they keep you warm.' Laurence smiled wryly and accepted another piece of meat.

Laurence had been given a bear claw by Baali and Kristian earlier that afternoon as a token of friendship and after the meal he pulled it out of his pocket and placed it carefully on the table. Traditionally the gift of a polar bear claw in the district was a great honour, and was often used as an amulet to protect the hunter and to give him heightened senses when he was hunting. Some believed that an amulet in the right hands could enable the man to shape-shift into the form of a bear. After a couple of glasses of fizzy wine Laurence was beginning to feel the same way, and his uncertainty about eating the meat of such an extraordinary animal had eased as Navarana had explained more about the attitude of the Inughuit towards the polar bear and other local animals, and now he seemed almost empowered by the meal. As he was told the significance of the gift of the polar bear claw his eyes gleamed. Navarana encouraged him: 'You big polar bear man now!' He laughed, but his back straightened and he held his head high.

Navarana was in high spirits and, spurred on by the talk of bear spirits, produced an angákoq's drum. I told her that I had seen Aata's old 'drum' in his house on Herbert Island and she smiled. 'I remember your grandfather and his drum,' she said, pushing her chair away from the table to give herself more room. 'In our family whenever we needed to use a dustpan and brush, we always used to say we were using Taitsianguaraitak's drum!' she added, giggling girlishly. 'We are lucky in Thule,' she continued, more seriously now, 'that we still remember our songs and are strong enough to hold onto our traditions, unlike further south or east where the missionaries took the songs out of the people.' She took a delicate sip of wine. 'The missionaries took away all our traditions just like that – *pfft!*' Her hands flew into thin air. 'I don't know why foreigners think that they can do that,' she added heatedly. In an act of defiance she started playing some drum songs. There was one in particular that I recognized. 'Yes, of course you recognize it!' she exclaimed. 'It was your Aata's song.

'These days,' she continued, 'there are great differences in the singing from people over Greenland; I sang at a festival in Iceland and the organizers were so happy when they heard me sing! They told me my songs were so varied and melodic, and the other singer they had brought over from East Greenland sang only the same song, again and again, just like this: *ajaja ajaja ajaja!*' Her voice was high and the melody repetitive. 'Every song had the same tune, just different words. But the women sing *very* sexy!' Navarana said laughing huskily, and imitated the smooth languid gyrations of the women of East Greenland. 'But it was never traditional for women to use the drum. It was the angákoqs who used the drum to call up spirits or to do their magic, and women were never the angákoqs. Women did sing, but it was more traditional that they just use their voices, like this . . .' Navarana's voice softened as she placed the drum back on the table and sang a lullaby of a mother dovekie who was afraid to leave her babies alone. We were mesmerized by her soft crooning rendition that rose and fell like the call of the dovekie as it caught the air beneath its wings.

We talked more of the old songs and stories, and I mentioned that I had heard so many of Amaunalik's stories from my father when I was growing up, and that it was a shame that she was no longer alive.

'Amaunalik was my mother,' Navarana responded casually. I was delighted and asked her if she remembered any of the stories. 'A few,' Navarana replied. 'Sometimes I wish I had written some of her stories down, she knew so many! Now I have forgotten nearly all of them. The children now are not interested in the old stories. I think maybe they will all soon be forgotten.'

The air seemed noticeably warmer as we walked home. The

sun was no longer dipping behind the mountains and the icy roads were becoming treacherous in places where the thick waxy ice had melted and refrozen into sheer slick cascades. We were fuelled by stories, drum songs and polar bear meat, and in a nod to the old traditions, we looked out across the ice and gave our thoughts to the polar bear's spirit, wherever it wandered.

18. Poles Apart

The world was frozen. The horizon rippled in a mirage of cold so intense that it imitated heat. Land, water and sky merged in a confusion of blue, white and grey, and against this cold backdrop sat the town of Qaanaaq. Its colourful sprinkling of huts looked like a gathering of forgotten dolls' houses abandoned in this vast frigid landscape. Looking out at this inhospitable land I marvelled at how anything could survive in it.

It was a peaceful Sunday morning; the tolling of the church bells barely reached our hut and the dogs kept on the ice had stopped baying. Outside children played in brightly coloured hats and coats, sliding on pieces of plastic or cardboard down any available slope avoiding the countless puppies that gambolled around them. Times had changed – when I was a little girl the children used the fur from the head of a polar bear to slide on. Slowly people appeared at windows or open doorways as they lit their first cigarette of the morning; the smoke merged with clouds of warm breath on the icy morning air.

It was 6 April 2003 – a special day: the thirty-fourth anniversary of Dad reaching the Geographic North Pole during his British Trans-Arctic Expedition – the expedition was the first to reach the Geographic North Pole by surface crossing – and I stood on the steps of the house holding a cup of imported Earl Grey tea, thinking how appropriate it was that on this particular date I was up in the Thule district, where Dad did much of his training for the trip.

There are, in actual fact, five North Poles, and all move enigmatically over the polar north. The North Pole, on which the dreams and ambitions of the greatest polar pioneers were fixed, is the Geographic North Pole: True North: 90°N, from which every direction is south. The Geographic North Pole is the northern axis on which the globe rotates. Considerably closer to land is the Magnetic North Pole, the point at which the northern end of the axis of the Earth's magnetic field intersects with the Earth's surface. In other words it is the Magnetic North Pole to which our compasses point. The Magnetic North Pole moves significantly more than its more illustrious namesake: since its discovery in 1831 by James Clark Ross, the magnetic pole has moved on average forty kilometres per year and is currently roaming the Queen Elizabeth Islands of the Canadian Arctic.

To confuse the issue further there is the Geomagnetic North Pole, the northern point from which the earth's magnetic field and magnetosphere radiates according to mathematical calculation. Currently the Geomagnetic North Pole lies approximately five hundred miles east of the Magnetic North Pole, hovering not far north of Thule, where the ocean is around four thousand metres deep, and is for most of the year covered by sea ice.

Most poetically appointed is the Northern Pole of Inaccessibility: the point on the northern sea ice furthest from land in any direction – a place that was for centuries beyond human reach. It was believed in the nineteenth century that the Pole of Inaccessibility was the pivot for the pack ice of the Arctic Ocean, thereby making it the most impossible place to attain either by ship or on foot. In 1968 my father passed within a few miles of the Pole of Inaccessibility on his journey across the top of the world. (There is also a Southern Pole of Relative Inaccessibility, the definition of which is the opposite of its Northern counterpart – namely, 'the point furthest from the *sea* in any direction'.)

The last North Pole – and most ironically the only pole that is the closest to having a visual marker – is the Celestial North Pole, which rests along an imaginary golden thread that passes through the axis of the earth – through both the Geographic North Pole and the Geographic South Pole – and stretches astronomically into infinity, skimming the 'Pole Star', Polaris, the brightest star in the constellation of Ursa Minor, otherwise known as the Little Bear. The nearest star to Polaris bears my father's name, in recognition of the fact that he and his three companions spent the winter of 1968/69 almost directly beneath it.

All the poles of the north are invisible; no natural edifice or structure marks the great spot, but for some of the greatest explorers of all time it was the ultimate prize, the expeditionary Holy Grail whose discovery would perhaps bring some kind of order to the chaos of the universe. Even across the threshold of the Scott Polar Institute in Cambridge there is an inscription that bears witness to this: *Quaesivit arcana poli: vidit Dei* – 'He sought the mysteries of the Pole; he saw those of God.'

The earliest explorers headed north not only to claim the pole, but actually to discover what was there, for until someone had set foot on that elusive part of the earth no one could be completely sure if the North Pole was on land or at sea, or even whether the North Pole was actually a gateway to another universe. One of the more bizarre theories of the early nineteenth century was dreamt up by ex-US army officer John Cleve Symmes, who believed that there were ice fields at either end of the Earth, but that at the poles themselves were two vast holes that led to a universe within the Earth itself, inside which seven other worlds existed. There was light enough, he declared, from the holes themselves to support life on each of these smaller planets. Symmes, regarded at the time as being both visionary and madman, was nevertheless convincing enough to warrant twenty-five members of the Senate to vote in favour of an expedition to investigate his theory in 1822, and just three years later he was offered passage on a Russian North Polar voyage, but due to lack of funds Symmes was unable to accept the invitation. Although Symmes's theory may seem outlandish now, it seems strangely coincidental that the Eskimos, somehow aware of an earthly pivot in the north, named it '*qalaherruaq*' –

navel of the north. When exactly the Eskimos discovered the existence of the pole is not certain, although most modern Inughuit believe that it was a concept brought to them by visitors from the south, for the discovery of the North Pole was a white man's dream.

Although various forays had been made into the Polar Regions since St Brendan and Pytheas of Massalia, curiosity and inspiration were not enough to fund expeditions to the Arctic, and so the early expeditions, led by merchant explorers such as Davis, Hudson and Frobisher and supported by sponsors such as Queen Elizabeth I, flew the flag of commercialism, with their primary purpose to find a quick and safe passage between Europe and the fabled riches of the East. From a commercial point of view these expeditions were very successful; Henry Hudson's intent to sail across the North Pole – if indeed there was an ocean there – to the East resulted in the discovery in 1607 that the waters off Spitsbergen were resplendent with whales. The theory of a passage across the North Pole was abandoned, and for the next two hundred years whaling ships and their brutal men overran the polar seas and made a bloody fortune.

The nineteenth century, however, brought with it a different breed of explorer, and soon the quest for the North Pole began in earnest. Some of the greatest names in polar history joined in the race: there are too many failed expeditions to mention, but the most impressive, and the most controversial, were the claims to the North Pole of Robert Edwin Peary and Frederick A. Cook.

Peary, after numerous failed attempts, finally claimed he reached the North Pole on 6 April 1909 along with four Eskimos and his black manservant Matthew Henson, who had been his faithful companion and fellow traveller in the Arctic for many years. Little did he know at the time that only a few days before he sent home his message of triumph, Dr Frederick Cook had announced that he, along with two Eskimo guides, had reached the pole almost a year before, on 21 April 1908. Peary was

furious. On his return he and his supporters viciously attacked
Dr Cook's claim and poured slander upon his character. Cook's
claim was quashed and he was labelled a liar; in his place Peary
was pronounced the winner of this ultimate race.

The Peary–Cook controversy still rages to this day between
the Peary family and their supporters and the Cook Society,
despite numerous well-researched explorations into the records
of both men that conclude that neither man reached his goal –
including my father's own book *The Noose of Laurels*, said to
be the definitive work on the subject by both historians and
adventurers who have spent any notable time in the Arctic
regions. It would be impossible for me to go into the controversy
at length in this book. But what I have learnt from my father is
that enormous respect and admiration should go to both men
who even if they did not in the end reach their ultimate goal,
nevertheless contributed greatly to the world of exploration, and
were in the truest sense remarkable pioneers of their field. Peary
in particular, my father still believes, by virtue of his dogged
determination and drive deserved the luck to reach his dream.

My father was well aware of the role that the Polar Eskimos
had played in the expeditions of the Polar North. Explorers
such as Peary and Nansen were his inspiration and he had read
extensively about their reliance on the knowledge of the local
hunters; even though he had spent a considerable time in the
Antarctic driving dogs and making maps, he knew that the only
way to complete the journey with any chance of survival was to
refine and test his equipment and techniques in an extreme
environment, and to learn the skills of the greatest polar hunters.
There was only one place he could do this: Thule. Little did he
know when he first came to Thule as an inspired young man
that thirty-five years later his daughter would be celebrating the
success of his project in the same place where he did his training.

For centuries the Polar Eskimos have been the indispensable
guides and erstwhile supporters of expeditions to the North Pole,
all the while wondering at the folly of such expeditions, for there

was nothing *at* the pole; as it was devoid of animals it was, as far as they were concerned, devoid of treasure. They could not understand why setting foot on one unremarkable piece of ice – which looked like any other – was worth dying for. To this day the older generations of Inughuit talk in wonderment about the expeditions that their relatives participated in; they relate tales of the determination of the white men who hired them, and the hardship and loss they were prepared to endure in order to skewer a piece of ice with a harpoon, with a flag tied to it.

The attainment of the North Pole was not the primary reason for my father's expedition; at that time the Peary–Cook controversy had not reached its climax and although my father did not entirely believe Peary's claim of priority, nevertheless he felt that the pole was no longer the prize it once was. Instead he came up with an ambitious proposal, which many viewed as both foolhardy and impossible.

My father said in July 1967 as he prepared for the start of his epic trek: 'Man has crossed all the deserts, climbed the highest mountains, and made his first cautious probes into the oceans and into space and there is only one pioneer journey left to be made on the surface of the planet – a journey across the top of the world.' He believed that, 'Such a journey . . . would bring dramatically to an end the third and final act in the trilogy of Mount Everest and the two "super-mountains" at the top and bottom of the world.'

The journey across the longest axis of the Arctic Ocean would take my father and his companions Allan Gill, Dr Roy 'Fritz' Koerner and Ken Hedges from Point Barrow in Alaska to Spitsbergen: a distance of 3,620 route miles across constantly moving pack ice. Luckily their dogs had arrived in time for their departure: Allan Gill and Ken Hedges had flown the huskies from Thule just two weeks before the B-52 crash; had they left it any later they would not have had any dogs with which to start their journey, and the whole expedition would have been cancelled. But even at the start the completion of such a project seemed unpromising for they were confronted at Point Barrow by a belt of ice the consistency of porridge, beyond which were miles of fast-moving ice and wide stretches of water. It would have been suicide to set out in such circumstances. My father and his companions nervously waited for the conditions to change, watching the men at Point Barrow placing bets with one another on their survival and listening to disaster tales of people who had never returned from the ice, and of hunters who had been lost to 'Hell's Hole' two hundred miles to the north: a notorious whirlpool that had claimed many lives. The local Inuit population advised the men to give up then and there. The British press caught scent of the delay in departure, and started gearing up for a field day: the greatest expedition of their time that never even began. The pressure on the men was enormous, and to complicate matters further, Dr Fritz Koerner's daughter Eva was born just days before they were to set out. The need for success of the expedition, which had taken four years of preparation, was never more poignant. My father later said: 'It was like the eve of a battle – still, cold, silent, with no one sleeping; an atmosphere heavy with private thoughts.'

They departed Point Barrow on 21 February 1968, leaving behind them only the tracks of four sledges and a trail of vapours from the panting dogs. As they made a wild dash over the seething rubble of young ice towards the stronger polar pack each man huddled into his furs, feeling perhaps more lonely and vulnerable than he ever had before; nursing a silent terror that they would not return. It was a dread that not one man would divulge to his companions for fear of seeing it reflected in their eyes. They could only trust in the belief that once they mounted the polar pack the going would be easier. But when finally they reached it they were greeted by a chaos of pressurized ice through which there seemed no route humanly possible. Their journey had just begun.

The men soon fell into a routine: waking at 6 a.m. covered in ice and hoarfrost, they took it in turns to light the Primus stove and cook a breakfast of porridge, bacon and biscuits while the temperature in the tent climbed from $-42°$ to $-37°C$. 'We moved around outside with lamps and fumbled through the twilight, breaking camp and loading the sledges, untangling the dogs and hitching them up; and by 8 a.m. with our wolf-skins frozen as solid as suits of armour, we were on the move, cutting through the cold, with each footstep jarring the body back to the misery from which it had been released by sleep only seven or eight hours before.'

In between travelling, eating and sleeping the men also had to collect scientific data. Fritz in particular was responsible for this side of the expedition; his project was to provide an insight into how the ice of the Arctic Ocean was being influenced by the world's changing climate. For this project Fritz had to calculate 'the mean thickness of the old floes and what percentage of the 5 million square miles of the Arctic Ocean was covered by them'. He had to decipher what proportion of the ocean was ice-free at different stages in the year, and how much incoming radiation was absorbed and how much reflected by the many different ice forms. He also had to discover how the ice that was circulating differed from the ice of the trans-polar stream. This meant that he was required constantly to measure the thickness of the ice, the temperature profiles of different depths of ice and the minute variations in temperature, humidity and wind-changes in the air column five metres above the melting surface of each floe he studied. The data he collected from the expedition has contributed greatly to the world's understanding of glaciation and global warming, and is still the baseline from which almost all calculations of the polar melt begin.

Around them the ice groaned and splintered and drifted. Several times the ice split silently just a few yards away from the camp; opening like a zip with deadly precision through the imprints of the men's bodies in the ice as they scrambled away, hurling dogs and equipment to another floe in the darkness. At other times the Primus stove could not be heard over the screeching and moaning of the ice as it rose up above them, threatening to engulf them in an icy tomb.

On 6 April 1969, after thirteen gruelling months on the polar pack ice, including five months of pitch darkness, my father and his three companions became the first men to reach the Geographic North Pole by surface crossing. 'But it was an elusive spot to find and fix,' my father said, '. . . that place where two sets of meridians meet and all directions are south. Trying to set foot upon it was like trying to step on the shadow of a bird that is hovering overhead, for the surface across which we were moving was itself a moving surface on a planet that was spinning about an axis beneath our feet.' The men were exhausted. They had had to contend with the unrelenting force of the winds and currents of the High North, which fractured and buckled the ice around them, causing the skin of constantly shifting ice to rise up into elephantine pressure ridges or split into vast open leads around which no passing place could be found. They then had to convert the sledges into makeshift rafts and ferry equipment, men and dogs across, often only to encounter another crippling adversary: mush ice, which bore the weight of neither man nor dog. In order to make use of the good winter ice they were travelling for ten or more hours a day in temperatures down to $-45°C$ or lower. The elation and relief of reaching the North Pole – the goal of many other heroic explorers throughout history – was tempered for the small party: Fritz and Ken were suffering from hypothermia, Allan was recovering from a slipped disc, and they knew that they still had another two or three months of ice-travel before their journey would be completed.

By 20 May the men were concerned: the ice conditions were rapidly deteriorating and mush ice was starting to appear all around them. For the first time since the previous summer they began to smell the sea. By my father's calculations they should have spotted land on 23 May – fifteen months after losing sight of land on the other side of the Arctic Ocean – but the day seemed to promise no rewards. Finally at 10.50 p.m. on 23 May

1969 my father climbed atop a pressure ridge and, looking through the telescopic sight of his rifle, he saw to his relief and amazement, land. He scrambled back to his sledge and quickly made a note of the time, and with his heart screaming with excitement shot off to tell his companions.

Six days later, after facing the excruciating disappointment of finding open water, mush ice and gyrating ice pans three-quarters of a mile wide between them and the land they craved to set foot on, the men completed their journey across the longest axis of the Arctic Ocean with a wild scramble to a small rocky island known as 'Vesle Tavleøya' – the most northerly island in Svalbard, on which the mountain was given the name 'Herbertfjellet' by the Norsk Polarinstitute in 1979 in honour of my father's pioneering journey. After another 105 miles' travel south-west to their rendezvous with HMS *Endurance*, they greeted the first men that they had seen for nearly a year and a half, and sailed home.

The journey was a remarkable moment in the history of exploration, but the public's enthusiasm was channelled else-where. The world was captivated by the progress of spacecraft *Apollo 11* and its mission to the moon. But strangely the two very different goals were poignantly linked: at the very moment that Dad spotted land for the first time in fifteen months, astronaut Jack Young took the legendary photograph 'Earth Rise' – it was the first time that humankind had seen their planet from space. The success of the British Trans-Arctic Expedition fell into the shadow of the moon.

I called Scotland on my mobile phone and sent anniversary congratulations back. My parents too had been appreciating the coincidence of time and place and we scrambled through our excited conversation hiccupping with the time delay. Their voices were light and cheery as they talked over one another, and I could picture them in my mother's study, surrounded by the books and memorabilia gathered from around the world: gifts from Eskimos, Lapps, Native American shamans and Australian healers and photographs on the wall of Pascale and my parents with friends in southern France, of me in my mother's peacock-blue-and-gold sari standing beside a banyan tree in India, and of my father and Geoff Renner (who had experienced the storm of 1972 with my parents on the way to Herbert Island) in New Year party hats with rosy cheeks and glasses of red wine in the lounge of a ship bound for the Antarctic. In a moment of clarity I understood that my journey to Thule was not just about rediscovering my connection with the place and its people, it was also a chance to glimpse my parents' connection to it. Throughout my stay I had heard countless extraordinary stories from respected hunters who had travelled with my father and had seen pictures of my mother and me pinned to walls or stuck in cherished photo albums. Then through Laurence I had seen the place with fresh eyes, and realized for the first time what an amazing undertaking it was to live and work in such a remote place for so long a time with a small child. I felt honoured, and humbled to be a part of it.

As I finally hung up, sunlight broke through the low cloud and fell in hot spots on the ice. In the distance the mountains fell away to nothing and a lone husky raised his head to the sky and howled.

19. The Last Place on Earth

Laurence left in a flurry of hasty packing and last-minute shots on the ice where weeks before he had experienced for the first time the thrill of walking on water. The ice moaned and whispered as if it were echoing my wish that he wasn't leaving but he had to return to London for another assignment. I had travelled alone many times, but as the plane disappeared with him over the horizon I felt bereft, and overwhelmingly lonely. I hadn't seen the Qaerngâq family for days – they were either ill or busy, and suddenly I felt the cold and desolation of Thule more acutely than ever before. The Arctic was mirroring my emotions and the day which had looked promising at its start drew into itself and grew sombre and grey.

I threw myself into putting our simple hut back as it originally had been before it had turned into a production studio and writing den. Silence wrapped itself around the isolated house; the place seemed deadened with the weather and even the dogs had ceased calling to one another. A worker from the municipal office appeared and took away the television, the clock ceased to work, and I felt as though I was trapped in a vacuum.

I longed to leave Qaanaaq and head north – beyond all civilization – and was frustrated that I didn't have my father's skill and experience of driving dogs so that I could travel alongside the hunters that left Qaanaaq daily. But I knew that the ice was deteriorating. Fewer hunters were leaving town and those that did strapped kayaks to their sledges. I was told that due to the increase in open water over the last couple of years it was now impossible to travel by dog-sledge to Etah – where Kritlaq the Angákoq had landed with his followers, or the old hunters' hut at Neqe, which many hunters talked about with great fondness;

yet I still hoped to reach Siorapaluk at least. Siorapaluk was the most northerly continuously inhabited community in the world, and was the one place, I imagined, that could give me an indication of how the Herbert Island village of Qeqertassuaq would be now if it were still inhabited.

But the ice edge was gaining on Qaanaaq; you could see it with the naked eye from the hill above the town. All the talk at the store was the same: the ice was melting faster than ever. It was like nothing they had ever seen. The sea ice, which always appeared like clockwork as a fine frosted membrane over the local waters on my father's birthday – 24 October – was forming later and later. (The previous winter the first patches of ice did not appear until December, and even then it was so thin that the hunters dared not use their dogs on it. The ice broke up and re-froze three times before it was stable enough to travel on.) It was the real long-range hunters who were affected the most; instead of travelling from the first onset of winter to the far reaches of Northwest Greenland or even towards Canada, the hunters were obliged to hunt for what they could in the local area. But the main walrus and musk oxen hunting areas were already almost impossible to reach. The hunters shook their heads and raised their hands in frustration. What if this continued? Their eyes flicked to one another in fear of its implication.

The only way to get to Siorapaluk by sledge was to travel on the ice foot – a lip of ice that clings to the shoreline once the ice has broken up – which was an arduous way to travel, and would take at least four times as long as travelling on good ice, and no hunter was willing to risk taking me as a passenger. My only option was to take the twice-weekly helicopter that shuttled passengers, mail and groceries between Siorapaluk and Qaanaaq.

The helicopter ride was spectacular. We skimmed over the ripples of glaciers nosing their way down to their release into the fjord and over wild barren expanses of dark rock fissured with ice. From the air it was clear why the hunters were in such disarray. Large cracks lay across the sea ice like dark welts. Herbert

Island was now almost entirely surrounded by dark water, and any ice that remained was being shredded into ribbons by the waves of the dark northern waters and drifting perceptibly into Smith Sound. It could be a matter of only a week or two before the ice completely disintegrated.

Siorapaluk was considerably smaller than Qaanaaq, and was little more than a sprinkling of homes and a couple of warehouses on the edge of a small fjord. And with only around sixty inhabitants, of whom several were out hunting, the village seemed virtually deserted. Those hunters who were left behind were either too old to go out on the ice, or were casually tending their dogs or polishing the runners of their sledges between hunting trips. Huskies were tethered throughout the village all the way down to the beach and out onto the ice. I was greeted with throaty grumbles as I scurried between different teams. These were real working dogs, with thick healthy fur, albeit matted with grime and excrement, and bright wolf eyes. Sealskins dried on stretchers strung up on the outer walls of the prefab houses, and rubbish spewed from bags all over the village among discarded pieces of gristly meat and dried blubber.

The snow was starting to melt in the spring warmth, and as I scrambled over the hills behind the small settlement I relished the springiness of grass beneath my feet. Relative heat rippled off the black rocks and I stopped to take in the disembodied sounds that floated up the hillside from the village below. School had finished and the children played freely in the ice rubble of the tide crack. Excited by their presence teams of dogs howled, barked and whined, their plaintive cries blending with the hum of generators.

Wanting to escape any signs of civilized life, I walked further out until I was a mile or two north of the last hut. I sat on a lichen-blemished rock for a minute and reminded myself that at that moment the only people between myself and the North Pole – the very top of the world – were a handful of hunters and pole seekers, and I felt strangely drawn to it. For the first time I understood the passion of so many to reach it. It wasn't the actual prize of the North Pole that inspired me so much, as wanting to experience standing on top of our precious globe as it rotated silently through space.

I felt a thrill course through me, reminiscent of how I felt at summer camp the year before – the feeling one can only get when your eyes and mind are open in the vastness of Nature – and felt as though I were vibrating like a tuning fork that had just been struck on the side of a piano. The land was alive underfoot, and I could feel it thrumming with an insistent energy. It was no wonder that the ancestors believed that there were spirits in the rocks and the mountains. The hillside shimmered darkly and I trod softly, not wanting to disturb whatever it was that was giving me this eerie sensation. I wondered whether the light was playing tricks on me and making me delirious. More and more the coarse black moss looked like the hide of ancient animals. Long strands of bleached tundra grass moved softly in the breeze like the brittle locks of an ageing blonde, and the ground-hugging Arctic willow looked more and more like exposed arteries, red and plump and matted together in tightly woven patterns. I bent down and traced the entire length of a tree with my finger, just a couple of feet long; its trunk was only the width of my thumb. This tree was likely to be two hundred years old.

The temperature started to drop and I walked back to the village and took a guess on the schoolteacher's house. I had been told that it was the 'big red house *tuavani, avani* – way over there'; although there were several red houses, there was one that stood on its own, slightly bigger than the rest, sitting on the foot of the beach. I knocked on the door and heard someone hollering to me from one of the neighbouring houses: an old man hung out of a window, smoke billowing from his cigarette. He waved for me to go in.

I was overrun by children when I opened the door, all eagerly asking my name in a chaotic jumble of Greenlandic and Pidgin

English. 'Kina, who is it?' I heard someone call from beyond and then a distant 'Welcome, come in!' over the giggles of the children who were tugging at my clothes and helping me with my camera bag.

Eva Hunsballe was the schoolteacher from Siorapaluk – 'although,' she said with heavy irony as she welcomed me inside, 'we don't actually have a school'. Eva's home was very Danish, clean and tidy with Greenlandic memorabilia lovingly displayed around the walls. She showed me where the tea and coffee was and urged me to help myself: 'that is the way here in Siorapaluk, you are expected to help yourself, otherwise you go without. There is some musk oxen stew on the stove if you are hungry.'

It was as though Eva and I had been friends for years, and we were soon engrossed in conversation, listening greedily to one another's stories and views on the politics and education system of Greenland. Then the door opened and an Inughuit woman, who looked familiar to me, walked in. With a start I realized that she was the spitting image of the woman who had been keening at the funeral last summer. Without a word she walked around the small table and pulled me into an emotional embrace.

'I am Patdloq,' she said in a thick Thule accent, holding me away from her for a moment before hugging me again and talking quickly, reminding me that she had also lived on Herbert Island when we were little. She squeezed my arm tightly urging me to remember. The years had taken their toll on Patdloq, who looked some twenty years older than her thirty-seven years, but I suddenly realized that in front of me was standing the girl who had left me out on the ice when I was nine years old. My mouth fell open with surprise and she laughed excitedly, her smile revealing several missing teeth, with the others dark and rotten. She had a big family now, she told me as she pulled up a chair. Several of her children surrounded her now, looking at me with undisguised curiosity.

'Do you remember,' she gabbled quickly, 'when I took you dog-sledging to collect some ice?' She hurried on before I had a chance to answer: 'You fell off the sledge as we left and you cried out for me to stop.' She cackled as she told the story, encouraging the children to laugh with her. I distinctly remembered her leaving me on the ice on purpose, but I didn't correct her. 'Tomorrow,' Patdloq continued, 'I will take you out dog-sledging again, and maybe you will fall off and cry out for me to stop again!' She threw back her head and hooted in glee, revelling in the memory. Her face fell as she quickly got up to leave again, gathering two of her children behind her who had been prodding me for attention. 'Visit me,' she said simply and disappeared.

Patdloq's house was one of the smallest and oldest houses in Siorapaluk, which she shared with her husband and seven children. Patdloq was perched on a narrow platform that was used as both bed and sofa in the larger of the two rooms. Her eyes lit up as I bundled through the door with my entourage of children that I had gathered in the few steps between Eva's house and hers. Her husband looked up and grinned broadly, welcoming me with a flash of his knife.

'*Uanga* Nukagpiannguaq,' he said in a thick Siorapaluk dialect, '*Patdloq uie*; I am Nukagpiannguaq, Patdloq's husband.' He stood up and hovered behind her right shoulder in a gesture of unity with my childhood friend, before returning to the reindeer head sitting on a blue plastic bag on the floor, off which he cut the last remaining slivers of darkened meat and popped them in his mouth. The eyes of the reindeer seemed to follow me around the room as I settled next to Patdloq on the sitting bench. Nukagpiannguaq scraped a bit of gristly meat from around the eye-socket and generously offered it to me, I hesitated briefly, and he laughed and swallowed it quickly to spare me the embarrassment of refusal.

Patdloq and Nukagpiannguaq's home was a happy jumble of family chaos. To one side a bin overflowed with bloodied ends of pelts and unusable fur from the reindeer head and just a couple of feet away across ageing linoleum a pile of clothes threatened to take over the entire floor space. The children ran in and out, helping themselves to biscuits and squash and making pot noodles for themselves in between pulling at my clothes and hair to get attention. Patdloq looked tired and was nursing the youngest member of her brood on her lap with a plastic milk bottle. The child clutched at the bottle and watched me unblinkingly with one podgy hand gripped around the colourful plastic necklace that rested on Patdloq's exhausted breasts. Jackie Chan flew across the ancient TV screen but the audience paid no attention. I looked about me and smiled. In Siorapaluk I had finally found a place reminiscent of my childhood home.

Thick cloud silently overtook the dark mountains and lay in soft grey rolls over the icescape, completely obscuring the distant reaches of the fjord. It was a startling change from the cobalt skies of the last couple of days. I watched mesmerized as a single beam of platinum light teased the icecap and roved over its surface in a startling expression of delight on such a gloomy day.

I had another reason to come to Siorapaluk. I had been charged by my father to deliver a letter to a Japanese acquaintance of his who was living in the village with his Inughuit wife and children. Ikuo Oshima was well known in the district, and I was intrigued to meet a man who had, like my family, been seduced by Thule.

Hunting debris surrounded Ikuo and Anna Oshima's house: sledges in mid-repair, boat parts, dog harnesses and broken parts of machines and tools. A big wooden crate by the front steps had 'Oshima, Siorapaluk' stamped on its side alongside faded Japanese script. I knocked on the outer door and entered, squeezing past sealskins and old jackets, plastic buckets and large bowls filled with yellowing gristle and animal fat. It smelled like a hunter's hut. Anna was sitting at the table and called me in with a casual '*Ihirit*', and invited me to sit down with a smile that disappeared into her plump cheeks. The house was busy with people, although their voices were light and quiet; Ikuo had just returned from hunting that morning, and was crashed out in the only bedroom. The rise and fall of his sleep could be heard through the open door.

Ikuo first came to Thule in the 1970s with Naomi Uemura, a world-class Japanese mountaineer whose passion for the wilderness also turned him to polar exploration. Naomi had mounted an expedition to Greenland at the same time that we moved to Herbert Island, and as a matter of courtesy called upon my father to 'divide up' different areas of Greenland so that they would not step on each other's toes. They came to a mutual understanding that Naomi would have the interior to explore, and my father would stick to the coast – Dad was at that time just starting to plan the first circumnavigation of Greenland. A relationship of great respect and friendship between the two men grew out of that first meeting. Ikuo Oshima joined Naomi on his expeditions and fell in love with the hunting way of life. He finally moved to Siorapaluk permanently, took an Inughuit wife, and is now regarded as one of the best hunters in the whole of the Thule district.

The Oshima family lived in basic happy disarray and mismatched furnishings. It was a hunting household and was more practical than elegant, with the Japanese influence only really visible in a small lacquerwork and glass cabinet displaying two traditionally dressed Japanese dolls, a bottle of soy sauce on the floor next to a plastic bowl of meat, and a fanatically neat bundle of whip ends hanging on the wall. But it was homely. Anna had cultivated two small creeper plants over the years, and the sparse green foliage was strung all over the ceiling in between hanging beadwork decorations. She pushed two boxes of imported biscuits towards me over the plastic tablecloth.

Ikuo made an appearance a few minutes later. He greeted me with a sleepy smile, asked politely after my father and apologized for his state of exhaustion. 'We came back from hunting walrus this morning, my son and I,' he said casting a hand towards his adult son who sat in patched lime-green thermals, playing with

Ikuo's grandson, 'and we haven't slept for two days!' He laughed, his face crinkling in bleary amusement. 'It was a difficult trip, yes yes. Everything went wrong!' He described a long catalogue of mishaps and frustrations. 'But we managed to catch a large female, which will keep us going for a while.' He got up and searched for a clean cup in the kitchen among a pile of dirty crockery.

Ikuo was preoccupied, like most of the hunters in the district, with the deteriorating ice conditions, which affects the hunters around Siorapaluk more than those based in Qaanaaq. 'The last few seasons have been like never before,' he said gazing out of the window. 'Years ago we could travel by dog-sledge no problem to Qaanaaq, but now it is so dangerous. In the last two days there have been big movements in the ice; it is a big problem for us. We need to sell some of the meat and the skins to the store in Qaanaaq, but we can't get it there now.'

Ikuo's weathered face crinkled around his eyes with permanent good humour, and three perfectly round pale pink discs of weather-sore skin highlighted the apples of his cheeks and the tip of his nose from where he had frozen his face on one of his long hunting trips. You could tell how much time he spent outdoors from the tan line across his forehead, common to all hunters from where they have worn their knitted woollen hats when travelling. I smiled at the lightness of his character and saw that he was a child of the wilderness, which something inside me recognized and warmed to.

'The ice conditions are very bad,' Ikuo said again, gazing across the narrow fjord. 'Today I went on my bicycle over there to check my traps and the ice was breaking up just over there!' He pointed midway between us and the dark mountains on the other side. These days, he said, no one knew whether the ice was going to be safe to travel over or not. 'We didn't know whether to take our sledges or kayaks out hunting! And the snow is different too, there are hard ice crystals on the ice that are cutting the feet of the dogs. On a hunting trip recently we saw polar bear tracks but we couldn't follow them because the dogs were bleeding.'

'Maybe you should make them kamiks,' I suggested pointing at the sealskin boots hanging on the washing line.

'We did!' Ikuo said with wide eyes. 'But they won't wear them. Always they are just biting them off, they don't like wearing shoes.' Beside us on the sofa his daughter sat in a Stars and Stripes vest, vigorously softening a white sealskin with her fists. Ikuo gave her a paternal smile, looked back out of the window and quickly raised his binoculars to his eyes.

'Is a hunter coming?' I asked, straining to see what he was looking at.

'No, water is coming!' Ikuo said laughing, his eyes twinkling. 'Last year the ice broke up on the 6th of May. In four hours! In the morning there was ice, and in the afternoon there was only water, not even little bits of ice in the fjord. I think maybe this will happen again.'

The children were distracted and excited when I visited the 'school' the next day. Dog-sledge races for the children had been planned, and it was an event the small community had been looking forward to for some time. Concern over the state of the ice had had people buzzing over the route since early morning, but the designated area of the race was safe, and the competition would go ahead.

'It's chaos!' Eva cried in happiness as I stooped under the doorframe. 'I was worried that there weren't going to be enough dog-teams for the race as a few of the men had gone out hunting walrus, but a team came back in the night so now we have enough.' She sighed and fanned herself with strong thick fingers. 'Some of the children have been complaining of stomach-ache because they are so nervous. We are all so excited we cannot concentrate on anything!'

There were to be three dogs to each team, with two pupils

per miniature sledge, ranging in age from six to twelve. Teams were marked up on the small school blackboard, and names kept being swapped about as the children changed their minds about whom they wanted to race with.

The door flung open and the eldest of Patdloq's boys came crashing into the schoolroom. One of the sledges for the race needed modifying, he told Eva; the sledge was used for ice-collecting and had a wooden box screwed onto it – it was impossible to sit on the sledge as it was. They needed tools. Eva told them where the toolbox was and offered to help but the twelve-year-old boy dismissed her with a wave. 'No, just wait,' he said brusquely. 'We will fix it.'

'You see,' Eva turned to me laughing, 'he tells me to "just wait" because I am a woman and I cannot possibly know about these things! The boys are all like their fathers; there are things that women can do, and things that only men should do. They sometimes talk to me like I am this big,' she indicated the height of a small girl and added cheerfully, 'but I don't mind, it is their culture and they should be allowed to express themselves that way. Within reason of course.' Boys' voices rang off the ice outside as they shouted orders to each other, and we abandoned the schoolhouse to join them.

The excitement was infectious. Fathers started trickling out of houses and with bear-like yawns started preparing the small sledges for the race. Nukagpiannguaq waved as he was jostled down to the beach by his many children, and smiled indulgently as two of his boys pulled on his sleeves wanting to help him file the runners. As soon as they were bored of the hard work they called out to me 'Kaarignii, watch me!' as they practised with small child-size whips. As soon as they have learned to walk the children start learning how to use the whip – I have even seen babies in pushchairs flinging their right arm in the air with an imaginary whip as if they are preparing a dog team. The whips are small to begin with, made from a discarded short length of dog trace or something similar, but by the age of six or seven some of the children have developed an astonishing skill with even adult whips.

Already one team had been prepared and was waiting out on the ice and the rest of the dogs were straining at their leashes, whining and barking and wagging their tails. The dogs uniformly had coats matted with dirt. Eva pointed at the grubby teams and laughed gaily: 'I told the children in jest that they all had to go and wash their dogs so that they would be clean and smart for the race; they were incredulous! They told me that they had never heard of such a thing and all looked so worried that the dogs would freeze – it took me a while to convince them that I was joking.'

At ten minutes to twelve a large swathe of pale blue sky appeared over the fjord and with startling punctuality sledges and dog teams appeared from all over the village. The children, who up until now had been full of exuberance, were suddenly pale and quiet at the prospect of the competition as their fathers led their teams with great solemnity down to the ice. The women gathered in bright groups of colour chattering and arguing amicably over whose children would be the winners.

The fathers kept the dogs in a ragged starting line, waiting for the signal. The tension mounted. Without warning a woman's voice galvanized all the teams forwards and the dogs flew across the ice towards the horizon with the fathers sprinting alongside for a few feet before handing their sons or daughters their whips in a flourish. The speed of the sledges was astonishing, and within seconds most of the teams had streaked out across the ice, the dogs fired up by the excitement of the village, and unencumbered by the usual heavy sledges. Two sledges stopped just a couple of hundred yards into the race as the dogs became entangled and confused, not recognizing the commands of their charges. The women and the old people laughed as the men ran to help them: 'Ah, they will learn quickly this way.' The sound of children bawling with frustration carried on the breeze. But there was one team that raced a team's length in front of the others. The women made high-pitched bird-like calls to encourage them, the fathers shouted directions to their dogs, Patdloq shrieked wildly beside me in excitement with her arm linked through mine, and all the eyes of Siorapaluk, shaded against the sun by dark and calloused hands, were fixed on the race.

After completing the circuit of two large oil-drums in the distance the first sledge finally careered to a stop at the makeshift finishing line. The crowd ran to the winners, grasped the sledge firmly and thrust it into the air with the boys wobbling on top, waving small Greenland flags with one hand and clinging on for dear life with the other. The other sledges followed in their wake and all were applauded. I marvelled at the skill of the youthful drivers, and wished that the children of Qaanaaq had the chance to learn these traditions instead of sitting transfixed in front of the television, playing the same films over and over again. But at least there was a glimmer of hope here in Siorapaluk that the ways of the ancients would be remembered for at least another couple of generations to come.

'We won, we won!' the younger of the two winning boys cried as he ran towards his father, who was a bear of a man with kindly eyes. But the six-year-old boy stopped just short of his dad, not knowing what to do next. His father shook his son by the hand: '*Pidluarit* – congratulations,' he said solemnly. The boy swallowed hard. '*Qujanaq* – thank you,' he replied quietly, his hand disappearing into his father's paw, and his mouth trembling with emotion. The father bellowed with pride, threw the boy into the air above his head as if he were a trophy himself and then gathered him into a huge rough embrace and carried him back to the crowd on his shoulder. The boy's eyes shone like stars.

A few days later, after visits back and forth to the houses of my new friends and spontaneous dog-sledge rides with Patdloq and her family, the helicopter finally arrived (four days late) and I left

Siorapaluk. Almost all the village, as usual, gathered at the helipad in curiosity to see who was leaving or arriving, and if there was any post from friends and family elsewhere in Greenland. The children clung onto my legs and whimpered as I walked towards the open door of the helicopter, and dragged me back to the throng as Patdloq arrived, just in time to say goodbye. She hugged me stiffly. Her face was blank and unmoving. It was the same expression Maria was wearing the last time I saw her. I squeezed Patdloq's hand, and it triggered her emotions. I was pulled into a fierce hug as she wept inconsolably on my shoulder. 'I love you,' she whispered hoarsely and pushed me towards the helicopter.

A dog team weaved along a large lead in the ice outside Qaanaaq, unable to cross its width, going back and forth trying to find a passing place so the hunter could get back home; eventually the hunter disappeared way off towards the horizon to find a safe route. Later, two other sledges in convoy crossed the same piece of ice. The ice was opening and closing as if it were breathing.

I quietly prepared to leave Thule, and as I slowly packed my bags my mind lingered on the moments that I had recently shared with the Qaerngâq family and my other Inughuit friends. The twins had celebrated their thirty-ninth birthday a few days before, and it had been a rare moment when the whole family had gathered together. A red candle had been lit as always in the centre of the coffee table, but it seemed just another day in Magda's household. Gideon sat in a torn white T-shirt and stained jeans, growling playfully at Louisa's newborn daughter Sila. Magda and Baali sat either side of me bright-eyed and chatty. Naduk and Little Tekummeq wrestled playfully with Ilannguak, Orfik and Rasmus played with puppies on the floor and the hunters exchanged stories about their fear of spiders amid shrieks of laughter from the women, who teased them mercilessly for their cowardly ways, knowing full well the strength and courage of their husbands and brothers. We had left each other in high spirits after I had been made to promise that I would be back again soon. I knew that there would be no great emotional goodbyes, just as there had not been the last time I left. In many ways it was a relief not to face the turmoil of my emotions, for although the family were convinced that I would be back within the year, I could not be sure when I would next be able to return.

Then I was thrown into limbo. The plane was delayed due to bad weather and then mechanical difficulties, and I languished in Qaanaaq, visiting the sisters and other friends, but their manner was cool and awkward as we continually avoided saying goodbye over and over again. As I had grown to know my Inughuit friends and family as an adult I had found it increasingly frustrating not being able to communicate with them on more than a childlike level, and in turn that had made the feeling of isolation from the whole community tangible. Over the last few weeks I had felt as though I was marooned on a small ice floe, drifting ever further from the Qaerngâq family; in truth, the distance between us was breaking my heart.

Then Louisa, the most constant in her affections towards me, had visited me in a touching gesture of sisterhood. 'My family misses you,' she had said in a jumble of English and Greenlandic as she held my hand gently. 'You here, but not here.' And then she fixed me with a liquid gaze that held within it an ocean of feeling. It had dawned on me then that perhaps we were all struggling with not being able to communicate properly.

I was the first to admit that my relationship with the Qaerngâqs was confused. There was no doubt in my mind that we would always have a life-lasting affection and respect for one another, but I was still unsure how deep the friendship went. We were after all very different people, and although I did not want to give up on the idea that I belonged with them in some way, I wondered whether I was being foolish to nurture the thought.

The airport was gradually filling up, the plane was finally on its way and all seemed well. Kristian walked in the door looking slightly out of his depth in a new airport uniform still creased from having just been removed from its plastic packaging. It was his first day at the new job and he smiled bashfully at me as I called out to him. He waved at me surreptitiously and then came over to give me a brief hug before he was called into the office for his instructions.

I was talking to two Danish tourists when a large group of women flew through the doors with their children, making an impressive entrance in the tiny airport lounge.

'Surprise!' the sisters cried, all eyes bright and gleaming. I was speechless.

I swung in and out of their arms squeezing them all tightly, not wanting to let them go. They were in a boisterous mood, and quickly commandeered a table and all the spare seats nearby. Baali eagerly looked out for Kristian who was busily unloading the plane's cargo onto the tarmac. She took my arm and pointed to him and smiled with pride as he worked.

'Next time you come,' Louisa said loudly, taking centre stage, 'you will be carrying a baby.' I coughed with surprise but she continued with a serious look on her face, the girls studying my reactions: 'And it has to be a boy,' she decided firmly. The girls giggled.

'I think you should have a baby with an Eskimo,' Najannuaq pronounced dramatically, setting off a chain of jokes from the other girls.

'Marie and Wally will wonder why the baby has straight black hair.'

'And black eyes.'

'And maybe is a little short!'

We were so wrapped up in our laughter that we didn't notice that people had already started boarding, and in a moment the laughter had turned to tears and I was passed from one tight embrace to another, hot wet cheeks smearing against one another. Louisa helped me pull on my rucksack and I was hurried out by Eviaq the airport manager, who commiserated as I walked through the door towards the plane. Behind me the girls tried to smile, but tears streaked our faces.

Kristian was standing beside the little Dash 7 and quickly hugged me goodbye again, and whispered to look behind me; the girls had all run around the airport building and were waving goodbye behind the tall fence.

I struggled to hold back the tears as I made my way to a free seat. I had barely sat down when the plane started taxiing down the runway. The red-cheeked hostess struggled to keep her feet as we bounced down the ice-covered runway, valiantly trying to act out the safety procedures but looking nervous in case the pilots took off before she finished. She completed the mime with a hasty 'you know it all anyway' flourish and quickly scrambled to her seat.

Outside a sharp wind was whipping veils of loose snow into the air, but my sisters did not give up their post. The small plane turned, and as the Dash 7 took off I pressed my hand and forehead against the window and watched as that little knot of women, still waving, disappeared into the vastness of the Arctic.

Acknowledgements

Foremost my most deep and heartfelt love and thanks go to my extraordinary parents – my youthful mother, fellow writer and best friend Marie Herbert, and my dearest father, my creative mentor and hero Sir Wally Herbert – without whom I would never have had such a vibrant foundation. Thank you for introducing me to a world of possibilities and wonder, and for your love, patience and support throughout. Your passion for adventure, and your endless quest for truth and beauty have always been an inspiration to me.

Deep gratitude goes to those that have given me a second home in the Arctic, in particular the Qaerngâq family who opened their arms to me again. Their love and generosity will always be cherished. Also many thanks to others whom I met and befriended along the way; in particular Hans and Birthe Jensen, Navarana for her great conversation and hearty polar bear stew, Nuka and Jacobena for helping me with my Greenlandic, and to Pauline Peary and Qissunnguak, and Uusaqqak Qujaukitsoq. Thanks to Kjeld Kemp in Ilulissat for his boundless hospitality, Eva Hunsballe for her warmth, and for teaching me how to make bread and Danish meatballs; Patdloq, Nukagpiannguaq and the children for the hours of companionship and laughter, and Ikuo and Anna Oshima for their prize gift. Many thanks also to all those from Thule mentioned in this book who gave me their time and friendship.

There are some without whom this project would have never been possible. Immense gratitude to those that took a chance on me: Nuna Fonden, Greenland Bank for their generous sponsorship, Greenland Tourism for their support – in particular Siw Møller Kristensen who took it upon herself to get me to

Greenland; Kodak for film, Hardy Haase at Hasselblad for the loan of the superb panoramic XPan camera, Helly Hansen and Rab Clothing for keeping me warm, O2 for the XDA communications device that allowed me to share my adventures with my family while on the ice. Thanks to Lene, Ulla and all the staff at the Hilton Hotel Kastrup, Copenhagen, who gave me great comfort en route to the High Arctic.

I am most privileged to have a hugely positive and supportive agent, Lesley Shaw at Gillon Aitken Associates; may we have many more celebratory cocktails together. I also have a gifted editor, Mary Mount at Penguin – thank you for your tremendous help and guidance. And thanks to Nigel and Shane Winser at the Royal Geographical Society for their advice and unflinching encouragement. At home, I thank Laurence Blyth for being a wonderful companion and an all-round star – it would have been a lonely experience without you. And thanks to all of my closest friends who have been a great source of light and happiness throughout my life; sorry I can't thank you all individually. A big thumbs-up also to all those who have gone before me who have championed the uniqueness of the Inughuit people.

I would like to pay tribute to a few important people with whom I wish I could have shared this experience: Pascale – sister, friend and guiding light – Aata and Aana, and Maria and Avatak.

Lastly, I would like to give a profound nod of the head to the Inughuit people themselves.

Notes

Part One: A Long Way Home

Chapter 1 – The Beginning

Page 9 Extract from Marie Herbert, *The Snow People.*

Chapter 2 – A Long Way Home

Page 30 Pytheas of Massalia: 'This seems to be a description of the breathing of sea-mist, or frost-smoke cold and dank along the ice boundary of a frozen sea – indeed he reported after one day's sail north of Thule he met "sluggish and congealed sea which could neither be travelled over nor sailed through" – a condition often met by sealers in Icelandic north-coastal waters and by polar explorers, among whom Pytheas was undoubtedly the first.' Wally Herbert, *Polar Deserts*, p. 68.

Page 31 In October 1854 Dr John Rae, on his return to England from the Canadian Arctic, reported the first evidence of the gruesome end to the crew of the Franklin Expedition. In his report to the British Admiralty Rae wrote: 'From the mutilated state of many of the corpses and the contents of the kettles, it is evident that our wretched countrymen had been driven to the last resource – cannibalism – as a means of prolonging existence.' Six survivors of the Greely expedition of 1881 also gave evidence that some crew members had resorted to cannibalism.

Page 31 Arctic aborigines treated like children: Elisha Kent Kane refers to the 'Esquimaux' as being 'strange children of the snow', 5 October 1854.

Page 35 Amundsen and Byrd: There had already been other visitors to the fringes of the Arctic, notably the Irish abbot St Brendan who sailed north from Ireland in the sixth century AD with a small company of monks in frail oxhide-covered willow coracles in search of a place of rugged isolation in which they could meditate in peace. Their journey took them to Iceland, where he penned an eloquent description of his sighting of an iceberg as a 'floating crystal castle the colour of a silver veil, yet hard as marble, and the sea around it was smooth as glass and white as milk'. Three centuries later, in the middle of the ninth century, the Norseman Rabna Floki discovered the small colony of Irish monks after finding his way across the North Sea by periodically releasing ravens and following the direction they flew as they searched for the nearest land. Other Norsemen followed 'Floki of the Ravens' – noblemen evading the tax man – and colonized Iceland. It was this new Icelandic colony from which Eric the Red was exiled.

Chapter 6 – The Reluctant Angákoq

Page 106 Kritlaq was filled with so much nostalgia for his homeland that he only stayed in the district for a few years before he and a small group of faithfuls tried to make a return journey. It was a disastrous trip: many of the group died of starvation, including the great Kritlaq himself.

Page 109 The flood they speak of may be the flooding of the grounds surrounding the Bering Strait – now known as the Chukchi Sea – but this was very gradual, with the level of the world's oceans rising over several hundreds of years.

Page 109 However, according to Peter Freuchan, the Eskimos 'are taller than the Mongolians, and they are long-skulled where the Mongolians are short-skulled, a point too important to be overlooked'. *Book of the Eskimos*, p. 22.

Page 111 Unlike the Inugsuk who were hungry for knowledge, the Norse felt that they had nothing to learn from these primitive-looking hunters: their belief in their intellectual superiority was to be their downfall. The Norse relied heavily on supplies from Iceland and Norway, but supply lines were severed by the Black Death. With no skills to fall back on, and stranded in this inhospitable land, Eric the Red's once flourishing colony of some ninety farms was utterly deserted by AD 1345. The Norseman's animals returned to the wild and no trace of humans, alive or dead, could be found.

Chapter 8 – Twilight Years

Page 147 Walrus hunting: quotation from Richard K. Nelson, *Hunters of the Northern Ice*, p. 363.

Chapter 10 – Arrival at Summer Camp

Page 180 Peter Freuchan talks about his experiment with lice in his *Book of the Eskimos* in which he discovered that lice did not die from exposure to water, nor from being kept outside for several days in a test tube in temperatures of minus forty.

Chapter 11 – Narwhal Song

Page 209 Permafrost is permanently frozen ground: the ground in the High Arctic has been frozen for tens of thousands of years, and scientists have measured the depth of the permafrost to be well over 2,000 feet. The surface layer, which melts and refreezes according to weather conditions, is called the 'active zone', within which the roots of all vegetation are confined as neither roots nor water can penetrate the frozen ground beneath.

Few species of plant are able to complete a full life cycle this far north, but the rest have evolved so that they complete a single stage of their development during the summer, pause during the frozen winter months, and then resume their activity; therefore a plant can produce buds one summer, but not actually flower until the following summer, or even in some cases, two years after the bud has been formed. It takes many plants ten years from their seed germination to mature enough to produce buds.

Page 212 Jean Malaurie, *The Last Kings of Thule*, p. 80.

Chapter 12 – Leaving Camp

Page 221 Barry Lopez discusses light and ice effects in his book *Arctic Dreams: imagination and desire in a northern landscape*.

Chapter 13 – In Search of Happiness

Page 241 Minik spent twelve years in America, during which time all his companions, including his father, died of tuberculosis and influenza. Shortly after his father's death, Minik discovered his father's skeleton on display in the American Museum of Natural History. Minik was sent back to Greenland in 1909 and had to relearn the skills of the hunter, but he returned to America seven years later, and died in 1918 of influenza.

Page 246 Resolving disputes and the Eskimo psyche: to this day, mockery is still used as the most powerful instrument to discipline a child. The fear of being ridiculed will make an Inughuit child look to his or her peers and mentors to guide them; in this way their ego is subdued, and the child is pulled back to the safe norm of behaviour. It is extremely rare for children in Thule to be reprimanded verbally or physically.

Part Two: Return

Chapter 17 – Nanuq – the Ice Bear

Page 301 By all accounts the polar bear has a highly developed intellect. When waiting for its prey beside a seal's breathing hole – sometimes waiting patiently for hours beside a single blowhole – the polar bear is said to use its paw to cover its black nose, and both Greenlandic and Canadian Inuit insist that the polar bear sometimes uses tools such as rocks or blocks of ice to hit its prey over the head; many carvings across the Arctic depict polar bears doing this. My father also told me as a child that hunters will never stand with their backs facing open water as polar bears have been known to swim under the water, grasp the ice-edge with the claws of their back paws and swing themselves upright onto their hind legs before launching a deadly silent attack upon the surprised hunter. And even as early as 1857 polar traveller Sir E. Leopold M'Clintock noted that, 'in the capture of their prey [polar bears] display a degree of instinct almost akin to reason . . .'

The people of the North were not the only ones who revered and desired the offerings of the great white bear. The courts of the world prized five treasures from the North: the ivory tusks of the mammoth, the walrus or the 'unicorn' (the single ivory-tusked narwhal), the white gyrfalcon, and the polar bear. Legend preceded the cream-coated bear. Hans Egede, the eighteenth-century missionary to Greenland, pronounced that polar bears spent their winter in luxury, living in palatial snow dens 'made with pillars, like stately buildings' (*The World of the Polar Bear* – Fred Bruemmer). Polar bears, or their furs, were presented at courts in Japan, China and Egypt: the contemporary Greek writer Athenaeus reported that Ptolemy II, King of Egypt (285–246 BC), had a polar bear in his private zoo, which was led on fantastic processions through Alexandria preceded by a 180-foot-tall gilded phallus. Polar bears also reached the Middle East and the courts of Europe.

Owning a live polar bear was the ultimate status symbol. Monarchs gave fellow monarchs gifts of bears. Norwegian King Haakon presented King Henry III with a polar bear – whereupon King Henry ordered 'the sheriffs of London to furnish six pence a day to support our White Bear in our Tower of London; and to provide a muzzle and iron chain to hold him when he was fishing in the Thames'.

It was not just for novelty or status that polar bears were captured and hunted by the whites. The gall bladder of the bear is still highly prized in Korea as a cure for stomach or liver complaints; ointment made out of bear fat was used to ease rheumatism in many countries and bear fat was even used by the Romans as axle grease. Today, the sale of furs has been outlawed in many countries, including the USA and many countries in Europe, but with a market value of $3,000 per gall bladder, and the increasing interest in big game (big money) hunting, the prize of the polar bear is still a lucrative business.

Page 304 In the 1980s there was an epidemic of distemper and almost all the dogs in Thule died. It was disastrous for the community and it has taken them years to recover. Still the hunters greatly fear any illness that affects the dogs.

Chapter 18 – Poles Apart

Page 317 In 2004 the Magnetic North Pole is calculated to have its location at 82°'N, 113°4'W. Curiously, the closer one gets to the Magnetic North Pole, the more inaccurate one's compass is.

Page 317 The location of the Northern Pole of Inaccessibility is 84°03'N, 174°51'W.

Page 317 The Celestial North Pole is currently 45 arc minutes from Polaris. Polaris has not always been the 'Pole Star', and in fact has only been close to the Celestial North Pole for around the last thousand years, and in the next millennium is likely to move further away from the Celestial North Pole – due to the wobble of the Earth as it is influenced by the pull of other bodies in the solar system. For the Egyptians their Pole Star was not Polaris, but instead was Thuban in the Draco constellation.

Page 318 More information on Symmes and the historical quest for the North Pole can be found in *Ninety Degrees North: the quest for the North Pole* by Fergus Fleming.

Page 319 'Navel of the north': some Inughuit believe that it was Matthew Henson, Robert Peary's black manservant and companion on all his major expeditions – who also spoke Inuktun well – who coined this phrase in his attempt to explain what the North Pole was to the Polar Eskimos.

Page 319 Between 1719 and 1915 the British and the Dutch took out around 120,000 bowhead whales. Scientists believe that there are only around 300 bowhead whales left in Greenland waters.

Page 323 Recent studies have found that the volume of the ice pack is 60 per cent of what it was when Dr Roy 'Fritz' Koerner conducted his studies on the Arctic Ocean during the British Trans-Arctic Expedition.

Sources and Bibliography

There are innumerable books on various aspects of the High Arctic, but there are a few that have given me a much deeper understanding of this place. Valued guides have been the works of Peter Freuchan which give a very entertaining and human viewpoint on the area before modernization took over and Knud Rasmussen's fascinating ethnographical studies and stories of his travels in the area.

More recent studies include *The Last Kings of Thule* by French ethnographer, eccentric and family friend Jean Malaurie, and his recent English translation of *Ultima Thule*, which is a magnificent tribute to the area of Thule. His painstaking research has been of great inspiration to me when writing this book.

The books written by my parents were of particular significance to my story and my understanding of this place. *The Snow People*, written by my mother Marie about our stay in the Thule area when I was a child, is a great story told with poignant freshness and innocence. Her more recent book *Healing Quest*, although not about the Arctic, nevertheless deals with ancient tribal wisdom and the journey through grief, which was something I encountered many times during my return to Thule.

The many works by my father were indispensable to me. In particular his beautifully crafted books *Eskimos, Hunters of the Polar North* and *Polar Deserts* inspired me to continue his project recording the evolving lives and environment of the Inughuit. His book *Across the Top of the World* gave me an insight into who he was as a young man and the beginnings of his affinity with the High Arctic and its people, and his masterpiece *The Noose of Laurels* about the Peary–Cook controversy gave me not only all the information I needed about their race for the pole and their journeys in the Thule area, but also was an example to me of how a book should be written.

There are many other great books written on the Arctic that I read during my research, and several of which I have quoted during the course of this book. All these, and those books that were of particular relevance are listed below.

Bandi, H. G., *Eskimo Prehistory*, Methuen & Co., London, 1969

Bruemmer, Fred, *The World of the Polar Bear*, Bloomsbury Publishing, London, 1989

Ehrlich, Gretel, *This Cold Heaven: seven seasons in Greenland*, Fourth Estate, London, 2001

Fitzhugh, William & Kaplan, Susan, *Inua: spirit world of the Bering Sea Eskimo*, Smithsonian Institution Press, Washington DC, 1982

Fleming, Fergus, *Ninety Degrees North: the quest for the North Pole*, Granta Publications, London, 2001

Fortescue, Michael D., *Inuktun: an introduction to the language of Qaanaaq, Thule*, Institut fir Eskimologi, Copenhagen, 1999

Freuchan, Peter, *Ice Floes and Flaming Water*, Gollancz, London, 1955

——, *Book of the Eskimos*, Fawcett World Library, New York, 1961

Freuchan, Peter & Salomonsen, Finn, *The Arctic Year*, Jonathan Cape, London, 1959

Giddings, J. Louis, *Ancient Men of the Arctic*, Alfred A. Knopf, New York, 1971

Gilberg, Aage, *Eskimo Doctor*, George Allen & Unwin, 1948

Harper, Kenn, *Give Me My Father's Body: the life of Minik, the New York Eskimo*, Blacklead Books, Northwest Territories, 1986

Herbert, Marie, *The Snow People*, Barrie & Jenkins, 1973

Herbert, Wally, *Across the Top of the World: the last great journey on Earth*, G.P. Putnam's Sons, New York, 1971

——, *Polar Deserts*, Collins, Glasgow, 1971

——, *Eskimos*, Collins, Glasgow, 1976

——, *North Pole*, Sackett & Marshall, London, 1978

——, *Hunters of the Polar North*, Time-Life Books, Amsterdam, 1981

——, *The Noose of Laurels*, Hodder & Stoughton, London, 1989

Kane, Elisha Kent, *Arctic Explorations in the years 1853, '54, '55*, Childs & Peterson, Chicago, 1856

Knox, Alexander, *Night of the White Bear*, Pan Books, London, 1972

Krakauer, Jon, *Into the Wild*, Macmillan, London, 1998

Larsen, Thor, *The World of the Polar Bear*, The Hamlyn Publishing Group, London, 1978

London, Jack, *The Call of the Wild*, Signet Classics, London, [1903] 1991

——, *White Fang*, Signet Classics, London, [1906] 1991

Lopez, Barry, *Arctic Dreams: imagination and desire in a northern landscape*, Macmillan, London, 1986

Malaurie, Jean, *The Last Kings of Thule*, E.P. Dutton, New York, 1982

——, *Ultima Thule*, W. W. Norton & Co., New York, 2003

McKinley, William Laird, *Karluk: the great untold story of Arctic exploration*, George Weidenfeld & Nicolson, London, 1976

Nelson, Richard K., *Hunters of the Northern Ice*, University of Chicago Press, Chicago, 1972

Peary, Josephine Diebitsch, *My Arctic Journal*, Longmans, Green & Co., 1893

Peary, Marie A., *Snow Baby*, George Routledge & Sons, 1935

Peary, Robert E., *Northward over the 'Great Ice'*, Frederick A. Stokes Company, New York, 1898

Rasmussen, Knud, *People of the Polar North*, Macmillan, London, 1908

——, *Greenland by the Polar Sea: the story of the Thule Expedition from Melville Bay to Cape Morris Jesup*, William Heinemann, London, 1921

——, *Across Arctic America*, Putnam & Co., London, 1927

——, *Collected Works Vol. III, No. 3. Report of the Fifth Thule Expedition 1921–24*, Gyldendalske Boghandel, 1928

Rink, H. J., *Tales and Traditions of the Eskimos*, William Blackwood & Sons, London, 1875

Rink, Henrik, trans. Helge Larsen, *Danish Greenland: its people and products*, C. Hurst & Co., 1974

Smith, Frances C., *The World of the Arctic*, Lutterworth Press, London, 1962